# T·H·E

# TOTAL
# NEGOTIATOR

# T·H·E
# TOTAL
# NEGOTIATOR

## STEPHEN M. POLLAN and MARK LEVINE

AVON BOOKS  NEW YORK

THE TOTAL NEGOTIATOR is an original publication of Avon Books. This work has never before appeared in book form.

AVON BOOKS
A division of
The Hearst Corporation
1350 Avenue of the Americas
New York, New York 10019

First Avon Books Trade Printing: April 1994

AVON TRADEMARK REG. U.S. PAT. OFF. AND IN OTHER COUNTRIES, MARCA REGISTRADA, HECHO EN U.S.A.

Printed in the U.S.A.

OPM   10  9  8  7  6  5  4  3  2  1

# Acknowledgments

The authors would like to thank Shannon Carney, Gabrielle Kleinman, Stuart Krichevsky, Jane Morrow, Jody Rein, and Ann Goodman for their help; Robert Cucullo, Howard Greene, Ernest Honecker, Dale Klamfoth, Emily Koltnow, Elysa Lazar, William Martin, Olivia Mellan, Michael Salzman, Kenny Tillman, Tessa Albert Warschaw, and Martin Yate for their advice; and Corky Pollan and Deirdre Martin Levine for their love, support, and understanding.

# Contents

## Part 3: Persuading People—
### *Negotiating Actions*

## Part 4: Two-Part Tussles—
### *The Rules of Hybrid Negotiations*

# T·H·E

# TOTAL
# NEGOTIATOR

# BECOMING A TOTAL NEGOTIATOR

## Confessions of a Hired Gun

My formal title may be attorney/financial consultant, but when it comes right down to it I'm a hired gun. Clients come to me to handle situations and resolve problems they don't think they can handle on their own.

In our frontier past (or at least in the movie version of our frontier past) when the homesteaders needed help defending themselves they'd send for a hired gun. They'd hire a professional gunslinger who'd ride into town, rout the bad guys, collect his fistful of dollars, and ride off into the sunset. I serve the same role, albeit a lot less dangerously and glamorously, for my clients. Sometimes they need my help in buying a home or asking for a raise. Other times they want advice on how to deal with parents or partners. In my role as CNBC's Answer Man, television viewers write and call me, asking how to resolve consumer complaints and make financial decisions. While the word itself is rarely used, all these people are asking me to help them negotiate.

My clients come to me because I've developed a reputation for being able to solve problems. That reputation comes, in large part, from having successfully (and publicly) negotiated everything from the return of faulty toaster ovens to corporate mergers. Because I've negotiated so many different problems, from the monumental to the mundane, people have called me a total negotiator. But for a long time I've been embarrassed by this reputation. Sometimes, after finishing a successful deal, a client would turn to me and ask "How did you do that?" My embarrassment came, not because I'm modest, but because I couldn't answer the question.

It wasn't that I wanted to avoid revealing professional secrets. I couldn't answer because I truly had no idea how I did what I did. All my life I've been an entirely instinctive negotiator. Don't get me wrong: I don't believe there's a negotiation gene that you either have or don't have. I'm convinced my negotiating skill was learned. I just didn't know how or from whom.

My inability to answer my clients' question led to my becoming a negotiation book junkie. I read everything written about negotiating, not just because it was my business, but because I was looking for a way to turn my technique into a formula. Some of the books I read were scholarly works, written by experts who, through careful analysis and study, developed a negotiating theory. While these books have always fascinated me, I've found that none of the theories addressed all of my negotiations. I looked further, reading psychological works that divided people into different personality types. While I was invariably impressed by the authors' insights into human nature, I could never quite match up all the people I knew with the character sketches, or vice versa.

Then there were the dirty trick collections. I really loved these. Generally written by other hired guns, these offered all sorts of neat suggestions like having people sit with the sun in their eyes or turning up the heat . . . literally. Although they're fun to read about, I've never had the guts to use these tricks myself. I'm afraid they may backfire.

Since no one seemed to have written the book I was looking for, I thought I might as well do it myself. I sat down with my co-author, Mark Levine, who has helped me write about everything from buying a home to surviving in a recession, to define my theory of negotiating. We assumed there must be some underlying theory behind what I've been doing all these years. We spent five years trying to find a theory that worked where others had failed: in addressing all the thousands of negotiations—large and small—that I've been part of. After banging our heads against the wall for five years suddenly a light bulb appeared over both of our heads: Why did we need a theory?

I've always tried to address problems in a pragmatic manner. Whenever there has been some goal I needed to accomplish—whether for myself, my clients, or my readers—I've determined exactly what steps needed to be taken, in what order, and then have taken them. This step-by-step approach to problems has worked in both my personal and professional lives. Why not try to apply this approach to negotiating and treat it in a practical, rather than theoretical, manner? Rather than examining what worked and then figuring out why, we would simply outline exactly how to do it and leave the theories to the philosophers. The more we thought about this the more sense it made. If we could reduce negotiating to a series of simple, common-sense steps applicable to any and every situation, we'd be able to teach everyone how to do what I do and turn each of our readers into a "total negotiator."

I believe that in this book we've succeeded in doing just that. By following the steps we've outlined and explained you'll be able to serve as your own hired gun in every situation from buying a home to talking your way out of a speeding ticket. And you'll be able to turn your life from one filmed in black and white to a Technicolor extravaganza. That's because, as I'll explain in chapter 1, negotiating enhances your life.

# PUSHING THE ENVELOPE

## Getting More out of Life Through Negotiating

*"Let us never negotiate out of fear. But let us never fear to negotiate."*

—JOHN F. KENNEDY

I believe the ability to negotiate effectively is, after reading and writing, the most important skill required to become successful personally, financially, and in business. Being able to negotiate effectively with family, friends, spouse, employer, employees, superiors, subordinates, professionals, tradespeople, salespeople, and everyone else you come into contact with can change your life from mundane to glorious. It can transform you from one of the "mass of men who lead lives of quiet desperation" into an individual who takes charge of his life and lives every moment to the fullest. That's because negotiating is a tool to help you get what you want, as opposed to settling for what you're being given.

## NEGOTIATING CAN IMPROVE THE QUALITY OF YOUR LIFE

People are either reactive or proactive, non-negotiators or negotiators. Those who are reactive don't negotiate. They settle for the status quo, content to shuffle through life accepting their lot, apologizing for the space they're taking up. Those who negotiate are proactive. They never willingly settle for less than what they want. Negotiators don't accept things as they are without first asking why they couldn't be made better. Negotiators go after what they want.

I like to think of negotiators as life's test pilots. Back before the space program, test pilots described current technology as an envelope around the earth. Each time the test pilots flew higher and faster than ever before, each time they stretched the limits of technology, they were pushing that envelope. Negotiators are always pushing the relationship envelope. They're always looking to get the most out of every interaction with others. That doesn't mean negotiators are greedy, pushy, or manipulative. It simply means they're driven. And most times that drive leads to success. Being a negotiator isn't a piece of cake—it's hard work. It's a lot easier to accept things the way they are than to try to change them. But I think the results you get from negotiating far outweigh the added effort required. As a rule, negotiators lead richer, fuller, more rewarding lives than non-negotiators. That's because in reaching for more, they almost always get it.

Tycoons and entrepreneurs aren't the only negotiators. The employee who gets larger and more frequent raises than her peers is a negotiator. The husband who has more honest and successful dialogues with his wife is a negotiator. The great teacher and the successful coach are negotiators.

## THEN WHY ARE THERE SO FEW NEGOTIATORS?

Since being a negotiator has all these advantages, you might wonder why there are so few of us. There are three reasons. First, most people simply don't know how to negotiate. Our parents don't teach us how to negotiate, probably because their parents didn't teach them how to negotiate. And despite the fact that negotiating is a vital skill, we're taught nothing about it in school. That leads to the second reason there are so few negotiators: people don't think it's possible to learn how to become one. Since we're not taught how to negotiate we just assume it cannot be taught. The third, and I believe most powerful, reason is fear.

Most people look on life as a zero-sum game—that for someone to win someone else must lose. If you believe there must be a loser and a winner in every situation you can rationalize not trying to win (that is, not negotiating for more) because if you try to win you risk losing. That's nonsense. In most cases, when a negotiation isn't successful you simply must settle for the status quo—which is what you would have gotten had you not bothered negotiating in the first place. If you ask a policeman not to give you a speeding ticket, and he persists, all you've lost is the time involved in asking. You still have the speeding ticket, but you're no worse off than if you hadn't asked. By asking, you give yourself the possibility of winning (not getting the speeding ticket) without taking on further risk.

To compensate for the fear and lack of knowledge about negotiating, some people paint it as a mysterious art beyond normal abilities. They think those who know how to negotiate must have been born with the skill. That's absurd. There's no special negotiating gene. When faced with the evidence that others are able to do something they cannot—in this case, negotiate—some people react by denigrating the skill they lack. They say negotiating is a shady, underhanded way of doing business. They claim to be "straight shooters" who are beyond pretense and posture. Nonsense. What they're really saying is that since they don't know how to negotiate, there must be something wrong with those who do.

## YOU MUST CHANGE YOUR DEFINITION OF NEGOTIATION

These attitudes and fears are needlessly cutting people off from a technique that can help improve their lives immeasurably. How can you get past these mistaken notions? First, change the way you look at the word *negotiate*. The word has taken on a formal, businesslike meaning, conjuring up images of gray-haired men in blue suits sitting around a conference table debating matters of high finance. Most people apply the word to their own lives only to describe the few times when they actually engage in such a premeditated, formal process—buying a home, asking for a raise, or buying a car. By concentrating on these monumental instances, which most of us dread, we reinforce the image of negotiating as a mysterious art. Actually, it's no more mysterious than having a conversation, and it happens just as often.

Whenever you hear or see the word *negotiate* from now on, replace it in your mind with the phrase *asking for more*. That's all negotiating is: asking for more than you'd otherwise receive. Assign this new definition to *negotiate* and you'll soon realize that most of your negotiations take place outside of business. You negotiate with your family and friends far more frequently than you do with your employer or with some hot shot executive. Every time you preface a question to a friend with "Could you do me a favor," and every time you begin a request of your spouse with "Would you mind terribly," you're negotiating.

Once you realize that negotiating is part of your everyday life you can shake off those images of rooms filled with smoke, suits, and talk of mergers. Free of your misconceptions, you'll be better able to follow the step-by-step approach to negotiation that I'll be offering in this book.

I want to help you get the most you possibly can out of life. I'm not looking to turn you into a professional negotiator, nor do I want to turn you into an obnoxious individual who tries to negotiate everything from the price of a cup of coffee to the amount of money the kid next door charges to mow your lawn. I simply want to turn you into a proactive person—someone who sets goals, pursues them, and generally reaches them—rather than a reactive person who just accepts circumstances as they're found. As I said earlier, I believe negotiating can transform black-and-white life circumstances into Technicolor. It's the exploration of what's available, but hidden, rather than the acceptance of only what's visible. It's digging deeper and learning more about a situation to gain a better understanding and create new choices.

By the way, I don't have a set of rules for you. As I said earlier, total negotiating isn't a philosophy with a series of commandments, it's an approach with a series of steps. That said, there are some fundamental truths you'll come across in the step-by-step process of negotiating. I call these the "axioms of total negotiating." Whenever one comes up in the book you'll find it set off from the rest of the text in a box. Don't worry about writing them all down—they're collected in Appendix B.

I've included these axioms in order to speed up your transformation into a total negotiator. You see, these truths are the fruits of my years of experience as a hired gun, the results of thirty-five years of negotiating. You would realize them yourself after going through repeated negotiations. I'm just saving you some time and gray hairs. Consider them a crash course in the school of hard knocks. Rather than rules to follow, they're things you should bear in mind when going through the three steps in negotiating.

## HOW USING THIS BOOK CAN MAKE YOU A TOTAL NEGOTIATOR

Let me tell you how, by using this book, you can become a total negotiator. In the remainder of this first part of the book—chapters 2, 3, and 4—I explain the three main steps you need to take in each and every negotiation, and I go over exactly how you go about taking them. Once you have a handle on the steps you can move on to the subsequent chapters of the book, in which I show you how to apply those steps to specific situations.

In each of those chapters covering specific situations I'll refresh your memory about the three steps in negotiating. That's because, while I hope you'll read this book straight through from beginning to end at least once in future months and years, when you're facing a particular situation I don't want you to need to reread the entire book in order to benefit from it. Each chapter that covers a specific situation can stand alone and serve as your guide.

That doesn't mean you should just skip the next three chapters and jump right into whichever chapter covers a situation you're facing today or will be facing tomorrow. In order to become a total negotiator you need to understand and absorb the three steps on their own, separate from specific situations. Only after you've become comfortable with them will you be able to apply them instantly to whatever situation you're facing. When you can do that you'll have become a total negotiator.

# — 2 —

# KNOWING YOURSELF

## Analyzing Needs and Weighing Options

*"Self-reverence, self-knowledge, self-control,
These three alone lead life to sovereign power."*

—ALFRED, LORD TENNYSON

All negotiations have three elements to them: the two parties who are doing the negotiating and the situation they're negotiating about. These three parts lead directly to the three steps in negotiating: know yourself, know your opponent, and know the situation. The first and most important step in negotiating is to know yourself. That's because you are the only element in the negotiation that you have complete control over.

As we will see in chapter 3, you can learn about, and try to influence, your opponent. But since he or she is an independent adult human being you can never totally control his or her actions. And as we'll see in chapter 4, you have even less sway over the third element, the situation itself.

Since you are the one element of the negotiation you do have absolute control over, self-knowledge and self-understanding can become your most effective tools for being successful in negotiating. Being your most effective tools, they're the ones you should focus on first. That's why knowing yourself must be the first step of any negotiation, regardless of who it's with or what it's about. Before you can start worrying about the nature of the specific situation or the motives and mind-set of your opponent, you need to examine your own.

Philosophers and poets throughout recorded history have reflected on and written about the path to self-knowledge. But in the context of negotiation this path is actually quite short and fairly easy to follow. In order to complete the first step and know yourself you must answer three questions: What do I want? Is it worth my time? Is it important to me?

**11**

## *WHAT DO I WANT?—SETTING A SPECIFIC GOAL*

Far too often we enter into negotiations without a well-thought-out, specific goal in mind. If we've any goal, it's usually something general like "I want to get it cheaply" or "I want to come out on top." Neither of these is an effective goal.

"Cheap" is an ill-defined concept. What exactly does buying something cheaply mean? Does it mean buying a particular type of item at the lowest price possible? Does it mean getting the most for your money? Does it mean buying a particular item at the best price you possibly can from a particular seller?

Let's look at an example. The World Series is around the corner, and Michael just can't bear watching it on his ten-year-old television set. He decides it's time to buy a new TV. His goal in the upcoming negotiation with the television salesperson will depend on his circumstances. If buying a new television presents an economic strain for Michael, his goal may be to get a TV set, any set, as cheaply as possible. If his finances are a little bit more stable, but not limitless, his goal may be to get the best TV he possibly can for the amount of money he can comfortably spend—in other words, the best he can afford. Finally, if money really isn't an issue for Michael, and he has his heart set on buying a particular television— the Zenon Model X11 with the twenty-foot screen and quadraphonic sound—his goal may be to buy that particular item for as little as possible.

Winning isn't an adequate goal either. What does winning mean? Will any movement on your opponent's part constitute a win for you, or do you need to humiliate or bankrupt the other side? "Winning" implies the other side's "losing." What do you gain from having the other side lose? Pure and simple, winning is an ego boost. Of course there are people out there who negotiate to boost their egos. However, I don't encourage it. Negotiating is too important and too difficult to be entered into for such petty motives. Negotiate when you're looking to achieve something that enhances your life or the lives of those important to you, not just to make yourself feel superior or secure.

Most of the theoretical books written on negotiation stress the need to look for solutions offering both sides a chance to be victorious. These works correctly note that negotiation need not be a zero-sum game: every victory doesn't require an equivalent loss. Unfortunately, most people you negotiate with will neither know nor care about such things. They'll want to win simply because human nature makes them competitive. So while you need to abandon any notion of winning, you must remember that your opponent will be trying desperately to win. This knowledge can be an advantage in individual situations, but for now, suffice it to say you shouldn't be looking to win but merely to achieve a specific goal that enhances your life or the lives of those important to you.

> ## The more specific your goal, the more likely you'll be to achieve it.

This first axiom—the more specific a goal you set, the more likely you'll be to achieve it—works because by setting a very specific goal you free up more areas for possible concessions.

Let's say you're buying a house. If your specific goal is to buy it for the best price you possibly can, you're able to use other issues, such as timing, terms, and personal property, as areas for concessions. On the other hand, if you're the seller and your specific goal is to transfer title by a certain date, you'll be able to use the price, terms, and personal property issues to make concessions.

You'll know you've succeeded in developing a specific goal when you can ask yourself the question "What do I want?" and answer it in a single sentence that offers no room for further refinement. In Michael's case:

- "My goal is to buy a color television with a screen that's thirteen inches or larger for as little money as I possibly can," or
- "My goal is to buy the best television set I can while staying within my budget of $500," or
- "My goal is to buy the Zenon Model X11 for the lowest price I possibly can."

> ## If your preparation time is limited, you should only set limited goals.

Sometimes you may be forced into a negotiation without having enough time to think out your goals carefully. Let's go back to Michael. He's driving home from the store with his new television in the trunk. He's anxious to set it up and watch tonight's ball game, so he's going a little bit above the speed limit. Suddenly he sees a state police car, lights on and siren blaring, filling up his rearview mirror. He didn't plan on getting involved in this negotiation, and he probably isn't going to have time to carefully think about and dissect his goals in the upcoming negotiation with the state trooper. In such instances the key is to immediately move to a specific achievable need. If your preparation time is limited, you should only set limited goals.

Michael's goal should simply be to legally avoid being issued a *speeding* ticket. All thoughts of getting away with no ticket at all should be banished from his mind. He doesn't have the time to prepare the kind of substantial defense that would be required to talk the trooper into letting him go with a warning. If he's able to get the trooper to write a ticket for a lesser offense than speeding, he'll have succeeded in this unplanned negotiation.

## IS IT WORTH MY TIME?—
## DECIDING IF IT'S READILY NEGOTIABLE

I believe that, theoretically, everything is negotiable. Philosophically speaking, I don't think there are two positions or people so far apart that it's impossible to reach a negotiated settlement. That said, there are situations I believe aren't *readily* negotiable. For example: There's obvious common ground between every buyer and every seller. Both sides want a sale to take place. However, if you walk into a furniture store and you see a sign that says WE DO NOT NEGOTIATE tacked up on the wall, you can assume any attempt to engage in a negotiation will result in the common ground being pulled out from under you. In effect, such a store is saying: "Sure we want to sell our furniture. But if we can't get our price we won't sell it at all." In most mercantile situations, such an obvious impediment to negotiating is backed up by very low prices to begin with. In many instances, however, the lack of mutually accessible common ground won't be obvious; it'll take some examination and thought.

Let's look at the case of Bill and Barbara, who are looking to buy a home in a lovely picturesque town. The real estate broker has taken them to see all the properties up for sale except one: a beautiful little Victorian nestled on a picture-perfect half acre two blocks from the center of town. Bill and Barbara have been driven past the house at least three times, and they can see the For Sale sign on the front lawn, but the broker hasn't even mentioned it. On the fourth drive past, Bill finally turns to the broker and asks, "What's the story with that house? Why have you avoided it?" The broker tells them the house is owned by a very stubborn old couple who have decided they want $100,000 for their house, regardless of what the market dictates it's worth, and are content to hold out for their impossible price.

> ## Don't bother negotiating for things that aren't readily negotiable.

Theoretically, the seller of a home could reach a settlement with a potential buyer—after all, they both want a sale to take place. But in this case, the possibility of reaching an agreement has been almost entirely eliminated by the sellers' irrationality. Rather than setting a specific achievable goal—such as "We want to sell our home within one year for the most money we possibly can"—this couple has set an impossible goal: "We'll only sell our home for $100,000."

Does this mean the purchase of their home isn't negotiable? Not really. Such a couple probably has a hidden goal that a skilled negotiator could uncover and then try to satisfy. For instance, they may have their heart set on buying a particular retirement home and need $100,000 to do it. Their goal is actually to buy that retirement home. This goal doesn't necessarily preclude the sale of their present home for less than $100,000, but they'll need to be convinced. And that could take a great deal of time and effort on Bill's and Barbara's part, time and effort that could probably be more productively spent looking for another home to buy. So while the price of the home is negotiable, it's not readily negotiable, and therefore probably isn't worth the effort.

What's true for homes is also true for almost everything else being negotiated. Although in some situations you may think you'll never have another opportunity like this again, believe me, you will. Opportunity doesn't knock only once; it returns over and over. And quite often, the feeling of facing a once-in-a-lifetime opportunity is generated by skilled salesmanship. There will be other houses. You'll get other job offers. There are other televisions out there. And once you realize you're not negotiating a "do-or-die" matter, your power in the negotiation increases dramatically—you'll be willing to walk away from a deal.

Of course, there's a caveat to this rule—as there is to all rules—but it's extremely rare. If the object or service in question is truly unique, and you must acquire it to maintain your life or the life of someone you love, then negotiate for it regardless of how difficult and time-consuming the process may be. For example: The demands of the kidnappers who are holding your spouse for ransom may not be readily negotiable, yet you wouldn't walk away from the negotiations. Sure, that's an extreme example. But it's only in such an extreme situation that I suggest you negotiate for things that aren't readily negotiable.

How will you know whether something is or isn't readily negotiable? While I'll get into specifics in subsequent chapters, generally it will be apparent, either by some definite statement, such as the sign in the furniture store, or by an obvious problem, such as a house that's on the market at the same price for a very long period of time.

### IS IT IMPORTANT TO ME?— MAKING SURE IT'S WORTH DOING

Just because you've successfully defined a specific achievable goal, confirmed something is readily negotiable, and discovered who has the power to make the decision, that doesn't mean you should necessarily engage in the negotiation. As you might have started to figure out, successful negotiating isn't simple. It requires a great deal of time and effort to prepare for and actually engage in negotiations. That means you shouldn't negotiate just for the sake of it. The process I'm outlining in this book should only be used when it's important.

> **To decide whether it's important enough to negotiate, consciously weigh the potential rewards and the outcome of not negotiating against the costs.**

What makes something important? Well, to some degree that depends on your personal circumstances. Negotiating the price of a new winter coat could be very important to someone on a fixed income. On the other hand, negotiating even the price of a new car might not be important to a wealthy individual. Negotiating with a spouse over where to buy a house may be of little importance to someone who works from a home office. On the other hand, to a commuter, the location of the house is very important.

The relative importance of a negotiation also depends on its potential ramifications. If you're a resident of New York with an otherwise clean license and you're about to be issued a speeding ticket in Montreal, it probably isn't worth trying to negotiate down the fine. Sure, it'll cost you some money, but it won't appear on your driver's license and affect your insurance rates. On the other hand, if you're pulled over in New York it might be worth negotiating since not only will you need to pay the fine but your insurance rates will rise as well. And if you already have a couple of offenses on your license, and this could be the ticket that results in its being suspended, it's certainly worth negotiating.

Deciding whether or not to negotiate is a mental balancing act. On one hand you've the potential reward—a savings of dollars, a shorter commute to work, or having a driver's license, for example. On the other hand you've the potential costs—the cost of negotiating in time and effort and the cost of not negotiating in potential outcome.

You'll be surprised how quickly and instinctively you'll be able to make this judgment. That's because you already regularly engage in this mental balancing without even being aware of it. Aren't there times when someone does something that annoys you and you let it go? You're saying to yourself, "It's not worth getting into a fight about it." Aren't there times when you know you could buy something for a few dollars less somewhere else but, because it isn't convenient, you make the more expensive purchase? All I'm suggesting is that you take this process one step further and make it a conscious judgment.

Let me give you an example. Allison is a free-lance graphic artist. She's scrupulous about getting her magazine clients to sign contracts before she does any work; her contracts always state she will be paid when she hands in the work. One day she gets a call from a regular client who tells her the accounting department has instituted a new policy. Rather than paying her for her work right away, the magazine now wants to pay for it when it's published. The problem is that the accounting department wants to make this policy retroactive, delaying payment for a couple of invoices Allison submitted the week before totaling $100. Allison points out that while she's not happy about the new policy she understands it. But since she has signed contracts predating the new policy she believes the two invoices should be paid. She's told the accounting department refuses. What should she do?

Allison does her mental balancing act. What's the reward? Superficially, it's receiving her $100 sooner rather than later. But underlying that is the integrity of her contracts with the client. If she allows the magazine's staff to violate the contracts now, what will stop it from happening again in the future? If she doesn't negotiate the matter now, on her next assignment the accounting department may say that another policy has changed and it can't reimburse her expenses at all. At some point the magazine may even refuse to pay what was agreed to in the contract. On the other hand there are potential risks and costs to negotiating further. This is her major client and she doesn't want to jeopardize her relationship with the staff. And dealing with the bureaucracy in the company will take time and is bound to generate some stress, which will take away from her work productivity.

Allison thinks about her relationship with the client. The editorial and art departments have always loved her work, and in fact, recently agreed to a hike in her fee. The problem doesn't seem to be with the people who hire and work with her but with the accounting department. She decides the underlying reward of having a contract with integrity outweighs the potential risk of damaging her relationship with the client, which actually appears to be very low. She decides to negotiate.

After asking yourself, and answering, the three questions I've outlined in this chapter, you'll have completed the first step in negotiating: you'll know yourself. Next you're ready for the second step in the process: knowing your opponent. That's the subject of chapter 3.

## Step #1

### Know Yourself
### Analyzing Needs and Weighing Options

- What do I want?—Set a specific goal.
- Is it worth my time?—Decide if it's readily negotiable.
- Is it important to me?—Make sure it's worth doing.

# — 3 —

# KNOW YOUR OPPONENT

## Leveling the Playing Field

*"Only a peace between equals can last."*

—WOODROW WILSON

The second step in negotiating is to know your opponent. That doesn't mean you need to become intimately familiar with every aspect of his life or that you must understand the way his mind works. In the context of negotiating, knowing your opponent simply means determining whether there's a discrepancy of power between the two of you and then working to minimize it. Let me explain.

I believe that a discrepancy of power between the parties—whether real or perceived—is an obstacle to a successful negotiation. When one person has a definite advantage over another, any negotiation between the two will result in failure: either failure to reach an agreement or failure to reach an agreement truly acceptable to both sides. That's because when unequal parties get together side issues such as ego and status consciously or subconsciously take on more importance than the actual issues in the negotiation. The good news is that, while the real or perceived discrepancy of power between the parties may never be absolutely eliminated, it can be minimized.

> # Eliminate or minimize any discrepancies between the real and perceived power of you and your opponent.

Let me explain this further with an example. Dave, an accountant who works for a telemarketing company, has a busy, stressful day ahead of him. He has an appointment with his supervisor this morning, at which he plans to ask for a raise. During his lunch break he needs to bring his car to the local auto mechanic to have the air-conditioning unit fixed. Dave is wearing his standard work outfit: a button-down shirt, a tie, and a nice pair of pants. His discussion with his supervisor begins well. His boss, wearing her omnipresent blue suit, agrees that Dave has been doing an outstanding job but suggests his division hasn't been generating sufficient profits for there to be pay increases. Dave, not knowing the facts, can't refute her assertion. His boss sends him back to his desk with a promise to discuss the issue again . . . once profits pick up.

More than a little upset, and feeling powerless, Dave heads over to the service station. When the friendly, grease-covered mechanic offers to show Dave the problem, Dave declines, saying he doesn't want to get dirty. He then testily says, "I don't care how it works, just fix it." The mechanic curtly says he'll call Dave later that afternoon. Dave's bleak mood darkens when the mechanic telephones an hour later to tell him the repair will cost $500 and will take at least a week.

Dave had two unsuccessful negotiations, both of which were derailed by unequal power. When negotiating with his boss Dave was in a naturally inferior position; after all, he's beneath her in the hierarchy. He isn't routinely privy to all the information she and the other supervisors possess. His boss, subconsciously reacting to Dave's less formal appearance than her's, and consciously drawing on her greater access to information, was able to brush off Dave's request easily. Dave, by not directly addressing and compensating for the discrepancy in power, in effect accepted his inferiority and acted as a supplicant begging for a morsel, rather than as an equal asking for adequate compensation.

As I'll discuss later in this chapter, and in the chapter on negotiating raises, Dave should have thoroughly researched the company's and his department's financial health prior to the meeting in order to minimize an actual discrepancy in power: in this case, access to information. Dave should also have minimized a perceived discrepancy in power by dressing in a way similar to his boss. That doesn't mean he should have dressed up on the day of the meeting—that's too obvious and wouldn't work. Instead, he should always have dressed similarly to his boss as possible. That way he'd have decreased both the real (information) and perceived (appearance) gaps in power between them.

The same held true for Dave's negotiation with the auto mechanic. In that situation, Dave was in a naturally superior position. But here the discrepancy in power is due to much less obvious reasons. In the American cultural hierarchy, an auto mechanic, regardless of how well paid or how highly skilled, is deemed lower on the totem pole than an accountant . . . particularly when the auto mechanic is covered with grease. In addition, Dave is a potential customer and the auto mechanic is selling a service. And since the repair isn't an emergency, Dave has plenty of opportunity to take his business elsewhere. While Dave may not have the technical knowledge of the auto mechanic, his higher place in the hierarchy and his status as a customer definitely place him in the position of dominance. But rather than this working to his advantage it actually worked to his disadvantage.

Dave subconsciously and consciously flaunted his real (status as a customer) and perceived (social stratum) power advantages—partly because he himself was made to feel inferior earlier that day. This enraged the auto mechanic, leading him to ruthlessly wield his only power (technical expertise) as a weapon of revenge. Dave's appearance marked him as being in a different social stratum immediately. But the auto mechanic probably didn't hold that against him. However, when the mechanic offered to show Dave the problem, and Dave responded that he didn't want to get dirty, the mechanic sensed that Dave looked down on him. Then when Dave minimized the importance of knowing about the workings of his car and demanded rapid service, it was clear that Dave looked down on the mechanic. In response, the mechanic used his power to cut Dave down to size: he charged Dave top dollar for the work and made sure it was done at a snail's pace. As I'll discuss later in this chapter, and in the chapter on negotiating with service providers and professionals, Dave should have done everything possible to minimize the discrepancies in real and perceived power between himself and the auto mechanic, even though he was in the superior position. In both situations, regardless of whether he held the inferior or superior position, Dave wasn't able to negotiate successfully because of the discrepancy of power.

The way to achieve this equality is to know your opponent. I like to think of this as "leveling the playing field." In the early days of American football, since there weren't any perfectly manicured gridirons around, teams used whatever open fields could be found. But few of these fields were perfectly level. That meant one team had an advantage since they'd be playing downhill, while the other was disadvantaged by having to play uphill. In order to mitigate any inequity, the rules were changed so that after every score the teams switched sides of the field . . . in effect, leveling the playing field.

When negotiating, you can't do anything as simple as change sides of the field, but you can learn about your opponent and mitigate whatever discrepancy in power exists by asking yourself four questions: What information do I need? With whom should I negotiate? Are there any side issues that could cause trouble? What do I share with my opponent?

## WHAT DO I NEED TO KNOW?—
## GATHERING INFORMATION

The first and perhaps most important question you must ask yourself in getting to know your opponent is "What do I need to know in order to level the playing field?" Then you must go out and gather that information. In many negotiations you'll be at an automatic disadvantage because your opponent will have a great deal more information than you do. Some of this is information about your opponent himself or herself. For instance, someone selling a home clearly knows *why* he is selling, but you won't.

You'll also need to gather information about the item under negotiation. For example, a television salesperson knows all about her products, including what the store paid for them and at what price she can afford to sell them, while you know nothing other than what's written on the price tag.

In general, it's easier to find out information about the item under negotiation than information about your opponent. In the case of a house, you can consult the listing records, investigate comparable home sales, hire an independent appraiser, walk around the neighborhood, and even have the house inspected. In the case of a television, you can read publications such as *Consumer Reports* that provide detailed information about various products, and you can shop at a variety of stores, asking the salespeople questions. While I'll be offering specific advice in subsequent chapters, for now all you need to understand is that to gather information about the item under negotiation you'll need to do some formal objective research.

Gathering information about your opponent, however, calls for investigation rather than research, which is a little bit more difficult. Remember, most of your opponents won't be interested in leveling the playing field. They're wrapped up in "winning." So unless your opponent is extremely naive or extremely enlightened (another reader of *The Total Negotiator*), he will attempt to remain a mystery. That will require you to rely on techniques intelligence agencies use to gather information: observation, infiltration, and analysis.

*Observation* means carefully taking in and recording the surroundings, attitude, and actions of your opponent. *Infiltration* means finding a third party, someone close to your opponent, who'll intentionally or unintentionally provide you with the information you need. And *analysis* means putting all the pieces together and making a sound, reasoned judgment. While I'll be going into this in greater detail in chapter 5, let's look at the purchase of a home as an example of the information-gathering process.

Jane has found what she thinks is the home of her dreams. She begins her information gathering by finding out all she can about the house. She learns how long the house has been on the market. She tours the neighborhood and studies recent sales of comparable properties. She has an appraisal done.

Next Jane needs to gather information about her opponent, the seller. Since, like most savvy sellers, he isn't present when Jane looks over the house, he can't be questioned directly. Jane first does her observing, taking note of everything she sees in the house: some of the rooms are almost empty; there are very few pictures still on the walls; there are lots of boxes in the basement. Next she tries to infiltrate the other side. In this case she has a ready spy: the real estate broker. Jane asks the broker some questions about the seller. What does he do for a living? (He's a college professor, she's told.) Why is he selling? (He has gotten a new job, she finds out.) Does he have children? (Yes, one six-year-old boy.)

Finally, Jane does her analysis. The home is priced very close to its market value and has just come on the market. Empty rooms, few pictures on the walls, and boxes in the basement seem to indicate the seller has thinned out his possessions and is preparing to pack—this means he already has a place to move to. This is somewhat confirmed by the fact that he has gotten a new job. Since he already has a new job, and he has a school-age child, Jane deduces he is under pressure. He probably wants to sell and be in his new home at least by late summer since he needs to be on the job in September, and he'd clearly like his son to be able to start in his new school at the beginning of the term. Combining the information gained from research with the information gained through investigation provides Jane with a very clear picture of her opponent's motivations. He is looking for a very quick negotiation, contract, and closing so he can be in his new home as soon as possible. This information will be invaluable to Jane's ability to complete a successful negotiation.

I learned the value of gathering information from one of the first big corporate deals I negotiated. I was president of a venture capital firm at the time. We were forced to take over a film-processing lab we had invested in that had gone under. All in all we had about $1 million invested in the lab, which at the time was a great deal of money. We were looking for someone to buy the lab from us, but there didn't seem to be any local takers.

While I was looking for potential buyers I read in a newspaper that a major movie studio was in the midst of a labor dispute with one of its own film-processing labs. I decided to go visit the head of the studio and suggest he shut his problem lab and buy ours instead. I was very nervous about the prospect of meeting with this corporate bigwig, so I did what my law school education told me to do: prepare exhaustively. One part of my preparation process was to learn everything I possibly could about the person I was about to meet. I consulted *Who's Who in American Business and Industry*. I ordered a report from Dun & Bradstreet. And I went to the library and dug up all the magazine and newspaper stories about the company I could find.

In the process of my investigations I found out that the fellow had been married twice, had been a Boy Scout leader, had graduated from West Point, had been a Rhodes Scholar, and was a gourmet cook. I loaded up on all the information I could, even memorizing the names of his kids. When I finally met the fellow I felt as if I had known him for years—I was much less nervous than I would have been if I had gone in cold. In the process of our meetings I was able to subtly allude to his good taste in food and his apparently military bearing, allowing him to bring up his hobby and his college years. Our relationship became less formal. We began speaking to each other without posturing. We closed the deal. Since that day I've been an obsessive information gatherer.

## WITH WHOM SHOULD I NEGOTIATE?— PUSHING THE UP BUTTON

The second question you must ask yourself in order to know your opponent is—ironically enough—''With whom should I be negotiating?'' I'm constantly amazed by how many potentially successful negotiations are derailed by the failure to ''push the up button'' and by how much time and energy is wasted in negotiations with individuals or groups who don't actually have the power to make decisions.

> # Find out whether your opponent actually has the power to make a decision.

Let me give you an example. Tom applies for a personal loan at his neighborhood bank. Since he's a longtime depositor with a good credit history he assumes he'll have no problem. He quickly fills out the standard application and drops it in the mail. He's shocked when he receives notification that his application has been rejected. Angrily he telephones the bank to complain. The operator connects him with a "customer service representative." Despite his pleas and mounting anger, the only response he gets is "I'm sorry, but your application didn't meet our requirements." In a fit of anger Tom tells the individual on the other end of the line he'll be changing banks tomorrow. When all his threat elicits is an unemotional "I'm sorry you feel that way," he hangs up the telephone. What went wrong?

In two instances Tom negotiated with individuals who didn't have the power to actually negotiate. Casually dropping his application in the mail was his first mistake. Submitting an application is, for all intents and purposes, the beginning of a negotiation. By going through the traditional channels, Tom placed his fate in the hands of someone who didn't have the power to negotiate. His application ended up on the desk of a loan clerk. Each morning this clerk is handed a scoring sheet—a paper that lists numeric values for every possible answer on the loan application, and gives a minimum total score for acceptance. The clerk simply assigned numbers to Tom's answers, added them up, saw that his total didn't meet the minimum score, and rejected his application. That wasn't much of a negotiation, and it was, in the final analysis, a waste of Tom's time and efforts.

Tom's second mistake was in the way he complained—or, in effect, tried to renegotiate his rejection. As soon as he telephoned and told the operator he wanted to complain he was connected with someone whose job it is to deal with complaints. The only power she has is to state and restate the bank's policy. Since she has no say in setting that policy she has no power to overrule it. Tom allowed this individual to block his desire to negotiate, making him feel powerless and leading him to issue an angry, ineffective ultimatum.

What should Tom have done? He should have made a more personal and studied approach, first investigating the bank's criteria for granting loans and then filling out the application with an eye toward highlighting how he met those criteria. In any areas where he didn't meet them, he should have explained why he still should be granted the loan. This customized application would have confounded the clerk and forced a supervisor—someone with discretionary power and therefore open to negotiation—to examine it. If the loan was rejected, Tom's complaint should have been made to an individual who actually had the power to change the decision. When he faced a roadblock he should have "pushed the up button" and asked to speak to a loan officer—someone who helps set policy and can therefore change it. And if necessary he should have kept pushing the up button until he reached the bank president.

Powerless individuals may be positioned as your negotiation opponents for a number of reasons. In Tom's case, they were used as buffers between the parties. Bankers don't want to negotiate individually with people since it will take up too much time, so they make it difficult for people to deal directly with decision makers.

In other cases, powerless individuals may be used as "decoys" to try to dilute your position, to encourage you to "fall in love." Auto dealers do this all the time. They'll have a salesperson negotiate price with a customer, getting the buyer to exhaust all his ammunition. When the deal seems to be finalized the salesman will back off and say he needs to have it approved by his sales manager. The sales manager comes back and tries to renegotiate the price up, hoping the buyer will have his heart set on the car and will no longer have any negotiating power left.

Finally, in some other cases, powerless individuals will engage in negotiations in an effort to keep from appearing powerless. This happens a great deal in the workplace. A manager won't want his subordinates to know he doesn't really have the power to decide on their raises, so he'll negotiate with them directly and then go on his own to the executive with the real power. In effect, the subordinates have wasted their time.

How can you determine whether or not you're negotiating with a person who has the power to make a decision? Actually it's often quite simple: you ask them. When complaining to the bank over the telephone Tom should have directly asked the other party if she had the power to change loan decisions. If she said no, or even hemmed and hedged, Tom should have pushed the up button until he found someone who clearly did have the power. When discussing price with a car salesman you should directly ask him whether he has the power to make a deal or must get it approved. If the deal must be approved by a sales manager, negotiate directly with the sales manager instead. Don't worry about being lied to by a powerless party. If you are, you'll be able to use that as a potent tool when you negotiate with his superior.

I learned all about pushing the up button when I was running a small business investment corporation. We had a technical regulatory problem with the Small Business Administration, which threatened to finish us. The local SBA representative wouldn't budge. In desperation I asked to speak to his supervisor. He said it wouldn't make a difference but gave me his boss's name. I flew down to Washington, D.C., to meet with this new opponent and couldn't believe the difference. The level of intelligence, insight, and flexibility jumped tenfold with just one move up the bureaucratic ladder. We were able to resolve our problem amicably. From that point on I learned to push the up button rather than giving up, getting out, and waiting downstairs.

## ARE THERE ANY POTENTIALLY DISRUPTIVE SIDE ISSUES?—REMOVING DISSONANCE

The third question you need to ask yourself in order to know your opponent is "Are there any side issues surrounding the negotiation that could cause trouble?" I call these potentially damaging side issues "dissonance." If there is dissonance present, you need to determine how to make sure it doesn't affect the negotiation. I've found three main types of dissonance that can muddy up my negotiations: past history, timing, and appearance.

*Past history* refers to anything that occurred before this negotiation but could still influence its outcome. Past history could involve previous encounters between you and your opponent, you and someone similar to your opponent, and/or your opponent and someone similar to you. Let's say you and your significant other are about to negotiate whether or not you should contribute to the financial support of your parents. Any previous negotiations the two of you have had (and I'm sure there were thousands) don't belong in this negotiation. Neither do any positive or negative feelings your significant other has toward your parents or vice versa. But you can bet that if you don't clean up that past history it's going to interfere with your negotiation.

Or perhaps you're about to negotiate a pay increase with your supervisor. All the previous negotiations the two of you have had—whether about salary, promotions, deadlines, or the quality of your work—don't belong in this negotiation. In addition, all the previous raise negotiations your supervisor has had with other employees are side issues as well.

So how do you get these side issues to stay on the side, where they belong? You use a technique psychologists call "bridging." This means building a bridge over the past. It's really very simple to do. Just mention the past situations, acknowledging their potential impact, but then ask that they be put aside so the two of you can concentrate on the matter at hand. For example, when negotiating with a spouse about helping to financially support your aging mother, directly address your mother's relationship with your spouse. Acknowledge that your mother made mistakes and was often wrong, but then ask your loved one to put the past aside for the moment. Does this completely eliminate the impact of past history? Not necessarily, but it brings it into the open, and that goes a long way toward moderating any negative impact. The acknowledgment of past mistakes or problems generally robs them of their power to break deals.

*Timing* refers, obviously, to the day and hour when the negotiation is to take place. While rationally timing shouldn't affect a negotiation, it almost always does. Children are instinctively good at knowing the right and wrong times to negotiate. No child asks for a raise in his allowance immediately after bringing home a bad report card. Yet many employees, for example, disregard what's going on at work, choosing instead to ask for a raise on the anniversary of a previous raise. While I'll offer specific timing guidelines for each negotiation I cover in later chapters, for now suffice it to say that, in general, you want to negotiate when you have enough time to present your case fully, your opponent isn't upset or angry, and the time pressure is on your opponent, not you.

*Appearance* refers to how you look: your facial expression, grooming, and garb. This can have a great deal of subconscious impact on a negotiation. Once again, while I'll offer specifics in each chapter, the general rule is to dress like the party you'll be negotiating with, or in accord with the image you want to project.

Let's go back to poor Dave, whom we used as an example earlier in this chapter. If you remember, Dave wore his normal work clothes—a button-down shirt, a tie, and a nice pair of pants—on the day he was going to ask his boss for a raise and bring his car in to the garage. That same day he learned that an important client was in town and would be available to meet with him over drinks. But, still upset with being turned down for a raise and receiving a high estimate on the repairs to his car, he decided that rather than go home first to change into a suit and tie, he'd just run over to the meeting after work. When he showed up to meet the client, who was dressed in a three-piece suit, Dave's less formal attire marked him as being inferior to his client. In addition, his client was annoyed that Dave didn't think enough of the meeting to dress properly. Obviously, he should have dressed appropriately.

It goes without saying that your personal hygiene should be perfect. Bad breath, noticeable body odor, or any other hygiene problem will add an element of dissonance that no amount of effort will overcome.

In some negotiations, your own attitude may contribute to the dissonance surrounding the process. For instance, when buying a home, having the mistaken belief that there's one and only one perfect home for you may cause you to add elements of fear and desperation to the negotiation, and these elements may prevent you from being successful. In subsequent chapters, whenever applicable, I've described ways to adjust your attitude so you don't engage in self-destructive negotiating.

## WHAT DO I SHARE WITH MY OPPONENT?—
## FINDING AND DEMONSTRATING COMMON GROUND

The fourth and final thing you need to ask yourself in getting to know your opponent is "What do the two of us share?" I call whatever is shared "common ground." Common ground doesn't imply agreement. It can simply be the absence of disagreement. I like to look at it as the "non-opposing" needs of the two parties. Don't be mistaken, there's always common ground between two parties, even if it's only the desire not to be an SOB.

In many situations the common ground is obvious. In mercantile negotiations the buyer wants to buy and the seller wants to sell; therefore the common ground is the desire for the object to trade hands. In most employment negotiations the employee wants to feel respected and valued, and the employer—if he or she is intelligent—wants the employee to feel respected and valued. When spouses or lovers negotiate, the most obvious common ground is their mutual love and respect and commitment to the relationship. In subsequent chapters I'll point out the common ground in various negotiations.

As you'll see in the specific negotiations that follow, once you've determined the common ground you share with your opponent, you need to bring it to his or her attention. This can be done either directly or indirectly. If you already have a good relationship with your opponent it's best to directly state the common ground. For example: If you've been a loyal and valued employee of your company for ten years and have a solid relationship with your supervisor, you might begin a raise negotiation by stating: "I think you know how strongly I feel about the company, how much I enjoy working here, and how much I respect you as my supervisor. And it's apparent from your words and deeds that my work has been appreciated and my skill respected."

If you're negotiating with someone for the first time, on the other hand, it's easier to establish common ground indirectly. This can be done by eliminating your opponent's fears and establishing an environment of trust. Surprisingly, both can be accomplished very simply. All it takes is for you to project warmth and caring. Smile. Look people in the eye. Avoid body language that projects confrontation, such as crossed arms. Sit on the edge of your seat and lean forward, demonstrating interest. Try to use the other party's first name. Don't hesitate to pay compliments to your opponent, such as "I couldn't have said that as well as you did" or "I love the tie you're wearing." If appropriate, use phrases like "I need your help" or "I've heard you're the perfect person to talk to about my problem."

Through your words and actions you're trying to show your opponent you're not out to kill him; you're just another nice guy and, parenthetically, you're just like him. What I'm suggesting isn't manipulation, it's just savvy negotiating. All I'm saying is that you shouldn't allow your being opponents in a negotiation to prevent you from showing warmth. Besides, you should treat your opponent this way even if it won't help your chances. He isn't your enemy; he's your partner in trying to reach an agreement. If you can internalize that notion you'll find your body language, dialogue, and actions automatically adjust, leading the other party to feel comfortable with you.

After asking yourself, and answering, the four questions I've outlined in this chapter, you'll have completed the second step in negotiating: you'll know your opponent. Next you're ready for the third and final step in the process: know the situation. That's the subject of chapter 4.

## Step #2

### Know Your Opponent
### Leveling the Playing Field

- What do I need to know?—Gather information.
- With whom should I negotiate?—Push the up button.
- Are there any potentially disruptive side issues?— Remove dissonance.
- What do I share with my opponent?—Find and demonstrate common ground.

# 4

# KNOWING THE SITUATION

## Learning the Lessons of Experience

*"Experience isn't interesting till it begins to repeat itself—in fact, till it does that, it hardly is experience."*

—ELIZABETH BOWEN

The third, final, and most problematic step in negotiating is knowing the situation. The reason for this step is obvious. There are three elements to every negotiation: you, your opponent, and the situation. Only by mastering each of these elements can you maximize your chances of successful negotiation. In chapter 2, I explained how you can know yourself, the only one of the three elements you have complete control over. In chapter 3, I demonstrated how you can know your opponent, at least to the degree possible and necessary in the context of a negotiation. Now it's time to look at the element you have the least control over: the situation.

Each and every situation is different. That's because not only are the circumstances of each negotiation unique, but the environment is changed by the interaction of the two parties. I can't provide you with a list of questions to ask that will help you know the situation because there are just too many variables. So how can you complete the third step in the negotiating process? You need experience.

Over time, as you face the same situation over and over again, you'll learn all the possible nuances and twists. After being in the same situation time and time again you'll know it inside out. There will be no surprises since you'll have played out every possible variation.

But since you're not a professional negotiator you won't have the opportunity to go through the same situation over and over. In addition, you won't have the luxury of being able to look at mistakes as lessons for the future. You may face a particular situation only once in your life, and when you do, it's your money or future, not a client's, that's on the line.

It's sort of a catch-22: you need experience to know the situation, yet you won't have the chance to become experienced. How can you get around this? You'll need outside help. But don't worry about finding that help—it's already in your hands.

## ABSORB THE INSIDER TIPS OFFERED THROUGHOUT THE BOOK

I've been negotiating professionally for more than thirty-five years. I've faced the same hundred or so negotiations over and over again. That experience allows me to know each and every situation I commonly face. And in the pages of this book I'll be sharing my experience with you in the form of what I call "insider tips." In negotiations where even I don't have enough experience to truly know the situation, I've turned to others who have the needed experience.

In most cases, these experts were the people you'll be facing as opponents. For example: I spoke with police officers to come up with the insider tips for the chapter on speeding tickets, and I spoke with administrators and teachers for the chapter on negotiating school disciplinary decisions. I literally have spoken with hundreds of different sources in preparing this book and have culled insider tips from each.

These insider tips are the lessons of experience that could only otherwise be learned from years of professional negotiating. They are the final ingredient you need to become a total negotiator, someone capable of skillfully negotiating every situation, whether monumental or mundane.

## BECOME A STUDENT OF THE PROCESS AND DO YOUR OWN RESEARCH

Don't be content just with the tips contained in this book, however. If you want to continue to expand your repertoire and increase your negotiating skill you'll need to become a student of the process. Besides learning from experience you'll need to do your own research. Speak to past, present, and possibly future opponents. Ask them about what they normally do in negotiations, what their goals are, and what techniques they use to get their way. You'll be surprised how open they'll be with you. That's because, as negotiators, they realize that this isn't a zero-sum game:

the knowledge they give you doesn't diminish them. In fact, the more informed you are, the better off they are.

The more two parties know about each other's needs and wants, the more likely a mutually acceptable agreement will be reached. When I know what will make you happy, and you know what will make me happy, it's easier for us to come up with a solution that works for both of us. That's why when two total negotiators come together both end up winning.

That's it, the whole negotiating process—the three steps to getting more of what you want out of life. All that's left is for me to explain how to use the rest of the book.

## APPLYING THE THREE STEPS TO YOUR OWN NEGOTIATIONS

The three steps outlined and explained in part 1 apply to every single negotiation, regardless of who it's with or what it's about. It's the universal quality of these three steps that makes it possible for me, and now you, to be a total negotiator. But in an effort to make the rest of the book easier to use, I've broken down all negotiations into three types, based on their content, and have tacked each type in a separate part of the book.

Part 2 covers number negotiations. Part 3 deals with persuasive negotiations. And part 4 addresses hybrid negotiations. Number negotiations are, simply enough, debates over a number, usually a price. Persuasive negotiations are discussions between two parties in which one tries to convince the other to adopt a course of action. Hybrid negotiations are complex dialogues involving both a persuasive element and a number negotiation.

Each part begins with a brief discussion of that type of negotiation and offers some axioms to remember. Since I couldn't possibly address every single situation you're likely to face, I've had to pick and choose which negotiations to include in each part. I've tried to tackle the most important, common, or educational situations in full-length chapters. These show you exactly how to apply the three steps to the specific situation through the use of an example. In an effort to be as comprehensive as possible, I've included a concluding chapter to each part that goes over the application of the three steps to other situations in a more abbreviated fashion.

If you're interested in negotiating a specific situation, and it's included in the book, simply turn to the appropriate chapter. If you're confronting a situation not specifically covered in the book, you'll need to determine what type of negotiation you're facing. To do that, simply ask yourself this question: "What is my goal?" If your goal is solely to reach an agreement on numbers or terms, you're about to enter into a number negotiation. If your goal is only to convince, you're about to enter into a persuasive negotiation. And if your goal is to both convince and then agree to the details, you're about to enter into a hybrid negotiation. You can then turn to the appropriate part of the book and read through the chapters extrapolating the information and advice you'll need to handle your particular situation.

Don't worry—that's a lot easier than it sounds. Since the book covers most of the common negotiations, by the time you come across something that's not covered you'll already have quite a bit of experience as a total negotiator. That will make it easy to apply your knowledge to a new situation.

## Step #3

---

## Know the Situation
## Learning the Lessons of Experience

- Absorb the insider tips offered throughout the book.
- Become a student of the process and do your own research.

# DOLLAR DEBATES

## Negotiating Numbers

*"There is no safety in numbers, or in anything else."*

—JAMES THURBER

Negotiations over numbers are what most people think of when the word *negotiation* is mentioned. These are discussions between two parties—generally buyer and seller—in an effort to agree on a common number—generally a price.

Clearly it would be impossible to cover all the numeric or incremental negotiations you'll face in your life since they are as numerous as the number of possible buyers and sellers of products and services. In selecting which number negotiations to highlight in the full-length chapters and concluding capsule chapter, I've tried to cover what I think are the most important, common, and/or educational situations you'll face. My hope is that these examples will both address your most pressing needs and serve as guides in those number negotiations I didn't have the space to cover.

Just to make sure you're prepared for any situation that's not covered, let me go over a few generalities I've discovered over the years about number negotiations. Remember, these are axioms, not rules; they're things to remember and think about when you're going through the three steps.

---

## Prices are invitations to buy, not statements of value.

---

It's important to understand exactly what a number, or price, really is. In our culture we've been brought up to believe that a price tag, whether spoken or written, is a firm and authoritative assessment of value. Nothing could be further from the truth. *A price is actually an invitation to buy.* It's often more a proposal than a declaration. Sellers rarely base their numbers on some exact mathematical formula. Instead, their numbers are generally hopeful guesses at what someone will be willing to pay. Sure, an objective seller will make sure his price is greater than his cost, but when it comes to how much greater he too will be taking a guess.

> ## Terms are just as important as dollars when negotiating numbers.

In addition, price isn't the only thing that enters into a transaction. Terms of payment can have as much, if not more, of an impact on actual value. This can work two ways. A seller may accept payment below his stated price if you offer sweeter terms in lieu of the extra dollars. For instance, an item priced at $150 may be bought at $125 if you pay the seller all cash, up-front. The money in-hand may be worth more to him than the additional $50 in six months, or even a week from now. Conversely, as the purchaser, you may be willing to meet the seller's price of $150, as long as the terms of the deal are in your favor. You pay the ''full'' price—but over a period of time, which effectively lowers the actual price since you continue to have the use of that money until you have to pay it out in the future.

> ## You must negotiate a number with the person who sets it.

Because numbers are generally so slippery there is almost always room for negotiation. I'd go so far as to say that the only time a number isn't negotiable is when you're unable to deal with the person who set the price.

However, that doesn't mean you should negotiate every number: the potential money savings may not be worth the time and effort involved in getting through to the person who set the price. But if you can get beyond the notion that price tags are etched in stone and are the only element in a purchase or sale, a whole world of possibility will open up for you. By viewing prices as declarations of value, rather than as invitations to buy, we allow them to become obstacles to negotiating and, therefore, obstacles to getting the most from life.

# 5

# WAITING FOR THE GREAT UNZIPPING

## Buying a Home

*"Selling is essentially a transference of feeling."*

—ZIG ZIGLAR

When Fran and Bob's new daughter, Dana, began to walk rather than crawl, it became clear they'd need to move into a larger place. And rather than continue to throw money down the drain and rent, it made sense for them to buy. They carefully figured out how much they could afford to spend for shelter each month, in order to come up with an estimate of how large a mortgage they could carry. They then added to that figure a 20 percent down payment—which they'd raise from their savings and loans from their parents—to come up with an idea of how much they could afford to spend on a home. Next, Fran and Bob scouted around for areas that fit their needs: good schools for Dana and not too long a commute for Bob. Luckily, one of the suburban towns they'd targeted had homes in their price range.

## THE HOME BUYER'S SELF-EXAMINATION

In buying a home, as in every negotiation, the first step in the process is for the buyer to analyze needs and weigh options, to know himself or herself. That's accomplished by asking three questions: "What do I want?" "Is it worth my time?" "Is it important to me?"

### WHAT DO I WANT?—SETTING A SPECIFIC GOAL

Home buyers often make the mistake of initially setting too mercenary a goal. They say, "I want to buy this house as cheaply as possible." This mercenary tendency has become even more prominent since the collapse of the real estate market. Today, too many buyers are looking at the purchase of a home as an opportunity to make a killing. It's ironic, since most of these same would-be killers, once hooked on a particular home, become as meek as lambs. All thoughts of a killing vanish once they've fallen in love with a home. At that point they do everything possible "not to lose" what has become the home of their dreams.

Rather than having such a mercenary and impossible-to-keep goal, you should establish two realistic goals for yourself, one general and one specific. Your general goal should be *to buy the best home you possibly can, in the area you're interested in, while staying within your budget.* That's not as simple as it sounds. When shopping for a home two things often happen: your price range starts creeping upward, and your target area starts expanding. These are natural reactions to the fact that there are only a limited number of properties for sale at any one time. Once a broker has shown you everything that fits your initial criteria and hasn't gotten a nibble from you, he understandably broadens the criteria so he can show you more. And just as understandably, since you're in the market to buy, you accept this broadening. However, my advice is to stick as closely as possible to your initial criteria. As time passes new houses will come on the market and homes that were once out of your price range will be reduced and become accessible. The secret is patience.

Once you've found a house that appears to meet your criteria, you should immediately set a new, more specific goal: *to buy this home, from this buyer, within a reasonable period of time, for the best price you possibly can.* This goal helps you focus on the really important factor in successfully negotiating the purchase of a home—the needs of the seller— rather than concentrating on getting the lowest price possible. Serious sellers are always selling for a reason and are always under some time pressure. Even if there's no external time factor, the time value of money will come into play: the sooner a seller has his money in the bank, the more interest he'll earn.

## IS IT WORTH MY TIME?— DECIDING IF IT'S READILY NEGOTIABLE

Home prices are negotiable as long as both seller and buyer truly desire to transfer ownership. Since real estate values are actually set by the market, an aware seller should understand that the value of his home is based not on what he thinks it's worth, or what he paid for it, but on what a buyer is willing to pay for it. But in the early stages of a negotiation you can only find out if a home is readily negotiable by learning as much as you can about the seller and the recent sales history of the home.

There are basically three types of sellers: flexible, firm, and virginal. A flexible seller is one who understands that you, the potential buyer, determine the value of his home. A firm seller is one who refuses to concede that power and is determined to obtain his price, regardless of whether or not it's realistic. A virginal seller is one who has just placed his home up for sale, and therefore there is no past history you can use to determine whether he'll be firm or flexible. I'll explain how to determine what type of seller you're up against in the section on gathering information. But for now, suffice it to say that homes being sold by flexible sellers are readily negotiable, homes being sold by firm sellers aren't readily negotiable, and homes being sold by virginal sellers may or may not be readily negotiable.

## IS IT IMPORTANT TO ME?—
## MAKING SURE IT'S WORTH DOING

It's almost always worth negotiating to buy a home since the potential financial savings can be substantial. In fact, I can think of only two cases when it's not worth negotiating. The first case is if the seller is so inflexible as to make negotiating a very long, tiresome process. I honestly believe, given enough time, you could successfully negotiate with even the most inflexible home seller. However, it may not be worth the effort. There isn't only one home that's right for you—there are many homes that could be right. Time wasted by trying to negotiate for an unobtainable "dream home" is better spent looking for another "dream home" that's more readily negotiable.

The second case when it's not worth negotiating is when you clearly cannot afford to buy a particular home. Sure, you may be able to talk the seller of that $500,000 country manor down to $400,000. But if your credit history, savings, and income add up to your only being able to afford $200,000, what's the point? Negotiating shouldn't be a game. It's hard work for everyone involved. That means it should only be entered into if there's a good chance of it turning out successfully.

Fran and Bob's self-examination helped them focus on the task ahead. They tried to refrain from recession-inspired greed and set as their goal to buy the best home they could, for $200,000 or less, in the community they'd selected. After a couple of weeks of shopping around, the broker tried to interest them in stepping up to the next price level, or to persuade them to consider another community. Fran and Bob stuck to their guns and one week later were rewarded by finding a home that seemed to meet their needs. It had just been reduced in price, indicating it was readily negotiable. And clearly it was worth negotiating since it was within their price range. Next, Fran and Bob moved on to the second step—know your opponent—and began to level the playing field.

## LEVELING THE HOME BUYING PLAYING FIELD

The second step in negotiating the purchase of a home is for the buyer to get to know his or her opponent and to use that information to level the playing field. This is done by answering four questions: "What do I need to know?" "With whom should I negotiate?" "Are there any potentially disruptive side issues?" "What do I share with my opponent?"

### WHAT DO I NEED TO KNOW?— GATHERING INFORMATION

Information is vital to successfully negotiating the purchase of real estate. First, you'll need to learn everything you can about the property itself. Then you'll need to gather all the information you can about the needs and wants of the seller. Luckily, when it comes to real estate, there are many sources of information.

Ask your broker for a list of comparables (recent sales of properties similar to the one you're interested in). The information on comparables will provide you with some idea as to how those houses stack up to the one you're looking at. Still, make it your business to stop by and look at them in person as well. You may not be able to get inside, but you'll be able to compare exterior conditions as well as locations.

Once you've got a good idea of how the property you're interested in compares to recent sales, you can move on to gathering information about the seller through observation and infiltration. In most cases, sellers will absent themselves from the scene when you come to look at the house—at least if they're smart. Still, you can gain a lot of insight into a person from the decor, style, and tidiness of his home. The best way to learn about the seller, however, is to use a spy—your real estate broker. Ask your broker about both the seller and the history of the listing. Is the seller married or single? How old is he? Does he have children? What does he do for a living? How long has he lived in the home? Why is he moving? How long has the house been on the market? Have there been any other offers? If so, why didn't they work out? How many people have looked at the house recently?

Don't feel that you're being excessively nosy. Your eagerness for information will demonstrate to the broker you're a serious, astute buyer—

and that tells him he'll eventually get a commission from working with you.

Once you've gathered all your information you can analyze it and try to determine the seller's primary needs and wants, what pressures are bearing on him, and what type of negotiator he'll be. For example: Someone who has been transferred to another area needs to sell as quickly as possible. If he has had the house on the market for some time and has reduced his price, he's clearly flexible. On the other hand, someone who's selling simply because he wants to buy a bigger home in the area, and who has had his home on the market for a long period of time without reducing his price, probably isn't a serious seller—he's just fishing for the right price. Without any pressure to sell he'll be content to wait for a sucker—excuse me, naive buyer—to come along.

## WITH WHOM SHOULD I NEGOTIATE?— PUSHING THE UP BUTTON

Logically you should be negotiating directly with the owner of the home you want to buy. However, logic doesn't always work in residential real estate transactions. In most cases you'll actually be working through a variety of professionals rather than dealing directly with the owner. Both you and the seller should have real estate brokers, who may or may not be the same person. And both you and the seller should have your own attorneys, who clearly won't be the same person. That makes for a possible four intermediaries between you and the seller. While this can lead to confusion, it can also be a blessing.

Intermediaries offer you an opportunity to gain information and float trial balloons. Brokers, in the final analysis, are concerned solely with closing a deal—that's the only way they make money. You can use this concern to your benefit. Brokers can be excellent sources of information about the other side, and can also be used as powerful advocates for your position. If a broker believes you won't go above a certain price, he'll turn around and put pressure on the seller to make a deal; he may even offer to cut his commission. Your attorney can often be used to float trial balloons. If you want to make an offer, or use a maneuver, that could potentially upset the other side, have your attorney do it. That way, if it backfires, you can turn around and disavow the maneuver, blame the attorney, and still be in a position to close the deal.

Another advantage of having intermediaries is their ability to help steer you past potential problems in the seller's camp. You'd be surprised how many times I've been involved in real estate negotiations in which the problem was the attitude of one spouse. For example, recently I was helping a client buy a home. The sellers were relocating and were under extreme time pressure. They'd bought the home at the peak of the market, had invested considerable money in renovating it, and now were selling at the bottom of the market. That meant they probably weren't even going to get their money back. They were wealthy enough not to have been overly concerned with the financial loss, but the husband refused to negotiate. He was fixated on getting back the money he'd invested, regardless of what the market was like. My client and I probed the real estate brokers for information. It turned out that it had been the husband's idea to buy and renovate this house, and it was also his idea to relocate. His pride wouldn't let him take a loss. In order to work around this problem, my client and I approached the sellers' broker and asked him to bypass the husband and approach the wife. He did, and we found the wife to be much more flexible and realistic. With the wife in effect serving as an advocate for us, we were able to successfully negotiate the purchase of the property. The message of the story is: Don't assume there's unity in the sellers' camp—and don't be afraid to reach out to the intermediaries for help.

Before we eliminate the dissonance in a home-buying transaction I want to warn you about virginal sellers. I mentioned that flexible sellers are readily negotiable, that firm sellers aren't readily negotiable, but that you can't really tell whether virginal sellers—who have just put their house on the market—will be firm or flexible. Because of their unpredictable nature, I encourage my clients not to deal with virginal sellers. If they find a house that has just come on the market, and that no one has yet bid on, I suggest they refrain from making an offer for at least one or two weeks (unless, of course, it's an active sellers' market and the house is priced properly). While it can be tough to do, there's a reason for this self-denial. Virginal sellers often respond very poorly to the first offer they receive. Since they're not used to the give-and-take process, and probably have an inflated idea of the value of their home (which was encouraged by brokers to get the listing), they tend to get angry at someone who shatters their illusion.

I've seen the scenario play itself out time and time again. The first offer comes in, the seller gets insulted, assumes there will be other offers, and the deal falls through. The buyer goes on to something else, while the seller waits for another offer . . . and waits . . . and waits. After a while the seller kicks himself for having thrown away the opportunity and lowers the price. Rather than having to go through this, I tell my clients to let listings sit on the market for a while so the seller at least gets a sense that people won't be banging down his door with offers. If I can't convince them to wait, I tell the broker of my worries and hope he can temper the seller's angry response to a lower-than-expected offer.

## ARE THERE ANY POTENTIALLY DISRUPTIVE SIDE ISSUES?—ELIMINATING DISSONANCE

Once you've analyzed your information about the house and the seller you'll be able to determine what side issues may cloud the negotiation and set about eliminating them. The most typical types of seller dissonance are depression over having to face up to the actual value of the home, an emotional attachment to the home reflected in a desire to sell it to "the right kind of people," and an irrational demand often brought on by not really wanting to sell.

Depression over having to face up to the actual value of a home is understandable. How would you feel if you'd bought a home for $150,000 in 1987, put another $20,000 in renovations into it in the past five years, and found, when you put it on the market in 1992, its value was still only $150,000 . . . or perhaps had even dropped to $130,000? That's become an all-too-familiar scenario for today's home sellers. The way you as a buyer eliminate this dissonance is to refrain from gloating. It helps neither you nor your negotiations to shrug off such news. Instead, be compassionate . . . and let the seller know you're compassionate. Let your broker pass on your message. Express your sympathy for the seller's plight. Of course, your sympathy isn't going to extend to offering him more than the home is worth, but simply showing compassion can help make the seller feel better. And it'll put you in a better light as well.

That can be important because for many people the sale of a home is a traumatic event. To you this is only a house, but to the seller it's a "home," with all the emotional baggage that word entails. You may see a marked-up door frame but the owner sees a height chart for his children. You may see a broken shingle but the owner sees his son playing basketball in the backyard. People don't part with such an integral part of their lives without wanting some emotional, as well as financial, compensation. Praise the character of the home ceaselessly. Talk about how you can tell it was loved and cherished, how you can see the care and concern that went into every detail of the decor—even if it looks as if it was thrown together overnight. Your goal is to demonstrate to the seller you're the kind of person who'll treat his home with the respect it's due. If you're planning on gutting the whole addition the seller painstakingly (but incompetently) constructed himself, don't tell him about it. Admire his work and keep your demolition ideas to yourself.

Finally, don't be surprised if at some point the seller brings up some seemingly irrational minor point, especially if he's being forced to sell. Many times people who don't want to sell their home, but must, subconsciously try to sabotage the deal. It's a last desperate grasp at preventing the unwanted from happening.

In one situation I recall, a deal was just about completed when the real estate broker called me up and said the owners had decided they needed to keep the washer and dryer. My clients, the buyers, were understandably upset. They were stretching their resources to make the buy, and the appliances had been included all along. What was actually happening was that one of the owners—the wife—didn't really want to sell. This was her final shot at derailing the process. I told my clients to simply agree to the sellers' demand but to say they'd then need to lower their price by $1,000 so they could buy a new washer and dryer. The sellers agreed even though the extra $1,000 could have bought them a much better washer and dryer than the ones they'd be taking with them.

The moral of the story is: When a seller becomes irrational, go along with him. Extract a price for your concession, but don't allow him to subconsciously derail the process. And in order to diffuse such dissonance early on, acquiesce to the seller's every whim. If he doesn't want to sell the light fixtures in the dining and living rooms let him keep them. If he says the switch plates in the bedrooms don't convey, let them go. Don't let minor matters stand in the way of a successful negotiation.

### WHAT DO I SHARE WITH MY OPPONENT?— FINDING AND DEMONSTRATING COMMON GROUND

The common ground you're looking to establish and demonstrate to the seller is that you're willing to pay a fair price for his home—and to do everything possible to make the transition a smooth one—in exchange for his accepting a fair price. This is demonstrated first by stating just that to your broker, having the message passed along to the seller, and then by continually being the proverbial "nice guy." Use every opportunity you have to compliment the seller and his home and to mention how much you love it. Agree readily to everything he asks for . . . within reason. And present your own needs as being "fair." By doing this you'll show you're an average "nice" person who happens to be trying to buy his home for a low, but "fair," price, not a shark taking advantage of his economic misfortune.

Fran and Bob began leveling the playing field by doing formal research on recent home sales in the area. They asked their broker for comparables and spent a day driving around to see them and then analyzing how they stacked up against the home they were interested in. They then asked the broker a great many questions about the seller. They found out the home was owned by a widow whose children had grown and left the area, and who now wanted to leave as well. She didn't seem to be under time pressure but was apparently flexible, since, after not getting any offers on her home for two months, she had just reduced her price. Fran and Bob analyzed their information and guessed the widow had decided to sell and just wanted the whole thing done with. She was represented by a real estate broker, indicating that while she was the person to negotiate with, the two brokers could be used as intermediaries. Sensing she might have been afraid of being taken advantage of, Fran and Bob made sure to eliminate dissonance by demonstrating they wanted to be fair and weren't interested in making a killing. They repeatedly mentioned they could tell this was a good place to raise a family, how much they loved the house, and that they were looking forward to raising their own family in the house. They passed word to the seller that they were interested in buying for a fair price and hoped she was interested in selling for a fair price. Then they began formulating their first offer.

## INSIDER TIPS FOR HOME BUYERS

The third and final step in negotiating the purchase of a home is to know the situation. That's accomplished by applying the lessons learned by those who are experienced with this particular situation. From my own thirty-five-plus years of experience in negotiating real estate transactions, as well as from the research I conducted for this book, I've culled five insider tips for you to remember when negotiating the purchase of a home.

First, the more you can take on the garb of an all-cash buyer the more concessions you'll be able to get from the seller.

Second, initial offers should be based on what *you* perceive the home's value to be, and should effectively set the parameters for the rest of the negotiation.

Third, the seller's response to your offer often indicates where he's willing to settle.

Fourth, your subsequent concessions should come in decreasing increments and be supplemented by nonfinancial concessions.

And fifth, rather than simply accepting a final offer, you should close the deal with a final ''but.''

### TAKE ON THE GARB OF AN ALL-CASH BUYER

All-cash buyers invariably pay lower prices for homes than those who must obtain mortgages. That's because an all-cash buyer represents a speedy and definite sale for the seller: there will be no delay while the buyer applies for the mortgage and no chance the deal will fall through due to the bank's rejecting the mortgage application. Unfortunately, not everyone can be an all-cash buyer. However, you can take on the appearance of an all-cash buyer, making yourself a more attractive purchaser, and hopefully gain more concessions. The secret is to prequalify for a mortgage.

Banks grant mortgages based on two factors: your willingness and ability to make the monthly payments, and the value of the property (most banks will only loan up to 80 percent of the value of a home). Its judgment on your character and financial status is based on your credit history and your net worth and income. Its judgment on the value of the home is based on an independent appraisal. That means a bank can readily and quickly make half the mortgage determination—that you're a good credit risk and are capable of paying back a loan of up to a certain amount—in advance of your actually finding a property and agreeing on a price. By having yourself prequalified you can turn to a seller and offer him the assurance that you'll be able to obtain a mortgage to buy his home, since you've already been approved. The only stumbling blocks remaining are the selling price and the appraised value of the home. This way you take on some of the advantages of the all-cash buyer without actually having to come up with the cash.

While many banks have formal prequalification programs, I suggest you avoid the fees and paperwork they entail and go through an informal procedure. Contact an officer or manager of a bank you've dealt with in the past. Explain to him that you're shopping for a home and would like his help. Ask him to informally look over your credit record and financial records and make a nonbinding judgment of whether or not you'd qualify for a mortgage and approximately how much you'd be able to borrow. Once he has made these judgments, ask him to write you a letter explaining them. This letter, while not a formal binding mortgage qualification, can be shown to brokers and sellers as proof that you won't have any trouble getting a mortgage.

### BASE INITIAL OFFERS ON YOUR PERCEPTION OF THE HOME'S VALUE

Being able to cloak yourself in the mantle of an all-cash buyer will be helpful when it comes to the second insider tip: your first offer. It's important to remember that you, as a buyer, determine the value of real estate. The seller's asking price is nothing more than a wish or a guess. It should have no bearing whatsoever on your first offer. Instead, your offer should be based on two factors: the appraised value of the home, and how much it's worth to you.

Real estate appraisals can cost anywhere from $100 to $300 and are, I believe, a sine qua non for savvy negotiating. A real estate appraisal is a mathematical analysis based on comparable recent sales that balances out the differences between those homes and the one being appraised. Being purely mathematical, appraisals don't take into account aesthetic judgments. The invariable result is that the appraised value of a house is below the actual market value—a fact you can use to your advantage. I suggest that you have an appraisal done before you make an offer on a home. Tell the broker to pass word to the seller that you'll be making an offer but only after you receive the results of an appraisal. If the broker tries to push you into making an offer sooner rather than later, resist. Explain that you don't want to make an offer that's too high and then have to take it off the table—or make an offer that's so low as to be insulting. If the broker says there may be competition, tell him that in that case you won't be making any offer.

Many times, sellers and brokers imply or actually say there are other buyers interested in a house. Whether or not it's true, competition is used by sellers to try to turn a two-way negotiation—buyer versus seller—into a three-way negotiation—buyer versus buyer versus seller. This almost certainly will guarantee a higher price since the natural competitiveness of the two buyers will come out. The house is suddenly more desirable since someone else wants it too. And now not only do you need to "beat" the seller, you first need to "beat" the other buyer. I saw this happen to a very affluent film star client of mine recently. He was looking for a summer home in a very exclusive area where few properties come on the market. The broker showed him a home that was terribly overpriced and really didn't meet his needs. Yet the broker also dropped a few hints that another film star was interested in the house. Suddenly it no longer became a matter of just buying a home—for my client it was a battle against this other actor. It was only after I did some digging and was able to prove that the competitor was a figment of the broker's active imagination that I was able to break my client of his desire to compete for the house.

My advice is to avoid competition at all costs. If you find someone else is bidding on the property, tell the broker you'll be stepping out of the process. Say that if the seller isn't able to close a deal with this other party he should contact you. Similarly, threaten to step out of the negotiation if the broker hints there may be competition. Tell him you're not about to enter into an auction and will refuse to bid on a house at the same time someone else is bidding. If he's fabricating the competition, all mention of it will soon drop. If it's true, and there is someone else interested, you'll do better not getting involved in a three-way negotiation.

While you're waiting for your appraisal, make a list of all the things you'd need to do to the property. If the kitchen must be renovated, write it down. Bathrooms redone, take note of it. Wallpaper removed, list it. Once your list is complete, take a look at one of the home renovation or home improvement books on the market that list the average costs of such work (my own book, *The Big Fix Up,* offers this information in chart form). Note approximately how much each project will cost and come up with a total. In order to come up with a bottom line for your first offer, subtract the total cost of fix-up projects from the appraised value.

This number, however, may not be your first offer. If it's so low as to be insulting (more than 20 percent below the sales of comparable homes) it could turn the seller off completely. What you're looking to do is seize the initiative with this offer. You want to clearly demonstrate that it's your judgment of value that counts, not the seller's or the broker's. And by using hard information, such as an appraisal and the costs of particular projects that need to be done, you demonstrate that your judgment is rational and objective. Remember, of course, this offer is just a starting point. It should be presented with the message that you're open to negotiation.

### THE SELLER'S RESPONSE INDICATES WHERE HE'S WILLING TO SETTLE

The seller's response to your offer brings me to the third insider tip, which I call "the great unzipping." Americans, uncomfortable as they are with negotiating and afraid of being perceived as unfair, reflexively seek to "split the difference" in number negotiations. If I ask $10 for an item, and you offer $5, the notion of settling at the midpoint—in this case, $7.50—almost instantly arises. In a real estate transaction, most sellers fall into this "split the difference" pattern and subconsciously demonstrate at what price they'd be willing to settle. Typically, the midpoint between your offer and his response would be an acceptable compromise for him. For example: If you offer $150,000 and a seller counters with $170,000, he's indicating his willingness to settle at $160,000. As long as you're aware of this "great unzipping" you can keep control of the remainder of the negotiation and bring the final price below that compromise midpoint you've uncovered.

By the way, you won't be guilty of making this same mistake with your first offer if it's based on what the home is worth to you, not the seller's asking price.

## CONCESSIONS SHOULD BE IN DECREASING INCREMENTS AND NOT JUST FINANCIAL

This is done through use of the fourth insider tip: concessions of decreasing increments coupled with nonfinancial concessions. Once a seller responds to your initial offer he's hooked. You see, in most areas—except for the rare sellers' markets—there are more sellers than there are buyers. There are literally hundreds of homes you could bid on, but there are only, at best, a handful of people who'll be bidding on homes up for sale. That means serious sellers must treat all but the most absurd offers as serious opportunities to sell. If the seller responds to your offer favorably, by lowering his price, believe me, he's hooked.

And once he's hooked the secret to obtaining a price close to your goal is to make continued price concessions but of decreasing size. For example: Let's say your first offer on a house that's listed for $200,000 is $150,000. The seller drops to $190,000. Your second price could be a $5,000 increase, to $155,000, which the seller responds to by dropping to $180,000. Your third offer should contain less than a $5,000 increase, and any subsequent increases should get progressively smaller and smaller. This signals two things to the seller: you're willing to negotiate, but there's a limit to how far you'll raise your price.

Once you've hooked the seller he's more likely to be willing to make steady decreases in his price. Rather than trying to "win," he's now trying not to lose you. He's happy someone has come around to buy his house and he's worried what will happen if this deal falls through. Will anyone else ever make an offer? Will he eventually need to reduce his asking price to get more interest? Why not just work with this offer? he tells himself. The voice inside his head, strengthened by tales he has been told by friends, relatives, and real estate brokers, is telling him one thing over and over: "Don't lose it."

In order to make these small price increases less uncomfortable for him, you should add nonfinancial concessions. For example: At a point where you feel your minute increase may be met with some anger, add a concession agreeing to close when the seller wants. The idea is to offer the seller other things he can take as victories, softening the apparent lack of financial victory.

Similarly, back up each increase you make with a reason. Remember, you've so far painted yourself as the arbiter of value and the epitome of logic. That means you must be increasing your offers for a reason. Go back to your list of repairs. When you increase your offer by $2,000, say you've decided you can live with the bathrooms the way they are. Or explain that the landscaping is so beautiful you think it's worth another

$1,000. As long as you give a reason for each new offer you keep your logical image. Lose that by increasing your offer without a reason, and the seller will assume you've begun bidding with your heart, not your head, and will sense you're willing to go much higher.

## CLOSE THE DEAL WITH A FINAL "BUT"

The best way to reinforce the idea that the negotiations are finite is to use the fifth insider tip: the final "but." Rather than simply agreeing to a final price, you should throw in a final "but" to close the deal. When you're ready to accept a seller's offer, or to propose a final offer of your own, add a condition to your acceptance. It could be anything from having him throw in the trash cans to asking him to put up the storm windows. The substance of the "but" is unimportant. What matters is that you're asking for one more concession. Otherwise, you leave the door open to further negotiations. An open-ended acceptance leaves the seller asking himself, "I wonder if the buyer would have gone higher?" By asking for something else, regardless of how obscure, you're saying, "I'll agree to buy at this price, but only if you agree to go along with my final request."

Now let's get back to Fran and Bob and see how they made out in their negotiation. The house they were interested in had an asking price of $220,000. Fran and Bob commissioned an appraisal that quoted a value of $175,000. Next, they made a list of all the work they'd need to do on the house, calculated what it would cost, and came up with a total of $5,000. They decided to make an initial offer of $170,000 along with their reasoning and a message that they were willing to negotiate. The seller responded with a counteroffer of $210,000, indicating to Fran and Bob she was probably willing to settle for $190,000. Fran and Bob next offered $175,000, saying they'd decided not to renovate the bathrooms right away. The seller responded by lowering her price to $200,000. Fran and Bob next offered $178,000 and said they'd be willing to close whenever the seller wished. The seller, thinking Fran and Bob probably wouldn't be willing to come much above $180,000, and afraid of losing the sale, dropped her price to $190,000. Fran and Bob then offered to settle at $180,000 as long as the seller threw in the lawn mower and other yard tools. The seller agreed.

# Waiting for the Great Unzipping
## Buying a Home

- Buy the best home you can, in the area you want, sticking to your budget.
- Buy this home, from this seller, quickly, for the lowest price possible.
- Use intermediaries to gather information.
- Don't assume seller unity.
- Learn the seller's needs.
- Appear fair, loving, and agreeable.
- Look like an all-cash buyer.
- Base initial offers on appraisals.
- First counter is the great unzipping.
- Increase offers in decreasing increments.
- Make nonfinancial concessions.
- Close the deal with a final "but."

# 6

# HOOKING 'EM AND REELING 'EM IN

## Selling Your Home

*"People don't buy for logical reasons. They buy for emotional reasons."*

—ZIG ZIGLAR

Freda wanted to sell her home. Since both her sons and their families had moved away, and her friends had begun to retire and move as well, she realized there was nothing holding her back from moving too— especially since most of her net worth was tied up in the home she and her late husband bought thirty years ago. But in order to both buy a nice home and retire, she needed to sell her present home for as much money as possible. With the real estate market in the doldrums that wouldn't be an easy task.

## THE HOME SELLER'S SELF-EXAMINATION

In selling a home, as in every negotiation you'll encounter, the first step in the process is for the seller to analyze needs and weigh options, to know him or herself. That's accomplished by asking three questions: "What do I want?" "Is it worth my time?" "Is it important to me?"

### *WHAT DO I WANT?—SETTING A SPECIFIC GOAL*

When setting a goal for the sale of your home, it's important to be realistic. Too many people set as their goal "to get as much money as possible." The problem with such an open-ended goal is you'll never know how much the next buyer will be willing to pay . . . so there's always the temptation to wait to find out. That's a recipe for disaster. The goal of a home seller must be both realistic and finite.

Every home has a definite market value. This value is primarily determined by location rather than the characteristics of the individual home. All the homes in a given area will have values within a range of approximately 30 percent. Let me explain. In an area where the average price of homes is around $100,000, the most magnificent home will probably sell for no more than $115,000, while the handyman's special around the corner will probably bring no less than $85,000. In another area, where homes hover around the $200,000 mark, the best house will go for $230,000 while the worst will fetch no less than $170,000. Therefore, the location of a home dictates the price range, while the characteristics of the individual house dictate where in the price range its value falls. So the first part of a home seller's goal should be to sell his home for a price at or near the top end of the value range. (Of course, the handyman's special will never sell for the very top, but through preparation and savvy negotiating it should be possible to bring it up to the middle of the range.)

But there's another factor involved as well: speed. Time truly is money . . . and when you're talking about a sizable sum such as the price of a house, time is a lot of money. Many home sellers fail to realize they'll often be better off selling quickly for a slightly lower price, and having the money in the bank earning interest or being put to a good use, than waiting and waiting for a slightly higher price. There's also a staleness factor that comes into play. When a house first comes on the market everyone comes to see it. The longer a house remains on the market unsold at a particular price, the fewer people who'll come around. It has become stale, and both buyers and brokers believe something is wrong with it or the owner—otherwise, they think, it would have sold already. So the second part of a home seller's goal should be to sell as quickly as possible.

All considerations taken together, then, a good goal for a home seller is *to sell his home for a price near the top of its value range as quickly as possible.*

### IS IT WORTH MY TIME?— DECIDING IF IT'S READILY NEGOTIABLE

Unless you price your home way above its value, everyone involved in the process, from buyers to brokers, will consider the number negotiable. In fact, home prices are considered perhaps the most negotiable numbers in America.

For some reason, the typical American reticence to haggle over numbers vanishes when it comes to buying a used home from its previous owner. Perhaps it's because the seller isn't a professional salesperson. The price tag put on the home is perceived by Americans as being more of a guess or wish than the logical, mathematical price tags put on items sold in stores. Of course that's nonsense. The prices of new homes—and everything else sold by professional salespeople, for that matter—are just as capriciously set as the prices on used homes sold by amateurs. But because they're developed by professionals and printed on computer-generated price tags, most Americans accept them as gospel.

The point I'm trying to make is most potential home buyers are going to see this transaction as eminently negotiable, and, in fact, wouldn't think of paying the price you're asking. That, of course, leads sellers in general to price their homes substantially higher than they'd be willing to accept. With buyers coming in intentionally low and sellers starting off artificially high you're guaranteeing a negotiation will take place.

The secret is to simply lure the buyer by signaling that you're in fact willing to move down in price. That's done by pricing your home just above its price range but just below a standard number. For instance, if your home is in the $85,000 to $115,000 price range, and merits a price at the top end of the range, you indicate flexibility by pricing it at $119,000 rather than $120,000. If it merits a price in the middle of the price range you could list it for $114,000 rather than $115,000. In effect, you're already cutting $1,000 from your price. It's the same psychology a store manager uses when he prices a television at $199 rather than $200.

## IS IT IMPORTANT TO ME?—
## MAKING SURE IT'S WORTH DOING

If you're ever tempted to forego the frustration and exasperation that often comes along with negotiating the sale of your home and to simply give in and sell cheaply, consider this: when you're talking about sums this large, even a small percentage translates into something important. The additional money you make by negotiating well can pay for furniture for your new house; it could finance the purchase of a new car; it could pay for a year's college tuition; it could pay for a fabulous vacation; it could mean being able to go out to dinner every week for a year; or it could buy a new wardrobe. In fact, it can be anything you want it to be—and isn't that worth the effort?

For Freda, negotiating was clearly important since she was counting on earning enough from the sale of her home to be able to both buy a new home and leave her job. Through investigation she knew her house was in the upper portion of the $170,000 to $230,000 range. She wanted to be able to move within four months. Her goal, therefore, was to sell her house for as close to $230,000 as possible within the next four months. She hired a real estate attorney early on and, in an effort to get near the top of the price range while still indicating flexibility, listed the home with a local real estate broker for $239,000. Within three days a young couple came by, and the broker told Freda they'd be making an offer. At that point, Freda began leveling the playing field.

## LEVELING THE HOME-SELLING PLAYING FIELD

The second step in negotiating the sale of a home is for the seller to get to know his or her opponent and to use that information to level the playing field. This is done by answering four questions: "What do I need to know?" "With whom should I negotiate?" "Are there any potentially disruptive side issues?" "What do I share with my opponent?"

### *WHAT DO I NEED TO KNOW?— GATHERING INFORMATION*

As soon as you learn you're about to get an offer on your house, start gathering as much information as you can. Gather all the facts on which you based your price, such as records of comparable sales and formal appraisals. If you haven't already done it, calculate how near it is to the closest school, house of worship, train station, bus stop, and shopping center. In general, gather all the positive information you can about your home and your neighborhood. With that in place, you can begin to gather information about your opponent—in this case, the potential buyer.

Since you probably weren't around when the buyer or buyers came to look at the house, observation won't do you any good. Instead, jump immediately to infiltration. As I mentioned earlier in this chapter, you've a ready-made spy on your team: the real estate broker. Ask the broker about the buyer. How old is he? Is he married? What does he do for a living? Does he have children? How old are they? Where is he living now? Does he currently rent or own? Why is he moving? Does he need to buy by a certain time? How will he be paying for the house—with a mortgage or cash? Is the broker sure he can afford to buy your house? How many other homes has he looked at? Has he made other offers? If so, what went wrong with the deals? Don't feel nosy. If your opponent is smart he'll be asking the broker just as many questions about you. Don't be afraid of asking open-ended or personal questions about the buyer: you never know what you might find out. One client of mine was quizzing her broker about a buyer and was about to finish when a light bulb suddenly lit up over her head. She had found out that the young man interested in her home was a first-time home buyer, in his early thirties, who was married with five children. He was an accountant and his wife was a full-time homemaker. Being Jewish herself, my client recognized that the buyer's last name sounded Jewish. That, coupled with the fact that they had five children at an early age, led her to believe they might be Orthodox Jews. The broker was also Jewish, so my client didn't feel too self-conscious in asking the question directly. When she found out her deduction was correct it placed the whole transaction in an entirely new light. You see, being Orthodox, the buyer wanted to be within walking distance of a synagogue. There was an Orthodox synagogue right around the block from her house. My client now knew her house had an added value to these buyers.

Your goal obviously is to learn everything you possibly can about the buyer with an eye toward figuring out his needs, wants, and motivations. Once you've gotten answers to all your questions, sit down and try to analyze what you've discovered. For example: Parents of school-age children generally want to be settled in a new home by the time school starts. The same goes for parents who themselves are involved in education. Buyers who have just been transferred to an area also have a tremendous time pressure—hotel bills are exorbitant. Young couples buying their first home may be eager to buy appliances and fixtures along with the house, since they may not have any money left over after closing. You're looking for any needs the buyer has other than money. The more you can fulfill those nonfinancial needs the fewer financial concessions you'll need to make.

## WITH WHOM SHOULD I NEGOTIATE?— PUSHING THE UP BUTTON

Obviously you're ultimately negotiating with the home buyer, but there may be many other parties involved. First, there may be a great many professionals standing between the two of you. Unless you're foolish, you'll have a real estate broker representing you. The buyer will probably also have a real estate broker, perhaps a different one than you're using. And both you and the buyer may have attorneys, like me, who get actively involved in the negotiating process. That means you may be involved in an elaborate and expensive game of telephone. Offers may originate with the buyer, go to his attorney, then to his broker, who relays them to your broker, who tells your attorney, who tells you . . . or some variation on this theme. While initially this indirect communication may seem like a handicap to successful and speedy negotiating, you can use it to your advantage.

Smart buyers will want to learn everything they possibly can about you, and will be using their brokers as spies to uncover your needs and motivations. You may similarly be using your broker as a spy to find everything possible about the buyer. As long as you're aware of the potential duplicity of real estate brokers you can use them to your advantage. It's not unlike the double-cross system that was used by British Intelligence in World War II. Rather than immediately arresting German spies, the British left them in place but fed them false information. In that way the British influenced what the Germans thought and did. By selectively passing along information to real estate brokers you can do the same.

Attorneys can also play a positive role in your negotiations. They can be used to float trial balloons that, if unsuccessful, can then be shot down. For example: Your attorney can play the bad guy and say you absolutely cannot accept anything less than $200,000 for your house—even though you'll be willing to accept $190,000. If the buyer believes it and pays up, you've earned yourself another $10,000. If the buyer balks, you can always step in and say, "My lawyer didn't know what he was talking about. Of course I'm willing to negotiate." So rather than avoiding all these professionals, my suggestion is to use them to your advantage.

But in order to do that effectively you'll need to know who's really making the buying decision. I've seen many deals go bad because, when push came to shove, someone other than the buyer or buyers was actually making the decisions. Often, although the young couple who'll be living in the house are prepared to buy, a parent who's supplying the down payment, co-signing the mortgage, or financing the whole deal vetoes the sale. If you're dealing with first-time home buyers I suggest you ask your broker to find out where the money is coming from. It may take some investigation, since the young couple may be embarrassed and might not want to admit their dependence on someone else, but it's vital to find out. You don't want to waste time and concessions negotiating with someone who doesn't have the power to say yes or no. If you discover there's a hidden power on the other side, insist your broker or lawyer negotiate with the source rather than the buyer.

## ARE THERE ANY POTENTIALLY DISRUPTIVE SIDE ISSUES?—ELIMINATING DISSONANCE

Much of the dissonance clouding the home-purchase transaction for a buyer can be dealt with prior to and after the actual negotiation. For example: The less your personality is present in the home when someone comes to look at it, the more they'll be able to project their own personality into the home; and the sooner after agreeing on a price you get the buyers' signatures on a contract, the fewer potentially dangerous second thoughts they'll have. You can find such information in books on home buying—including my own *The Field Guide to Home Buying in America*—but for the purposes of this discussion let me explain what you can do to eliminate dissonance during the negotiation itself.

The big fear of a home buyer is that he's going to be taken advantage of by a cunning negotiator—a shark. Since you probably won't see him or speak with him directly until after the negotiation is over, you won't be able to use your appearance or body language to put him at ease. And since you'll be doing some tough negotiating, he may fear you really are a shark. The solution to this dilemma is to pass innocuous but friendly messages to the buyer through the broker. Find nice things to say. For example: If the buyer has young children and your children are already grown, tell the broker to tell the buyer you're glad children will be enjoying the yard again. Say how good it was for your kids to be able to walk to school and how you're sure he'll feel the same. Say how much your children enjoyed being able to ride their bikes to the park at the end of the street and how you're sure his children will feel the same. Say how you're glad a family will be buying this house, which meant so much to your family. Don't worry about laying it on too thick. You want the buyer to worry about his possibly taking advantage of you rather than worrying about your taking advantage of him.

## WHAT DO I SHARE WITH MY OPPONENT?— FINDING AND DEMONSTRATING COMMON GROUND

This "we're all just plain folks" kind of atmosphere is the common ground you want to cultivate. By demonstrating that all you want is to get a fair price for your home, and by saying you're sure all he wants is to buy it for a fair price, you're laying out common ground that's safe and inviting. You're saying you're not a shark, and that, we hope, will be enough to keep him from acting like a shark. You're painting pictures of you and your children returning years from now to the ancestral home and sharing a cup of coffee with the new residents. Sure, it's all fiction. You may want to get out of there and never come back. But by playing into this warm, romantic vision of home ownership you're tapping into something that's deep within the heart of all but the most mercenary home buyer.

\*     \*     \*

Freda leveled the playing field by first gathering all the information she could about recent sales in the area, the school district, and the community in general. Once she learned the potential buyers were a married couple with two school-age boys, she knew they'd want to be in the house by August at the latest. When she learned the husband commuted by train into the city, she knew her proximity to the railroad station was an added value. She eliminated some of the buyers' dissonance by passing word to the buyers through the broker that she had raised two sons in this house, that they had loved playing basketball in the backyard and other sports at the school around the corner, and that she was sure the buyers' two sons would feel the same. She also passed word that she was glad a young family would be moving into the house, since that's what she, her late husband, and her two sons had done thirty years earlier. She established her common ground with the buyer by saying that since she was retiring and moving away all she really wanted was a fair price, and that she was sure he felt the same.

## INSIDER TIPS FOR HOME SELLERS

The third and final step in negotiating the purchase of a home is to know the situation. That's accomplished by applying the lessons learned by those who are experienced with this particular situation. From my thirty-five-plus years of experience negotiating real estate sales, as well as from my research for this book, I've developed four insider tips for you to remember when negotiating the sale of your home.

First, your initial counteroffer must hook the buyer.

Second, any financial concessions should come in decreasing increments and be accompanied by nonmonetary concessions.

Third, you must add a final "but" to close the deal.

And fourth, you must beware the predatory buyer.

### THE INITIAL COUNTEROFFER MUST HOOK THE BUYER

Your response to the buyer's initial offer is the single most important part of the home-selling negotiation. I call it "the great unzipping," meaning it exposes the seller's actual desires. Let me explain. As I've mentioned throughout this book, Americans are very uncomfortable about negotiating. As a result they try to make it as simple and, presumably, fair as possible. This leads to a "split the difference" mentality.

Rather than trying to "win" a negotiation, Americans almost instinctively seek to make an even compromise. If one party says he'll pay $5, and the other says she wants $10, both almost reflexively offer to "split the difference" and settle at $7.50. In a residential real estate transaction this expresses itself in the seller's first counteroffer. Almost invariably, a seller's counteroffer indicates where he's willing to settle. The seller picks a number that is the same distance above his desired price as the buyer's initial offer is below the desired price. That way he sets up a "split the difference" solution. For example: A house is on the market for $100,000. The buyer offers $85,000. The seller is willing to settle at $90,000, so he comes back with a counteroffer of $95,000, hoping the buyer will suggest splitting the difference at the desired $90,000 level.

As long as you're aware of this tendency you can use it to your advantage in the negotiation. The way to do that is to appear to send the message the buyer wants. By making a sizable first concession to all legitimate offers and seeming to indicate a split-the-difference approach, you effectively hook the buyer. Let me explain.

Buyers have been counseled by everyone, including me, to avoid falling in love with a home before they've bought it. That way they'll be better able to negotiate and less likely to overspend. This advice works well up to a point. A buyer is, of course, already in love with a home when he decides to make a bid—otherwise why try to buy it—but he tries to repress his feelings. Once you, the seller, respond to the buyer's initial offer with a substantial concession, apparently indicating a compromise solution the buyer can afford, the buyer is no longer able to repress his love for the home. As soon as you come back with a counteroffer that the buyer thinks indicates he can make a deal, the love affair with the house bursts into bloom. He begins picturing himself in the den, his wife begins picking out furniture, his kids see themselves playing in the yard, and you've got him hooked.

## CONCESSIONS SHOULD BE IN DECREASING INCREMENTS AND NOT JUST FINANCIAL

And once the buyer is hooked, you shift from "splitting the difference" to decreasing increments, the second insider tip. The secret to obtaining a price close to your goal is to make continued price concessions, but of decreasing size. For example: If your first counteroffer is a $5,000 drop from your asking price, your second price could be a $3,000 drop, your third a $1,000 drop, and your fourth a $500 drop. This signals two things to the buyer: you're willing to negotiate, but there is a limit to how far you'll drop your price.

Once you've hooked the buyer he's more likely to be willing to make steady increases in his offers since, rather than trying to "win," he's now trying not to lose. He considers himself a winner already since you made a substantial first concession. Now, his family, friends, and the voice inside his head are telling him one thing over and over: "Don't lose it."

In order to make these price increases less uncomfortable for him, you should add nonfinancial concessions to your decreasing financial concessions. For example: At one point where you feel your minute decrease may be met with some anger, add a concession agreeing to close when the buyer wants; at another point offer to include an appliance or fixture in which the buyer might have expressed interest. The idea is to offer the buyer other things he can take as victories, softening the lack of financial victory.

## CLOSE THE DEAL WITH A FINAL "BUT"

Your constantly decreasing concessions should be sufficient to convince the buyer the negotiations are finite. But just in case the message hasn't sunk in, there's another insider tip you can use to drive the point home. Rather than simply agreeing to a final price, you should throw in a final "but" to close the deal. When you're ready to accept a buyer's offer, or to propose a final offer of your own, add a condition to your acceptance. It could be anything from needing to close on a Wednesday to retaining possession of the mailbox. The substance of the "but" isn't important. What's important is you're asking him to make one further concession. Without this final "but" you leave the door open to further negotiations. An open-ended acceptance leaves the buyer asking himself, "I wonder if the seller would have gone lower?" By asking for something else, regardless of how obscure, you're saying, "I'll agree to sell at this price only if you agree to go along with my final 'but.' " It works every time.

## BEWARE THE PREDATORY BUYER

The fourth and final insider tip for home sellers is a warning about the tactics of some buyers in slow real estate markets. Unless you're prepared for the bullying tactics they adopt you may find yourself unable to deflect the assaults. Here are some things to watch out for.

The most predatory types of buyers that come out of the woodwork during slow markets are bottom fishermen and "all-cash" buyers. A bottom fisherman is an individual who is looking to steal a house. He preys on seller desperation and generally makes very low initial offers, which he implies are his final bids. A subspecies of the bottom fisherman is the "all-cash" buyer. The quotes I've placed around "all-cash" are intentional. This individual, realizing the power of all-cash offers, claims to be ready to pay cash, while actually all he's trying to do is get you to make a dramatic price concession. Once he has forced a seller down, his "all-cash" status disappears for one reason or another. By then, the seller has probably taken the house off the market and invested considerable time in the negotiation, often too much time to be able to back out.

The best way to deal with these real estate scavengers is to call their bluffs. When a bottom fisherman makes a ridiculously low offer—more than 20 percent below the value of your home—refuse to respond. Instead, say you're willing to negotiate and will respond to all "serious" offers, but that his offer isn't serious. If the potential buyer was just a wise guy, this should be enough to scare him off his bottom fisherman posture. If he truly is a bottom fisherman he'll vanish and start looking for other, more desperate, prey. When someone makes a relatively low offer, claiming it's "all-cash," ask for proof of his all-cash status before responding. This could be a letter from a bank stating he has been prequalified for a mortgage or some proof of the financial resources he claims to have at his disposal. If he actually is an all-cash buyer, he will respond accordingly. If he backs off his "all-cash" posture, respond with a very small concession—perhaps $1,000—indicating your willingness to negotiate but your awareness of his ill-conceived gambit.

Very often, a bold buyer will place a time limit on his offers or will pass word through the brokers that this is his "final offer." My advice is to ignore all such statements. Generally they're the sign of a frustrated negotiator. The buyer is probably angry at you for not making larger concessions, is feeling the pressure, and is striking out in an effort to make you as uncomfortable as he is. It's the negotiating equivalent of saying "Oh yeah? Well, I'll show you."

If an offer comes in with a time limit, respond as you would have if there were no time limit attached. My own pride would probably lead me to intentionally exceed the time limit and then respond with a counteroffer. But I suppose that's just childish. If you'd normally have responded within the time limit, do so. If not, don't worry. As soon as you respond the time limit will be forgotten. Similarly, any time you're given a final offer, treat it like any other. Respond with a counteroffer but add a simple message: have the broker tell the buyer that you're willing to negotiate. Your continued flexibility will be enough to turn that "final offer" into just one more offer.

Sometimes a bold buyer will try to make a seller wait for a response, hoping a desperate seller will bid against himself. *Never bid against yourself.* Once you've shown the buyer you'll lower your price without his raising his offer you've fallen into a bottomless pit. The buyer now knows he can simply wait and you'll drop your price again and again. Instead, if a buyer doesn't respond to one of your counteroffers, have the broker send him a message. Simply say that you remain willing to negotiate and that you're willing to make price concessions in response to serious price increases on his part. If the buyer doesn't come back he wasn't a serious buyer.

Let's see how Freda handled her negotiation. As I mentioned earlier, Freda listed her house in May at $239,000. Her goal was to sell for a price as close to $230,000 as possible within four months—or by September. She received an offer of $199,000 from a young couple with school-age children. In an attempt to hook the buyer she responded with a counteroffer of $235,000, a drop of $4,000, apparently indicating to the buyer she'd be willing to settle at around $217,000—the midpoint between the offer of $199,000 and her counteroffer.

The buyer, sensing victory, immediately came back with another offer, this time of $212,000, assuming Freda would come back with $217,000 and the deal would be done. Instead, Freda began reducing her concessions. She next came back with $232,500, a drop of $2,500. The buyer, afraid to lose the home he'd already pictured as his own, but unsure of what was happening, came up to $215,000. Freda wasn't deterred. She responded with another decreasing concession, down $1,500 to $231,000, but added a nonfinancial concession, a willingness to close within thirty days.

The buyer, now seeing what price range Freda was looking for, increased his bid to $220,000, rationalizing the increase by saying that at least he'd be in the house before school started in September. Freda, undaunted, dropped another $1,000 to $230,000, and offered to throw in the washer, dryer, and refrigerator. The buyer, thoroughly hooked, and happy he wouldn't need to go out and buy appliances, raised his bid to $225,000.

Freda came back with an offer to settle at $229,500 as long as the closing could be held on a Friday—a final "but." The buyer, convinced he'd won since Freda had come down a total of around $10,000, and tired of the back-and-forth negotiations, agreed.

# Hooking 'Em and Reeling 'Em In
## Selling Your Home

- Sell your home quickly for a price close to the top of its value.
- Set your price above what you're willing to accept.
- Negotiate with whoever is paying.
- Use intermediaries as spies.
- Learn buyers' needs, wants, and motivations.
- Demonstrate fairness and ask for it in return.
- Make a sizable first concession to set the hook.
- Subsequent price concessions decrease in size.
- Make nonfinancial concessions.
- Close the deal with a final "but."

# 7

# TURNING THE HEAT
# ON LANDLORDS

## Renting a Home or Apartment

*"A landlord is supposed to be brutal, stingy, insulting, and arrogant. Like the police, like the magistrates, like all the authority figures of white society. That's what we're used to. That's what we understand. We're accustomed to our enemies, we know how to deal with them. A landlord who tries to be a friend only confuses us."*

—KRISTIN HUNTER

When Robert agreed to take a new job on the other side of the country he knew finding a place to live would be difficult. His job took up most of his time, so it was tough to go apartment hunting. He was getting depressed living out of a hotel room, so he finally enlisted the help of a real estate agent. Still, it took the agent nearly three weeks to find an apartment Robert liked that was within his price range. The agent, who had just about exhausted his listings, breathed a sigh of relief. When he and Robert got back to the real estate office, the agent pulled a lease form out from his desk and asked Robert to sign. But despite his understandable eagerness to get settled in his new apartment, Robert stepped back from the situation and realized that by signing immediately he'd effectively close the door on a negotiation opportunity.

## THE RENTER'S SELF-EXAMINATION

In renting a home or apartment, as in every negotiation you'll encounter, the first step in the process is for the seller to analyze needs and weigh options, to know him- or herself. That's accomplished by asking three questions: "What do I want?" "Is it worth my time?" "Is it important to me?"

### WHAT DO I WANT?—SETTING A SPECIFIC GOAL

A tenant's main goal in an apartment lease negotiation shouldn't be to obtain a lower rent. When buying a home, people assume the price is negotiable, so they look at properties priced higher than they can afford. But with renting, it's generally assumed by both sides that the rent is nonnegotiable. Therefore, in most cases, the rent that has been quoted either by the landlord or the agent is obviously acceptable to the tenant, otherwise he wouldn't have looked at the apartment in the first place. If a landlord knows his rent is acceptable to you, you stand little chance of negotiating it down.

However, there are elements to the transaction that can be negotiated, such as the terms of the lease, the size of security deposits, and the way the rent is distributed. Wouldn't you like to have some money available to furnish and decorate your new apartment? Wouldn't you feel more secure if the lease protected you as well as the landlord? Therefore, a good goal in this negotiation might be: to conserve as much of your cash as possible and make the lease as evenhanded a document as you can.

### IS IT WORTH MY TIME?— DECIDING IF IT'S READILY NEGOTIABLE

Apartment leases are always negotiable—even though landlords and renting agents say otherwise. Rental agreements are almost always printed documents drawn up by attorneys who represent landlords. The fact that they're printed standard forms is often enough to keep some tenants from negotiating. But you shouldn't let their appearance deter you from altering them. These are truly one-sided documents, often containing clauses and provisions that are actually illegal. In an economic environment such as today's, with real estate sales lagging and apartment vacancies on the rise, tenants are in an excellent opportunity to negotiate lease terms. Once you demonstrate to the landlord you're not going to accept the lease contract as gospel, his pretense that the document isn't negotiable will vanish.

### IS IT IMPORTANT TO ME?—MAKING SURE IT'S WORTH DOING

There are three ways to look at the value of negotiating a lease. First, there's an economic value to reducing the amount of cash you must commit up front. Any cash expenditures you can defer or eliminate can then be applied to other needs, such as furnishing and decorating the apartment. In addition, cash is always better in your pocket than in someone else's—in this case, a landlord's—since it can earn you interest.

Second, there's a legal value to altering the terms of the lease agreement. While expanded landlord obligations and the right to sublet don't carry cash value, they're beneficial since your options are broader and your rights are more defined.

And third, there's a philosophical value to putting the landlord/tenant relationship on a more even footing. Landlords generally seek to establish a dominant position over tenants, primarily for defensive reasons. Possession of an apartment is a substantial right, one that carries tremendous power. It's extremely difficult to evict a tenant once she's in place. To compensate, landlords seek to strip tenants of every legal right they possibly can. By negotiating the terms of a lease you demonstrate to a landlord that you're an equal in the transaction, not a supplicant. And that can help set a better tone for the entire relationship—for you and for others.

In this first step of his negotiation Robert determined that his goal was to conserve as much of his cash as possible and alter the lease agreement so it more adequately balanced the rights and responsibilities of both parties. He realized that there were many apartments available in the area but few tenants, so the lease was clearly negotiable. He also understood that the agent had little power or reason to negotiate, so he'd need to get through to the landlord. And finally, he decided that the opportunity to conserve cash and expand his rights was well worth the effort required. His next step was to level the playing field.

## LEVELING THE TENANT/LANDLORD PLAYING FIELD

The second step in negotiating the rental of a home or apartment is for the prospective tenant to get to know his or her opponent—the landlord—and to use that information to level the playing field. This is done by answering four questions: "What do I need to know?" "With whom should I negotiate?" "Are there any potentially disruptive side issues?" "What do I share with my opponent?"

### WHAT DO I NEED TO KNOW?— GATHERING INFORMATION

Prior to negotiating the terms of a lease, it's essential for you to learn everything you possibly can about both the apartment and the landlord.

Information about the apartment can be easily gathered through formal research and observation. Compare the size, quality, and location of the apartment you're interested in to others you've seen and to advertisements in the local newspapers. Is it priced accurately? Is it smaller than others renting for the same amount? Is it better equipped? Has it been maintained well? Try to find out as much as you can about the rental market in the area. Are there many places for rent? Do they seem to remain on the market for a long period of time?

Information on the landlord himself is more difficult to obtain, but you've a ready-made spy: the renting agent. Use the agent to infiltrate the other side. Ask him about the landlord. How many buildings or apartments does the landlord own? How long has he been trying to rent this place? Has he had bad experiences in the past with tenants? What does the landlord do for a living? Where does he live?

Once you've gathered all the information you can, analyze it. Where does the apartment fit in the market? How active is the rental market? What are the primary needs of the landlord? What are his fears?

## WITH WHOM SHOULD I NEGOTIATE?— PUSHING THE UP BUTTON

This is one instance when you'll need to maneuver to get to the person with the power to negotiate. Rental agents are often hired to both screen tenants and close deals for landlords who don't want to be bothered with the task. Most will do everything possible to keep you from dealing directly with the landlord, since such face-to-face dealings tend to weaken the agent's position. However, rental agents often have no latitude to negotiate the terms of the lease.

You need to negotiate directly with the landlord. In some cases, you may need to tell the agent that your meeting with the landlord is a sine qua non for signing the lease. An effective technique is to tell the rental agent, "I want to meet the landlord, and I'm sure that the landlord would want to meet and speak with the person who's going to be in possession of his property for the next $X$ years." When push comes to shove the agent will usually relent, since most landlords really do want to meet their tenants—and since the agent makes money only when an apartment is actually rented.

## ARE THERE ANY POTENTIALLY DISRUPTIVE SIDE ISSUES?—ELIMINATING DISSONANCE

While they may strike a superior posture, landlords are actually very fearful. They may be having a hard time renting their place, and every day it remains vacant puts a further drain on their own resources. They may have had bad experiences with tenants in the past, so they're afraid of having someone damage or even destroy their property.

The way to eliminate this dissonance is to position yourself as a financially solvent and responsible person who wants to rent a landlord's property. This can be done by drawing on your own past history and dressing to fit the landlord's image of a dream tenant. Have available the addresses and telephone numbers of personal references, including your employer and previous landlords. Better yet, if you can, obtain generic letters of reference from these people. When you meet with the landlord, dress and act as you would for a job interview. You want the landlord to feel you're the most solid citizen imaginable—someone who would never damage his property or walk away from an obligation.

If you're negotiating to rent an apartment in a multifamily dwelling in which the landlord himself lives, you need to make an extra effort in eliminating dissonance. While every landlord is concerned with his tenants' character, a landlord who will be living downstairs from his tenants is especially concerned. Dress and act like a conservative librarian. You're trying to portray yourself not just as an excellent tenant but also as a wonderful—that means silent and invisible—neighbor. If need be, stress your willingness to help in the upkeep of the property and your desire to make permanent improvements. And it should go without saying that you should express your high opinion of the neighborhood—after all, it's the landlord's neighborhood as well.

### WHAT DO I SHARE WITH MY OPPONENT?— FINDING AND DEMONSTRATING COMMON GROUND

The obvious common ground between a landlord and tenant is that the former wants to rent the apartment and the latter wants to live in it. But there's also a more subtle common ground between the two parties, one that can serve as the foundation for a negotiation. The landlord is concerned with how his property will be treated, and the tenant is concerned with how he will be treated. A possible common ground between the two is that in exchange for the tenant's promise to treat the property fairly, the landlord promises to treat the tenant fairly. This mutual fairness can be put into concrete form by negotiating an equitable lease agreement.

## INSIDER TIPS FOR RENTERS

The third and final step in negotiating the rental of a home or apartment is to know the situation. That's accomplished by applying the lessons learned by those who are experienced with this particular situation. I've been representing tenants and landlords for more than three decades, and I've been both a tenant and landlord. From my own experiences, and from the experiences of landlord/tenant attorneys I've spoken with while researching this book, I've developed four general insider tips, four specific insider tips dealing with particular elements of the lease, and one insider tip for dealing with commercial landlords.

## TREAT THE LEASE AS A BUNDLE OF ISSUES

A lease agreement is a bundle of various items. Rent isn't the sole issue. There are also the size and makeup of security deposits, the rights of tenants to sublet and assign, and the legal language and clauses of the lease itself.

## LOOK TO MODIFY RATHER THAN CHANGE THE LEASE

You'll have the best chances to negotiate successfully if you look at the items individually and try to modify them, not completely change them. Whenever possible accept the landlord's numbers. You should present the negotiation as a request to add certain elements, not as a debate over the validity of numbers. This makes the negotiation seem less adversarial.

## CONTINUALLY DEMONSTRATE YOUR GOOD CHARACTER

Throughout the negotiation, repeatedly stress your sense of obligation for the care and maintenance of the property, and your stability and financial responsibility. These sentiments, coupled with your references, your attire, and your seeming acceptance of the landlord's numbers, should enable you to make some substantive changes to the terms of the lease.

## MAKE SURE YOU NEGOTIATE
## THE MOST IMPORTANT ISSUES FIRST

Tenants should always try to address the most important issue first, so that if they're successful in obtaining a concession they can give in on subsequent areas of lesser importance, letting the landlord feel that he has won some victories.

Now let's take a look at the insider tips dealing with the specific elements of a lease.

## *TRY TO ALTER THE STRUCTURE OF THE RENT*

Rather than trying to negotiate a rent reduction, consider altering the structure of the rent payments. Most landlords don't view rent as a monthly income but as an annual return. If you're renting for more than two years you can ask that the rent be graduated rather than a flat fee. For example: If the rent is $1,000 per month and you're renting for three years, state that you think the rent is fair, but ask that it be graduated as $850 per month for the first year, $1,000 per month for the second year, and $1,150 per month for the third year. Justify your request by explaining that you'd like to use the extra cash you save the first year to furnish and decorate the apartment, and note that the landlord will still be getting $12,000 per year averaged over the three years of the lease.

Don't be surprised if the landlord agrees to graduate the rent but asks for an increased average yield in return (that's what I would encourage him to do if he were my client). For example: $900 per month the first year, $1,100 per month the second year, and $1,300 per month for the third year, resulting in an average annual yield of $13,200. Since the landlord has agreed to your request for graduating the payments you'll be faced with having to decide whether having more cash in hand early on is more important to you than the total rent you'll be paying over the three years.

## *TRY TO SUBSTITUTE THIRD-PARTY GUARANTEES FOR SECURITY DEPOSITS*

After negotiating rent, move on to security deposits. Once again, the best tactic is to accept the validity of the landlord's number but to ask that it be handled a little differently. Say that you understand the need for a security deposit, but ask the landlord to accept a legal guarantee from a third party, such as a parent or an employer, instead of cash up front. If the finances of the guarantor are good, and the guarantee is legally binding, it'll serve the same purpose for the landlord. However, if such an arrangement isn't acceptable, make sure that the security is placed into an interest-bearing escrow account even if the landlord isn't required to do so by law. Bear in mind, however, that some landlords—particularly those who have been burned by tenants in the past—may stand firm on all issues surrounding security deposits.

## *ASK FOR MORE RIGHTS BUT OFFER SAFETY NETS*

Try to obtain additional rights under the lease, but for each right you request, offer a safety net to the landlord. For example: Ask for the right to sublet, but agree to remain personally responsible; ask for the right to assign the lease, but make it subject to the landlord's consent. If it's applicable, ask for the right of first refusal to purchase the apartment if it's put up for sale. Don't expect to win all these rights, especially if you've gotten other concessions. Still, they're worth trying for.

## MAKE THE LEASE MORE EQUITABLE WITH CAREFUL EDITING

Tenants should also address the clauses, provisions, and language in the lease document itself. Two simple techniques to make leases more equitable are to change the word *days* into the phrase *business days,* thus increasing the time you have to take certain actions; and after every use of the word *consent* adding the phrase *which will not unreasonably be withheld.*

## PURSUE NONFINANCIAL GOALS WITH COMMERCIAL LANDLORDS

Commercial landlords generally need to show a steady and sizable rent roll, since that's what their financing is based on. That means a commercial landlord may not be able to make many dollar concessions regardless of your negotiating skill. Therefore, your best bet is to negotiate for things other than money. When the market is flat, as it is now and probably will remain for the next five years, commercial landlords are willing to do most anything as long as it won't show on their books. Ask him to pay for improvements. Ask for an option to renew at the same, or a moderately increased, rent. You can even ask for free-rent periods, just as long as you don't quarrel with that monthly number.

Now, let's see how Robert did in his negotiation. His previous apartment-hunting trips and his study of the local newspapers showed that the $1,000 rent on the apartment he was interested in was a fair price. However, he also learned that the rental market was very slow. There were quite a few apartments available and very few potential tenants. Robert also discovered that the landlord was a retired teacher who depended on the income from her rental apartments. She had recently had a bad experience with a tenant and was therefore very concerned with security deposits and stability. Robert realized that if he could demonstrate his exceptional stability to the landlord, he could probably get quite a few concessions. He explained to the agent that he definitely wanted to rent the apartment but he needed to meet with the landlord first in order to feel comfortable. And he was sure, he added, that she'd want to meet with him as well. Before his meeting with the landlord, Robert obtained letters of reference from his employer and from his previous landlord. He dressed in a business suit for the meeting.

Robert began by presenting his letters of reference and stating his desire to rent the apartment. He said he had no problems with the rent being requested but would like it to be graduated over three years. After he explained his reasons, the landlord agreed. Robert next moved on to the security deposit. He asked the landlord to accept a personal guarantee from his father instead of the cash. The landlord, explaining her previous problems, insisted on the cash. Robert then asked for the cash to be placed in a separate interest-bearing account. The landlord agreed. Having won two major concessions, Robert moved on to ask for the rights to sublet and assign. The landlord balked, even with the additional guarantees Robert offered, and having already won his major points, he backed off. Finally, Robert went over the clauses in the lease he had problems with. The landlord stressed the importance of the lease to her, and how it was her only protection. Robert agreed to accept it as written. Both sides came away feeling good about the process. Robert had saved himself some money to furnish and decorate the apartment, and the landlord had a responsible tenant and a solid lease.

---

## Turning the Heat on Landlords
## Renting a Home or Apartment

- Obtain the most equitable lease terms possible.
- Terms are especially negotiable in slow markets.
- Negotiate with the landlord directly.
- Comparison shop.
- Learn all you can about the landlord.
- Stress personal stability and financial solvency.
- Address your most important concerns first.
- Ask for graduated rent payments.
- Replace cash security with a third-party guarantee.
- Ask for more rights, but offer veto power.

# 8

# HASSLE-FREE HAGGLING

## Buying Objectively Priced Items

*"Entrepreneurial profit . . . is the expression of the value of what the entrepreneur contributes to production in exactly the same sense that wages are the value expression of what the worker 'produces.' It is not a profit of exploitation any more than are wages."*

—Joseph Alois Schumpeter

Beth and her roommate, Kristen, began sharing their gripes one day over lunch. Beth was tired of writing her research papers on a typewriter. She thought a personal computer would not only make her life easier but might even have a positive effect on her grades. Kristen, who already had a PC, agreed with Beth. Her gripe had to do with the reception on her hand-me-down television. Sure it was better than nothing, but as a film student, Kristen thought she needed a better set. After convincing each other that their desires were truly needs, not just wants, Beth and Kristen made a date to go into town on the next weekend to shop for a personal computer and a television.

## THE OBJECTIVELY PRICED PRODUCT BUYER'S SELF-EXAMINATION

An objectively priced object is one that is initially priced based on its cost. Almost all traditional retailers, from the corner grocer to the new car dealer, sell objectively priced items. A subjectively priced item, on the other hand, is priced based either on what the seller perceives it is worth or on what the seller perceives someone will pay for it. Retailers of subjectively priced items would include artists, craftspeople, and sellers of antiques and collectibles.

In buying an objectively priced item, just as in every other negotiation, the first step in the process is to analyze your needs and weigh your options by getting to know yourself. That's accomplished by answering three questions: "What do I want?" "Is it worth my time?" "Is it important to me?"

## WHAT DO I WANT?—SETTING A SPECIFIC GOAL

While establishing goals is important in every negotiation, it's doubly important in the negotiation with an objective retailer since it will determine the tactics you'll use. Let me explain.

The goal most people instinctively come up with when thinking about retail purchases is to buy the object in question as cheaply as possible. That may be an entirely appropriate goal, but it does carry some risk. The amount of profit a retailer makes is, or at least should be, in direct proportion to the amount of value he adds to the products he sells. A store with expert salesmen who spend a great deal of time educating customers, and that services the products it sells, must make more of a profit than a store whose salesmen are strictly order takers, and that doesn't service its products. Businesses are well aware of this economic law. That's why many people live by the old adage of not buying a product from someone who doesn't make a profit on them. The logic goes like this: if someone makes a profit on you he or she will be around if there's a problem down the road. Businesses want to buy for a low price, but they also want to know that the seller will be around if service is required.

Consumers need to apply this same attitude to their own purchasing. If you'll need service on a product, or want to maintain an ongoing relationship with a retailer in order to draw on his expertise, you should be willing to pay a price that provides the retailer with enough profit to provide that service or with the time to answer your questions. If, on the other hand, you won't need service and don't need to maintain a relationship with the retailer, then you should look to cut as much profit from the transaction as you possibly can.

The decision of whether or not you'll need service, or whether or not you'll need to maintain an ongoing relationship, is an individual one. For example: If you're an avid photographer who takes pictures all the time it would make sense for your goal when buying a new camera to be: "I want to buy a camera with the features I need for as low a price as possible, while still ensuring I'll be in a position to get service and advice from the retailer." If you're a snap shooter who takes the camera out once a year when you go on vacation, you've no need for a continuing relationship, and you probably won't be buying a camera expensive enough to merit repairing. In that case your goal should simply be: "I want to buy a camera with the features I need for as low a price as possible."

Let's look at the two elements of this decision: service and advice. When should you be concerned with service? In answering this question I suggest you consider how much the item will cost to replace. If it costs close to the same amount to repair a product as to buy a new one, service isn't much of an issue. Let's go back to our photography example. If your simple snapshot camera broke it would generally cost you so much to repair it that you'd just go out and buy a new one. On the other hand, when a sophisticated camera breaks down it almost always pays to repair it.

When should you be concerned with advice? The answer to this question, I suggest, has to do with how easy the product is to use and whether you look on its use as a pleasant, unpleasant, or neutral experience. If a product is difficult to use, or at least requires some training, it will be essential for you to maintain an ongoing relationship with the seller. Going back to the cameras again, you'd be foolish to buy the sophisticated camera from a retailer you couldn't keep coming back to for guidance and advice, since the operation of it is very complex. If, on the other hand, all it takes to operate the camera is to point it and press the shutter release, you'll never need to come back to the retailer for advice.

Similarly, if you look on the use of the item as a pleasurable experience—as a hobby, perhaps—you'll be more apt to have an ongoing curiosity and interest in it, a curiosity and interest that can be encouraged and fostered by a knowledgeable retailer. If you look on use of the item as unpleasant or neutral—as a chore, perhaps—you probably have no curiosity or interest in it, and, therefore, no need for further information. Staying with the camera examples, if you're turning into a photo hobbyist, the camera retailer will be as much a mentor as a vendor. If all you ever do is take snapshots on your vacation, you'll never have any need or desire to stop in the camera store and talk photography.

## IS IT WORTH MY TIME?— DECIDING IF IT'S READILY NEGOTIABLE

As I've said many times in this book, while theoretically everything is negotiable, not everything is *readily* negotiable. As a general rule, in order for an objectively priced product to be readily negotiable it needs to be both widely available and priced high enough to make negotiation viable. Widespread availability provides for negotiability because it means dif ferent retailers have paid different prices for it. In almost every case, a manufacturer bases his price on the number of items a retailer buys and how quickly the retailer pays his bills. In other words, a retailer who buys a lot of products from a manufacturer and who pays his bills promptly will get a better price than another retailer. While a manufacturer may publicly advertise a ''suggested retail price,'' it's really meaningless. Each retailer bases his price first on what it cost him to buy the item, then on what it costs him to do business, next on what other retailers are selling the item for, and finally on what he thinks someone is willing to pay for it.

Let's say Joe's Camera Store buys 1,000 Nippon X20s, while Jim's Camera Store buys only 100. Joe may have paid only $60 for each camera, while Jim had to pay $100. The suggested retail price of the camera is $130. Both Joe and Jim advertise their cameras for $120. When a customer comes in to negotiate with Joe, there's a great deal of room since Joe can sell it for, let's say, $80 and still cover his overhead. Jim, on the other hand, doesn't have much room to negotiate. (Just for future reference, what Jim probably does is try to steer the customer away from the Nippon X20—which he had to pay a great deal for—and toward the Kanton F7, a comparable model that he bought in greater numbers and, therefore, at a better price.) As a general rule you can assume that the bigger the store and the larger the inventory, the less the store had to pay to obtain its wares.

Price also has a bearing on how readily negotiable an item is. That's because while percentages remain proportionate on lower priced items, the numbers themselves become less significant. Let me explain with another example using the two camera stores. Joe was also able to get a great deal on Dokad 35-mm film, buying it for $1 per roll, while it cost Jim $1.25 per roll, or 25 percent more. The film has a retail price of $1.50 per roll. Theoretically, that means Joe has more flexibility when it comes to his pricing and negotiating. But since the numbers themselves are low to begin with, it doesn't really matter much. No customer is going to come in and try to talk either Joe or Jim down in price for a $1.50 item. Joe's good deal will translate directly into a bottom line profit rather than increased negotiating room.

While obviously, I'm using a very low priced product to make a point, the rule is true across the board. Cars costing $20,000 are more readily negotiable than stereo systems costing $10,000, which are more readily negotiable than computers costing $5,000, which are more readily negotiable than camcorders costing $2,500, which are more readily negotiable than refrigerators costing $1,250, which are more readily negotiable than televisions costing $600, which are more readily negotiable than air conditioners costing $300, which are more readily negotiable than blenders costing $150. The rule of thumb in negotiating objectively priced items is: the more widely available an item is, and the more expensive it is, the more readily negotiable it will be.


## IS IT IMPORTANT TO ME?—
## MAKING SURE IT'S WORTH DOING

Whether or not it's worth negotiating a particular purchase is a judgment you'll need to make on your own. Ask yourself this question: "Is the amount of time and effort it will take me to negotiate worth the amount of money I could potentially save?"

Assume that by negotiating the purchase of a readily negotiable, objectively priced object from a legitimate retailer, you'll be able to save a minimum of 10 percent and a maximum of 20 percent. If the object has a list price of $10,000 that's a minimum savings of $1,000 and a maximum savings of $2,000. It's pretty clear that negotiating would make sense in that case. That's why nearly everyone, regardless of their income, tries to negotiate the price of a vehicle.

But what if the object is a refrigerator that lists for $1,000? Presumably you'd be able to save anywhere from $100 to $200 by negotiating. Is that worthwhile? Let's say it would take you one hour to prepare and one hour for the actual negotiation. Depending on how well you negotiated you'd be earning anywhere from $50 to $100 per hour. Not a bad fee, especially if it's done at a time when you wouldn't normally be working.

How about a $500 television? If you negotiated you'd stand to save from $50 to $100. It probably would still take you two hours, so your yield per hour would drop to $25 to $50. That probably still makes sense for most of us. It's when you get below $500 that things really start to become problematic. If you're looking for a camera that costs $250 you could save from $25 to $50 by negotiating. Once again, taking into account two hours of work, that would translate into a yield of from $12.50 to $25 per hour. I'd have to think long and hard about this one. In my business I work very hard and for very long hours. That makes my leisure time all the more valuable. If push came to shove I'd probably spend the two hours relaxing with my family rather than negotiating to save $25.

Of course, that's my judgment. Yours might be entirely different. I'm not saying you should come up with an ironclad rule. What I'm suggesting is that every time you're about to buy an objectively priced big ticket item you make a conscious judgment about whether or not it's worth negotiating. Sometimes you may be in a hurry and a savings of $50 won't be worth it. Other times it could be a rainy Saturday and you're bored and you don't mind spending two hours to save $25.

Let's see how Beth and Kristen did their self-examinations. In case you don't remember, Beth wanted to buy a personal computer for her school-work and Kristen wanted to buy a new television set. Beth had a little bit of experience with computers but knew she'd be needing ongoing advice. And since the computer was expensive enough to usually warrant repairing rather than replacing she knew she'd need after-sale service. Anyway, if she "got into" computers she'd like to have someone to turn to for advice. That's why Beth decided her goal was: "To buy a computer system with the features I need, for as low a price as possible, while still insuring I'll be in a position to get service and advice from the retailer." Kristen, like most teenagers, had a great deal of experience with televisions. She clearly knew how to operate them and, being a film major, even had some experience at hooking them up to VCRs and camcorders. She also knew that in most cases televisions lasted long enough that when they broke it usually was more economical to replace them than to repair them. Therefore she decided her goal was: "To buy a television with the features I need for as low a price as possible."

Beth knew she wanted either an IBM or an IBM-compatible computer system and that it would cost her anywhere from $1,500 to $2,000 excluding software. Since almost every store that carries computers carries IBM or IBM-compatible products, and since she was spending upward of $2,000, Beth knew her purchase would be readily negotiable. Kristen wanted a thirteen-inch color television. Clearly, since thirteen-inch color televisions are carried by almost every store that sells televisions, she'd be able to negotiate the purchase. But since the sets seemed to cost around $500 the purchase wouldn't be as negotiable as Beth's larger purchase of the computer system.

For Beth, it was clearly worth negotiating the purchase of her computer system: she earned only $5 per hour at the fast-food restaurant near campus and stood to save anywhere from $150 to $200 for a couple of hours of negotiating work. Kristen stood to save a little less by negotiating—from $50 to $100—but since she earned only $4 per hour at the same fast-food restaurant, her incentive to negotiate was just as strong. After both Beth and Kristen had analyzed their own needs it was time for them to level the playing field.

# LEVELING THE OBJECTIVELY PRICED PLAYING FIELD

The second step in negotiating the purchase of an objectively priced item is for the buyer to get to know his or her opponent—the seller—and to use that information to level the playing field. This is done by answering four questions: "What do I need to know?" "With whom should I negotiate?" "Are there any potentially disruptive side issues?" "What do I share with my opponent?"

## *WHAT DO I NEED TO KNOW?—GATHERING INFORMATION*

Gathering information about an objectively priced item is fairly straightforward. There are many excellent magazines that review consumer products and offer guidance to buyers. My suggestion would be to take a trip to the local library and read through back issues of both *Consumer Reports* and any specialty magazines that cover the product you're interested in. *Consumer Reports* is excellent in most areas (particularly cars) but I think it leaves something to be desired when it comes to reviewing more sophisticated products such as computers, component audio systems, sophisticated cameras, and high-end video products. For the sake of a more specialized opinion, I suggest you also read what the "buff" magazines have to say about the products you're interested in. Your goal is to make sure you'll be buying rather than being sold. Your purchase should be a proactive rather than reactive process.

However, don't look at your reading as a complete education. You're simply looking for an understanding of the important features of the product, the options, the price range, and the repair record. You're looking to gather enough information to keep the salesman honest. It's a mistake to read *Consumer Reports,* take its advice as gospel, and then enter a store demanding the single product it selected as the best buy. That's because manufacturers and retailers have learned how to deflect buyers with this type of tunnel vision.

Let's say you enter an appliance store intent on buying the Westag Model 70 refrigerator, which *Consumer Reports* rated as the best buy. You may be told the Model 70 is no longer being made. Magazines run at least six months, if not further, behind the retail market. By the time the Model 70 received its honors it might have been replaced by the Model 71. Or the salesman will tell you that the Maymore Model 50, which was rated second best, has been improved based on *Consumer Reports'* findings, so now it's probably even better than the Westag Model 70 you were asking for. Or perhaps the salesman will tell you that the Model 70 is only carried by department stores. Since he's a specialty store he carries the Model 77, which is different but of course better. Confused? That's the whole point. If you enter a store brandishing *Consumer Reports*—either physically or mentally— you're playing into the hands of the salesman.

Instead, you're going to get the salesman to give you an education. Once you've picked up the basics from your reading it's time to take a trip to the retailers you've selected as your negotiating targets. And while you gather more information you're going to simultaneously eliminate the dissonance from the situation.

## WITH WHOM SHOULD I NEGOTIATE?— PUSHING THE UP BUTTON

When it comes to negotiating the purchase of objectively priced items, the question "Who should I be negotiating with?" actually has two parts to it. First, you need to ask yourself, "In what type of store should I be negotiating?" And after answering that, you need to ask yourself, "Who in the store should I be negotiating with?"

### In What Type of Store Should I Be Negotiating?— Finding the Right Store

Most of the objectively priced items you'll be negotiating for fall into one of three categories. They're either vehicles (cars, trucks, motorcycles, snowmobiles, water craft, or aircraft), major appliances (refrigerators, freezers, stoves, ovens, ranges, washing machines, or dryers), or consumer electronics products (stereo systems, televisions, camcorders, VCRs, microwave ovens, or cameras). All of these are "durable big ticket" items, meaning they typically carry price tags of over $250, aren't subject to fashion changes, and are intended to last a long time.

Deciding what type of store you should buy from is really a moot question when purchasing vehicles. These items are so expensive that they're limited in distribution to specialty retailers who sell these items and nothing else. Sears doesn't sell cars, and you can't buy cars from a mail-order catalog. Your only choice is to go to an auto dealer.

However, when shopping for an item in one of the other two categories—major appliances and consumer electronics—you've got a wide range of retail outlets to choose from. These items are sold by department stores, discount stores, catalog showrooms, national specialty chains (such as Radio Shack or Egghead Software), regional specialty chains, and local specialty stores. For example: You could buy a stereo system at Bloomingdale's, Kmart, Service Merchandise, Circuit City, P.C. Richards (if you live in the New York metropolitan area), or at Kenny's Stereo Shack, the little audio shop around the corner from your house.

When selecting which type of retail outlet to negotiate with you should keep your specific goal in mind. If you're not interested in service or a continued relationship, and are solely concerned with price, you'll do best negotiating with regional or national specialty chains. If you're concerned with service and an ongoing relationship, stick with local specialty stores. Department stores, discount stores, and catalog showrooms don't offer much opportunity to negotiate. Prices at these stores are often fixed, and the sales staffs have little or no authority to deviate from the price tag. And even a national discount chain store may not be able to buy items at as low a price as a specialty chain.

### With Whom in the Store Should I Negotiate?— Finding the Right Person

Once you've decided what type of retailer you'll be negotiating with, your next step is to determine who in the retail outlet you should deal with. In all of the retail outlets that offer an opportunity to negotiate— auto dealerships, national specialty chains, regional specialty chains, local specialty stores—salesmen are given a certain negotiating latitude. The retailer may have set a policy of, for example, marking an item 25 percent over what it cost, and a salesman can, on his own, cut that to 15 percent. Any greater discounts would need to be approved by a store manager or the owner.

Since they don't have that many numbers to remember, auto salesmen can keep the figures in their head. Appliance and electronics salesmen, on the other hand, can't be expected to remember the costs of a hundred or so different products. To help them, retailers often put a special alpha-numeric code on their price tags, indicating either the cost of the item or the lowest price it can be sold for without management approval.

A great deal of consumer time and effort over the years has gone into trying to break these codes. However, I believe it's really not necessary. Your goal shouldn't be to break the code but to get the price down to a point where the salesman must go to his manager. That way you'll know you've negotiated a good price. Who in the store should you be negotiating with? Negotiate with the salesman first, but when he or she can go no further, negotiate with the manager or owner.

### ARE THERE ANY POTENTIALLY DISRUPTIVE SIDE ISSUES?—ELIMINATING DISSONANCE

Most of the salesmen who sell durable big ticket items work primarily on commission. They get paid a small salary, but the bulk of their income is generated by earning a commission on every product they personally sell. In order to become successful they must be both expert salesmen and expert in the product or products they're selling. Your goal is to eliminate the dissonance that causes them to emphasize their salesmanship side and to instead encourage their product expertise to dominate the process.

What causes a salesman to become an aggressive, possibly unethical, seller? Primarily it's pressure and ego. The more pressure put on a salesman to produce the more likely he is to twist arms, deceive, or obfuscate. In addition, the more his ego is put on the line, the more apt he is to rise to the challenge and try to come out on top.

While you're not going to be able to eliminate all the pressure a salesman is under, you can minimize it by timing your approach to coincide with his least-pressure-filled moment. That's why I suggest you shop for durable big ticket items on weekday mornings. Weekends are always much busier for retailers than weekdays, so a salesman will be under more pressure to both deal with more customers and close more sales. On a weekend the salesman isn't able to spend as much time with you, and therefore will have less of an investment in your making a purchase. On a weekday, when no one else is in the store, he'll be happy to spend as much time as you want telling you about his products. Mornings are always less pressure filled than afternoons and evenings for salesmen. In the morning they're not worrying about how many sales they didn't make during the day, but are optimistic about all the sales they will make. The boss isn't on their back about taking a long lunch and reminding them of their daily quota.

You can eliminate any ego challenge the salesman might feel by painting yourself as the confused nice guy looking for advice. Don't come in like a wise guy, armed to the teeth with articles and books on negotiation. That will just bring out the killer in the salesman. He'll see your posture as a challenge and will feel honor bound to somehow take advantage of you. Instead, explain to the salesman that you've read a little about what you're interested in buying but are confused and are hoping he can help you. By playing to his expert side rather than his salesman side you've boosted his ego rather than challenged it. And you're going to insure he's willing to spend time with you by next establishing common ground.

## WHAT DO I SHARE WITH MY OPPONENT?— FINDING AND DEMONSTRATING COMMON GROUND

The obvious common ground between a consumer and a retailer is the same as exists between any buyer and seller: both want ownership of the object in question to change hands. Incredibly enough, all that's necessary for you to form a common bond with the salesman is to directly affirm that you're a buyer, not just a shopper. In your introductory comments to the salesman, when you're explaining your need for information and advice, explain that you'd like to buy the item today. Those who are selling objectively priced items are only really interested in closing deals. They are initially focused more on short-term success than on developing a long-term relationship. Only after you've proven yourself to be a repeated buyer will that change. For now, your promises to buy "this week" or "soon" are meaningless to them.

# INSIDER TIPS FOR BUYERS OF OBJECTIVELY PRICED ITEMS

The third and final step in negotiating the purchase of an objectively priced item is to know the situation. That's accomplished by applying the lessons learned by those who are experienced with this particular situation. I've been negotiating purchases my entire life. And in preparation for writing this book, I spoke with dozens of retailers and salesmen. All that has helped me develop seven insider tips for you.

First, after you've reduced the internal pressure on the salesman by eliminating the dissonance, you must substitute external pressure.

Second, you must clearly ask for a lower price and offer possible ways and reasons for the seller to accommodate you.

Third, you should, if possible, try to obtain a cash discount.

Fourth, you should go through the same process with more than one seller.

Fifth, you can consider making a multiple buy in order to make a normally nonnegotiable item negotiable.

Sixth, you can try using the telephone as a shortcut.

And seventh, you should beware extended warranties.

## SUBSTITUTE EXTERNAL PRESSURE FOR THE INTERNAL PRESSURE YOU'VE ELIMINATED

The single best way to add external pressure to the negotiation is to comparison shop and make all the retailers aware of it. While it's an obvious ploy, I'm always amazed at the number of people who don't comparison shop. By shopping at only one store you eliminate your single greatest power—the ability to buy anywhere you want. There are few products that aren't sold in multiple locations. And, in fact, many of the same exact items will be sold in these multiple locations. Simply by going to two different stores, telling them you're interested in buying an item, and letting them know you'll be shopping at their competitor as well, you put pressure on them to come up with their best price.

## CLEARLY ASK FOR A LOWER PRICE AND OFFER REASONS FOR IT

Once you've let the salesman know you'll be comparison shopping, and will be buying today, ask for a good price. Here's how: your response to the quoted price shouldn't be either immediate acceptance or rejection. Instead, ask the salesman to do better. The best way to do that is to say that you'd like to buy the product, and you'd like to buy it from him, but you just can't afford it at that price. Follow up your statement by providing the salesman with one or more ways and reasons to lower his price further. You could:

- Ask if it's possible to get the full-featured model for close to the price of the stripped-down model. In effect, you're asking the retailer to throw in options free of charge.
- Say you need to save money to buy some extras and then mention what they would be. This gives the salesman the chance to throw them in for nothing if you buy at his price.
- Say appearance really isn't that important to you, so is it possible he could sell you a demonstration or floor model for a lower price. This provides him with an opportunity to either sell an actual floor model or to at least save face.
- Ask for last year's model, explaining you really don't need a state-of-the-art product. Again, this gives the salesman a chance to sell something he needs to get rid of, or to save face and give you a discount.
- Imply that you'll be coming back for other products and will become a regular customer, or that you somehow represent the lead element of a group of other potential new customers.

## TRY TO OBTAIN A CASH DISCOUNT

Another insider tip is to ask for a cash discount but to do so in such a way that the salesman is forced to bring his manager or the store owner into the negotiation. Once you've gone through the entire process up until this point you'll have probably brought the salesman down to the limit of his power. You can see if there's any further room for negotiating by thanking the salesman for his efforts and then asking him to ask his manager if paying cash would be at all advantageous. In smaller, single outlet stores, you'll often be able to get a cash discount, since that frees the store from having to pay credit card fees or may even enable the owner to hide some of his profits from the IRS. But even if there's no cash discount policy, by asking the salesman to approach the manager you've pushed the envelope to its limits and are insuring you're getting the retailer's best price.

### GO THROUGH THE SAME PROCESS WITH MORE THAN ONE SELLER

Once the salesman comes back with the answer from the manager, thank him profusely. Say that his price sounds good, but say you have something you need to do. Stress that you'll be back as soon as you can. He might be annoyed—but don't worry about it. He wants to make the sale, so he'll just grit his teeth and smile. Then repeat the entire process with another one or two retailers. Now that you've got two or three prices you have a choice.

If the prices aren't far enough apart to make a difference, and you're concerned with service and cultivating an ongoing relationship with the retailer, I'd suggest you return to the salesman whose expertise and honesty impressed you most and who stressed his store's ability to provide service to its customers.

If the prices are significantly different, and you're concerned with service and developing a relationship, I'd still return to the most impressive salesman/store, but in this case I'd offer him a chance to do a little bit better. Tell the salesman that you received a lower price at another store but that you'd like to buy from him. Then ask him if he can come close to the other price. He'll probably then return with a slightly lower price.

If the prices are at all different, and you're concerned primarily with price, return to the store or stores with the higher prices and present the salesmen with the lowest price quote you've received. Ask them to either meet or beat it. They'll either come back with a better price, offer to add something to the sale, or tell you they can't beat the lower price. In any case, if price is your primary motivation, buy the product from the lower priced seller.

### CONSIDER A MULTIPLE BUY TO MAKE A NORMALLY NONNEGOTIABLE ITEM NEGOTIABLE

Lower priced items (under $250) are generally not readily negotiable, nor are they usually worth negotiating over. However, it may be possible to turn these purchases into big ticket negotiations if you're prepared to buy in volume. If, for example, you're willing to buy ten pairs of $50 sneakers you may be able to negotiate a significant price reduction. There are two secrets to this technique. First, make sure you're buying a multiple of the exact same item. That gives the store the opportunity to pass along its own volume discount. And second, negotiate directly with a manager, buyer, or owner. Only someone who's in authority or who actually does the ordering will know how, or have the power, to come up with a volume discount.

## TRY USING THE TELEPHONE AS A SHORTCUT

If you're interested in purchasing only one particular product and aren't concerned with gathering information from retailers, you can use a negotiating shortcut. Compile a list of the telephone numbers of the relevant retailers in your immediate area. Telephone each, explain what product you're interested in, and ask for their best price. State that you'll be in later this afternoon to pay for and pick up the product. If they don't carry the product in question and/or if they try to talk you into another product, say you're not interested and move on to the next store. If they don't want to give you a price over the telephone, say you understand and move on. Once you've established a lowest price, reestablish contact with the other retailers on your list. Tell them you've gotten a lower price than they gave you and would like to know if they can meet or beat it. When you've established a new lowest price, give the salesman your name and tell him you'll be in later that day.

If when you appear at the store you find you've been misled—either they don't have the product in stock or they back off their price quote— don't bother engaging in a debate. You've been "lowballed." That means they've tried to take you out of the market by quoting a low price and then, now that you're hooked, they're trying to increase their price. Leave immediately and go to the retailer who gave the next lowest price quote.

## BEWARE EXTENDED WARRANTIES

While it's not strictly an insider negotiating tip, there's a technique salesmen use that I think you need to know. After you've completed the price negotiations on whatever you're about to buy you're often turned over to another salesman to discuss the purchase of an extended warranty. Beware. Extended warranties are a retailer's biggest moneymaker. These are insurance policies that have been designed to pay off handsomely for them, not you. And since they're so profitable for the retailer the firm's best salesman is often given the job of selling them. By all means listen to his or her pitch politely. But I suggest you never, ever, buy an extended warranty from anyone.

## COMPLAINING

Finally, since we're spending so much time discussing how to buy, I thought I'd add a few words about what to do if your purchase doesn't work out. There are five secrets to having bona fide retail complaints handled effectively.

1. Avoid weekends, holidays, and other busy store hours. You want there to be no time pressure on your opponent.
2. Negotiate directly with a manager or owner. He will have the power to resolve matters and also to avoid the complaint bureaucracy.
3. Stress that you're a regular customer, you intend to become one, or that you somehow represent a large number of potential customers.
4. Make sure you've got complete documentation, such as a register receipt, and have retained the original packaging.
5. Have a specific goal in mind, and present it clearly. Do you want the item repaired? Do you want a replacement of the same item? Do you want to exchange this item for a different item? Do you want a refund? As long as you don't expect to be paid cash back for what you purchased, and you've followed the other four points, you shouldn't have a problem.

If these five tips don't work for you, you'll only have one option left: small claims court.

Let's see how Beth and Kristen made out in their negotiations. They both went to the library one afternoon to do some research about their purchases. Once they had some understanding of what they were looking for they decided to go shopping the next morning.

Since Beth was concerned with service and expertise as well as price, she decided she'd shop the local independent computer store downtown, as well as the regional chain store in the mall. Kristen was concerned primarily with price, so she decided to shop the national appliance chain store downtown, and also go to the regional chain store at the mall. Both knew they'd be able to negotiate with the salesmen, but in order to get a really good deal they'd need to negotiate with a store manager. First they drove downtown so Beth could shop the local computer specialty store and Kristen could shop the national appliance chain store.

Beth explained to the salesman that she needed some help. She said she was looking for a personal computer system, primarily for word processing. She told the salesman her approximate budget, said she'd be looking at one or two other stores, but stressed that she wanted to go home with the system today. The salesman went over his line with Beth, explaining the pros and cons of each model. He quoted her a price of $2,000 for a system that he thought best suited her needs. Beth told him that she really wanted to buy the system but that she couldn't afford $2,000. Especially since she'd need to buy software, disks, and paper as well, offering the salesman an opportunity to throw in some extras. She said that normally she'd have been able to borrow these extras from her friends at the dorm, but that they were all waiting for her to be the first to buy a computer, implying that she'd be able to bring additional business to the store. The salesman told Beth he'd be willing to throw in a word-processing program, a ream of paper, and a box of disks for free. She then asked him if he'd ask his manager if there was any advantage to her paying cash, since she'd gotten the money for the computer as a birthday present and could draw it out of the bank and be back later in the afternoon. The salesman came back and said he'd be able to cut the price another $100 if she paid cash. She thanked him, told him she needed to meet her friend for lunch, but added that she'd definitely be back later that afternoon.

Meanwhile, Kristen was at the national appliance chain store up the street. She explained to the salesman that she wanted to buy a thirteen-inch color television. She said that while she knew how to operate a television, she really didn't know all that much about the different features or brands. She explained what her price range was, said she wanted to buy it today, and asked for his help. The salesman showed Kristen his products and quoted prices, explaining the features of each and letting her compare the picture quality. She selected one set that cost $500 and seemed to have the best picture, but told the salesman that she really couldn't afford it. She asked him if he had any floor models she'd be able to buy. He offered to sell her the demo model for $460. Finally, she asked him to ask his manager if it would be at all advantageous for her to pay cash. He said he didn't even need to check. The chain had a policy of not giving cash discounts. Kristen thanked him for his efforts, said she had to talk it over with her roommate, but would definitely be back later than afternoon.

Beth and Kristen met back at their car and then drove out to the regional appliance and electronics chain store at the mall. They both ran through the same scenarios with salesmen at that store. Beth was able to end up with a price of $1,500, but without the software, disks, and paper. Kristen was able to get a price of $450 on the same television. They met outside the store and discussed their options. Since Beth was concerned with service and ongoing support she was willing to pay a little bit more and buy at the local specialty store . . . especially since she was getting at least $200 worth of free extras. Kristen, on the other hand, was primarily concerned with price. They decided to go back downtown for one more round of negotiations.

Beth found the same salesman she had dealt with earlier and told him about the lower price from the chain store. She said that she really wanted to buy from him since she was concerned with service and advice, but asked if he could narrow the gap between his price and the other store. He went to talk to his manager for a minute and then came back with an offer. He couldn't lower the price any further, but he was now willing to throw in two free instructional classes and a couple of guidebooks. Beth agreed at once.

Kristen also was able to find the same salesman she had dealt with earlier. She told him the national chain at the mall had quoted her a price of $450 on the same set and asked him to either meet or beat it. He left for a minute, then came back and told her she could have the set for $450. She agreed.

## Hassle-Free Haggling
## Buying Objectively Priced Items

- If you'll need service, buy for a low price, but make sure you can come back.
- If you won't need service, buy for as low a price as possible.
- The more widely available and expensive an item is, the more negotiable it is.
- Negotiate with both salesman and manager.
- Gather general information from magazines and sales staff.
- Shop on a weekday morning.
- Boost rather than challenge the salesman's ego.
- Stress you'll buy today and you're comparison shopping.
- Ask for a lower price.
- Ask for a cash discount.

# 9

# ARGUING OVER AESTHETICS

## Buying Subjectively Priced Items

*"We might as reasonably dispute whether it is the upper or the under blade of a pair of scissors that cuts a piece of paper, as whether value is governed by utility or cost of production."*

—ALFRED MARSHALL

Lowell and Susan were almost done furnishing their home. It had taken them more than five years to renovate the lovely little Victorian, and another five years to furnish it, but they both felt the time and money were well spent. Susan had become a regular visitor to antiques stores, picking up pieces that fit her vision and her budget. She had left one purchase for last, since she knew it would present the biggest problem.

The problem was that Lowell and Susan kept their television, VCR, and stereo equipment in one of the front parlors. The only way they felt they could integrate all this technology into a Victorian interior was to buy a large armoire, drill sufficient holes in the back for all the wiring, and add enough shelves for all the equipment. Susan had priced armoires during her shopping trips and knew they were very expensive.

## THE SUBJECTIVELY PRICED OBJECT BUYER'S SELF-EXAMINATION

A subjectively priced item is priced based either on what the seller perceives it is worth or what the seller thinks someone will pay for it. Generally these items have an aesthetic rather than, or in addition to, a utilitarian value. Retailers of subjectively priced items would include artists, artisans, some highly skilled craftspeople, and sellers of antiques and collectibles. An objectively priced item, on the other hand, is initially priced through some concrete formula based on its actual cost. Almost all traditional retailers, from the corner grocer to the new car dealer, sell objectively priced items.

In buying a subjectively priced item, just as in every other negotiation, the first step in the process is to analyze your needs and weigh your options, getting to know yourself. That's accomplished by answering three questions: "What do I want?" "Is it worth my time?" "Is it important to me?"

## WHAT DO I WANT?—SETTING A SPECIFIC GOAL

The key to determining what you want from a negotiation with a subjective seller is to first determine why you're interested in buying the object in question. Basically, there are two reasons: either you've fallen in love with an object's beauty and decide to buy it; or you've a need you'd like to fill with an object of beauty. Think of it as a question of which came first, your need or your love of the object.

Let me give you an example. If you're in the market for a set of unique dishes and find such a set in a booth at a local crafts show, your need came before your love. On the other hand, if you were just browsing through the booths at the show when you came across the dishes, and their beauty sparked your desire to buy them, the love came before the need. In the former case, your goal should be to obtain *an* object that fits your need for the best price you can. In the latter case, your goal should be to obtain *this* object for the best price you can. The obvious difference is that if you're looking to fill a need you've more than one option. If you're looking to obtain an object you desire, rather than need, you're limited to a single choice.

## IS IT WORTH MY TIME?— DECIDING IF IT'S READILY NEGOTIABLE

As a rule, objects being sold by subjective retailers are readily negotiable. That's because, in most cases, the cost of either producing or obtaining the object has had no bearing on its price tag. Instead, pricing has been determined by perceptions.

A photographer selling his wares at a crafts show doesn't determine the price tag on his photos by calculating how much it cost him to develop and frame a print, then amortizing the cost of his equipment over the number of pictures he prints, adding in his overhead for renting the booth, and then finally adding in a profit. He's an artist and therefore probably prices the photos according to what he perceives they're worth aesthetically.

While he may be more of a businessperson, the antiques store owner is no more objective in his pricing. Somewhere back in his office he has a record of how much he spent on each item. And if he sat down with his accountant—if he has one—he could probably calculate how much it costs him to stay in business and maintain an item in inventory. However, he's an enthusiast and therefore probably prices his pieces based on what he perceives someone will pay for them.

Since in both cases the sellers' prices are based on perceptions of value, they're open to debate—and, therefore, negotiation. Your perception of an item's value is probably different from the seller's perception. If the seller wants to make a sale, he'll need to either convince you to accept his perception, agree to accept your perception, or offer a compromise somewhere in between. Therefore, as long as you realize that a subjective retailer's statement of value (the price tag) is a perception open to debate rather than an economic fact, the price is readily negotiable.

While every purchase from a subjective retailer is readily negotiable, some are more negotiable than others. If you're buying to meet a need and have a wide range of choices, the purchase is extremely negotiable since the seller and his product will be in competition with other sellers and other products. However, if you're in the market to buy a particular object from a particular seller, you've less negotiating room. In fact, unless you play the game right, you may even eliminate the negotiability entirely. Rather than the seller being in competition, you may actually feel you're competing with other buyers in the quest to purchase this rare item of beauty. This can be disastrous to a negotiation.

## IS IT IMPORTANT TO ME?— MAKING SURE IT'S WORTH DOING

Just as you needed to judge for yourself whether or not it was worth negotiating a purchase from an objective retailer, you need to determine whether or not you should bother negotiating for a purchase from a subjective retailer. Just because subjective retailers are, as a rule, more readily negotiable than objective retailers, doesn't mean you should always negotiate.

I know there are many people who disagree. They look on back-and-forth haggling as a pastime, a sport, or a hobby. They shop at flea markets and crafts shows not for the lower prices or the unusual merchandise but because they can negotiate with the sellers. For these people, negotiating is a thrilling game. Perhaps that's where my difference with them comes from. I see negotiating as a serious business, hard work that requires a great deal of time and effort. I don't look at it as fun or a game. Instead, I see it as something I need to do for either myself, a friend or family member, or a client. I know it sounds illogical, but deep down I feel there's a limited amount of negotiating power within me. I can't keep going to and drawing from that well of negotiating power all the time. If I do, I'm afraid one day, when I really need it, I'll find the well has run dry. I think this illogical fear of mine is actually a psychological defense mechanism. Somewhere deep in my brain there's an understanding that negotiating is time-consuming and intellectually draining. So in order to make sure I don't overtax myself, my subconscious paints this picture of the finite well.

Whatever the psychology of it, I suggest you, too, adapt the illogical idea of the finite well of negotiating power and give up all notions of negotiating as a game or pastime. Instead, look at all opportunities to negotiate as a time to ask yourself a question: "Is the amount of time and effort it will take me to negotiate worth the amount of money I could potentially save?"

Assume that by negotiating the purchase of a readily negotiable, subjectively priced object from its owner or creator, you'll be able to save a minimum of 20 percent. (I won't even hazard a guess as to the maximum possible savings, since a chair picked up at a junkyard for $10 could be an antique arguably worth $2,500, which ends up at an antiques store priced for $5,000, offering the seller an incredible amount of negotiating space.) If you negotiate the purchase of an antique table that has a list price of $1,000, there's a minimum likely savings of $200. It's pretty clear that negotiating would make sense in that case.

But what if the object is a photograph that lists for $100? Presumably you'd be able to save about $20 by negotiating. Is that worthwhile? Based on the tactics I'll be discussing later in this chapter, you can assume it's going to take you at least two trips to the seller, at least six hours apart, to conclude the negotiation, and there's going to be an element of risk that the object will be sold in the time between your two trips. Whether or not those two trips are worth the $20 depends on how long it will take you to get to the seller, what else you could be doing with your time, and how important that particular photograph is to you. How about a $50 ceramic bowl? If you negotiated you'd stand to save $10. Is that worth two trips?

For me at least, the magic number seems to come around at a savings of $50. Unless I'm at a flea market and will be spending the whole day browsing around, making it a simple matter to come back to a booth for a second stop, I don't bother negotiating for savings of under $50. Of course, that's my judgment. Yours might be entirely different. I'm not saying you should come up with an ironclad rule. What I'm suggesting is that every time you're about to buy a subjectively priced object you make a conscious judgment about whether or not it's worth negotiating. Sometimes you may be unable to make two trips and desperately want this particular item. In that instance a savings of $50 might not be worth it. Other times it could be a rainy Saturday you're going to spend wandering around an indoor flea market and you don't mind spending six hours to save $25.

Let's see how Lowell and Susan did their self-examination. Since they were looking for an armoire, any armoire, to use as a media cabinet, Lowell and Susan's need clearly came before their love for a particular object. That meant their goal was to obtain an object that met their needs for the best price they could find. In this case, their need was an armoire for $750 or less. Lowell and Susan knew that since they were looking for an old armoire, they'd be shopping at antiques stores, secondhand shops, and estate sales, which meant they'd be dealing with subjective retailers. Since subjective retailers base their prices on perception, they're automatically readily negotiable. And since Lowell and Susan weren't fixated on a particular item, their purchase offered even more negotiating space. Finally, Lowell and Susan knew that the purchase was worth negotiating. In fact, in their instance it was essential to negotiate in order to bring the price down to the level they could afford.

## LEVELING THE SUBJECTIVELY PRICED PLAYING FIELD

The second step in negotiating the purchase of a subjectively priced item is for the buyer to get to know his or her opponent—the seller—and to use that information to level the playing field. This is done by answering four questions: "What do I need to know?" "With whom should I negotiate?" "Are there any potentially disruptive side issues?" "What do I share with my opponent?"

### WHAT DO I NEED TO KNOW?— GATHERING INFORMATION

Aside from determining who's the owner or creator of an object you're interested in buying, the information-gathering process in this negotiation is more for show than effect.

Primarily you're looking to establish a rapport with the seller. You want to demonstrate you appreciate his artistry or his eye for beauty. You want to show you're not a "lowbrow" concerned solely with price but someone who admires beauty and wishes they could be a patron of the arts. A little bit of self-deprecation, coupled with admiring questions and rapt attention to answers, will draw enthusiasts and artists out of their protective shells. They'll try to take you under their wing and educate you in the ways of their art. Every enthusiast wants others to feel the same enthusiasm he does. Every artist wants an admiring audience. If through your attempts at gathering information you can answer these wants you'll be able to negotiate successfully.

I'm sure you're wondering why I'm not encouraging you to go out and research the value of objects in price guides and auction reports. I believe the market value of subjectively priced objects actually has little import for most people: it applies only to collectors since they're the ones who determine market value. If you're someone who's interested in the investment value of your purchase, or who's going to be reselling this item at a later date, its market value—the price other collectors are willing to pay for it—is important to you. But if you're purchasing something because you love the way it looks, or because it fulfills a need, its value to collectors is meaningless. What's important is its value to you, and that can't be determined from looking in a price guide.

Let me give you an example. I have a friend who loves building plastic models of airplanes. He's particularly interested in British aircraft of World War II. His birthday was coming around so I decided to buy him a model. I went to a very large hobby shop in New York City. I was browsing around when I found a stack of very old and rare kits of an unusual British airplane. They each had price tags of $35. Right next to the old kits I found a stack of new kits of the same unusual plane. They were each priced at $15 and looked to be just as good as, if not better than, the more expensive models. A man browsing nearby was ecstatic about the old, rare kits. He told me he'd been looking for one for years. I suggested he take a look at the new kit, which was less than half the price of the older one and looked to be even better. The other fellow said he didn't care for the new one. He didn't actually build the models, he told me. He was a collector. He enjoyed searching for them, and then stored them away in his basement, sure in the knowledge they'd increase in value. Building them, he told me, would destroy their value. He had a price guide in his pocket and looked up the value of the kit. The book said it could be sold for $50. He immediately purchased it. I, on the other hand, bought my friend the newer model for $15. To me, and to my friend, that particular model kit had a value of only $15. To the collector it was well worth $35.

## *WITH WHOM SHOULD I NEGOTIATE?—*
## *PUSHING THE UP BUTTON*

In order to successfully negotiate the purchase of a subjectively priced object you'll need to uncover who created it or who owns it. That's because since the object's price tag is based on either the creator's or artist's individual perception, you'll need to directly dissuade *them* of that perception. Surrogates or subordinates don't have the power to negotiate their superiors' perceptions.

It's not always obvious who's the artist or owner. Sure, if you're at a crafts show and a booth filled with photographs is manned by one individual you can be fairly certain he's the photographer. However, if there's more than one person in the booth, or if the booth contains a variety of objects, you can't be sure who created what. At an antiques shop you'll need to determine whether or not the person sitting behind the desk out front is the proprietor or merely a salesperson. And if you're browsing a booth or store with a wide variety of items you'll need to find out whether they're actually owned by the seller or are being sold on consignment.

Consignment is a retail system, common to the crafts and collectibles business, in which the retailer, rather than buying his inventory, agrees to pay the artist or owner only if an item is sold. The artist or owner asks for a particular price. The retailer then marks that price up to cover his overhead and make a profit. When an item is sold, the artist receives his price and the retailer pockets the rest. Since the prices in a consignment shop are initially based on a mathematical formula rather than an owner's or creator's perception of value, the store is an objective rather than a subjective retailer. In order to turn this situation into a negotiation with a subjective seller you'll need to bypass the retailer and get directly to the owner or creator.

The best way to uncover the truth about ownership and "creatorship" is simply to ask. If you're at a crafts display, simply ask the person, "Are you the artist?" That's a wonderfully flattering way to discern whom you should be negotiating with. If you're at a shop you can do much the same thing by asking, "Are you the owner of this magnificent store?"

To determine whether goods are being sold on consignment, check to see if information on artists is displayed near the items. Generally, one of the signs of consignment selling is that promotional material about the artist is provided. While this is done for marketing purposes, it also provides you with an opportunity to negotiate directly with the artist. (Don't be surprised if some objects in a store are being sold on consignment and others are not—that's a typical practice.) Once you find promotional material on the artist you can simply jot down his name, address, and telephone number, and then contact him directly.

## ARE THERE ANY POTENTIALLY DISRUPTIVE SIDE ISSUES?—ELIMINATING DISSONANCE

The dissonance surrounding a negotiation over a subjectively priced object is the very subjective nature of its pricing. The seller is afraid you won't appreciate the quality or aesthetics of his product and therefore won't respect his price. This is particularly true of creators. An artist or craftsperson considers his work to be art, deserving of a high price, but is afraid you'll think of it as mere decoration. In effect, his ego is wrapped up in the value of the product. The same is true, to a slightly lesser degree, for the enthusiast. While he didn't create the object, it has been his taste and judgment that has singled it out as being aesthetically valuable. Therefore, his ego is wrapped up in his price as well. That's why attempts to negotiate price are often viewed very negatively by enthusiasts and artists. They see them as attacks on their egos.

The way to eliminate this potential dissonance is to clearly demonstrate your appreciation of the object and to voice no objection to its stated value. You must present your effort at negotiation as being based on your inability to afford what the item is worth. That way, you assuage the seller's ego while still providing a reason for him to negotiate. For example: You should say something such as "I know this photograph is worth $100. In fact, it's probably worth more. I wish I could buy it, but I just can't afford to spend that much money."

## WHAT DO I SHARE WITH MY OPPONENT?— FINDING AND DEMONSTRATING COMMON GROUND

Unlike most mercantile transactions, the common ground between buyers and sellers of subjectively priced objects isn't always the desire for ownership to change. Since prices are based on perception, and are tied up in seller ego, appreciation is often just as important as money. Many subjective sellers actually aren't looking so much for price as they are for a validation of the value of their product.

I can't tell you how many antiques dealers I know say they wouldn't sell an item to a person who would do something "wrong" to it. It's as if they were parting with a limb. With creators this tendency is even more pronounced. They're parting with a vital organ. These sellers may want ownership to change hands, but they want that owner to be someone who feels about the item the way they do.

Throughout the information-gathering and dissonance-eliminating stages of this negotiation you'll be laying the foundation for your common ground: love of the object. You need to come out and state directly: "I love this item." Think of yourself as asking a parent for permission to marry his child. I know it sounds crazy, but if you clearly state your deep and abiding love for a seller's product, he'll feel much better about negotiating with you.

# INSIDER TIPS FOR BUYERS OF SUBJECTIVELY PRICED ITEMS

The third and final step in negotiating the purchase of a subjectively priced item is to know the situation. That's accomplished by applying the lessons learned by those who are experienced with this particular situation. I have extensive experience in negotiating the purchase of subjectively priced items, both for myself and for others. In addition, I've written on the antiques industry and have interviewed craftspeople, artists, and dealers for this book. All that has led me to offer two insider tips, which I call the "appeal" and the "bid."

## *THE APPEAL*

The appeal consists of cultivating a relationship with the seller, demonstrating your respect for his price, establishing your love of the item, but then pleading poverty and appealing to him to help you become the owner. It's basically a technique that will allow you to enter into a short back-and-forth price negotiation. Let me take you through it.

Let's say you're interested in buying a particular photograph you see at a crafts shop that's priced at $150. You ask the photographer about his technique, what kind of camera and film he uses, how long he has been taking pictures, and so forth. You then say you know the photograph is worth $150. In fact, it's probably worth $200. But unfortunately you can't afford to spend that much money. Next, you directly state that you really love this photo. And finally you ask if there's any way the photographer can help you become the owner of this photo.

In response, the photographer will in all probability ask you how much you can afford. Your offer should be based on how valuable the item is to you. Bear in mind, however, that offers seeking more than a 20 percent discount will probably destroy the common ground and goodwill you've built up. Let's say you sheepishly offer an apologetic $120, saying you know it's less than the picture is worth but that it's really all you can afford. The photographer will either grab the opportunity to sell his work or will offer a compromise figure. If he comes back with a price, tell him you need to think about it and will come back later.

Allow at least six hours to pass, if possible, before returning. You want enough time to go by for the photographer to realize that no one is banging down his door to buy the print, to begin to think that unless he sells it to you he won't sell it at all, and to fear that you will never return. Of course, you're taking a chance the item will be sold in that time, but that's the risk you must take in order to achieve the reward of a lower price. If the photo is sold upon your return, reiterate your love of the print and graciously tell the photographer you're glad he was able to sell it. If the photo hasn't been sold, offer a bit more than you did at first, but not as much as the photographer asked. Stress that this really is all you can spend. This minimal increase gives the photographer a chance to feel like a winner, reinforces your finite resources, and focuses the pressure. If the photographer doesn't agree, thank him and walk away. He may follow you or he may not, but in neither case should you move off your final offer.

Let me digress for just a paragraph and tell you about the first time I got up and walked away from a negotiation. About twenty years ago I was representing a father and son who wanted to buy a delicatessen in Brooklyn. From the very beginning the negotiations among the owners, the potential buyers, and the two attorneys were friendly. We used to meet at the deli and sit around a table in the back drinking beer, eating pretzels, and talking about the business. I genuinely got to like these people. After a few preliminary meetings we started to get down to details. Right away I could see that the two sides were so far apart that it seemed we'd never reach an agreement. Instinctively I stood up and started to put my coat on. The other side couldn't believe what I was doing. I explained that I didn't want to destroy what had been a wonderful relationship and that I was afraid we were so far apart that further discussions could only lead to bitterness. Why not just stop it here, I suggested. The owners, who obviously were anxious to sell, leaped to their feet, spitting out apology after apology, and immediately lowered their asking price without my clients' making a concession. We eventually closed the deal, but I had taken a big risk.

Speaking of risk, let's look at the second insider tip you could use when buying a subjectively priced item.

## THE BID

The bid is a little bit simpler and quicker technique, and it offers more potential reward—but at a greater risk. Let's use the example of the photo again. Go through all of the same early steps as you would in the appeal: demonstrate your respect for the photographer's price, establish your love of the print, and then plead poverty. But rather than appealing to the photographer to help you and looking to enter into an incremental negotiation, tell him you'd like to leave a bid with him. Explain that all you can afford to spend is a certain amount (approximately 20 percent less than he's asking). Acknowledge that this is less than the print is worth, but say that if he isn't able to sell the print for what it's worth, you'd like him to consider selling it to you for your bid. There's no reason for him to decline the offer—he has nothing to lose. Add a time limit to your offer—say, the end of the day—and give a reason for it: you're leaving town. Otherwise, the photographer can use your bid as a blank check he can cash anytime. You want him to feel pressured to lower his price.

After a reasonable amount of time has elapsed (the end of the day at a flea market, or perhaps the end of the month at an antiques shop), and just prior to the expiration of your deadline, return to the photographer. If the print has been sold congratulate him and reiterate your appreciation for his work and your wish that you could have afforded to buy his product. If the item hasn't been sold, once again ask if he's willing to sell it for the price you mentioned. If he tries to enter into another number negotiation, graciously refuse. Explain again that this is really all you can afford to pay, keeping the pressure on him. If he refuses, thank him and then walk away. Whether or not he follows you, refuse to come off your original price.

While there's no hard-and-fast rule, the bid gambit seems to work best with creators who are already under time pressure—such as artists and craftspeople displaying their wares at sidewalk shows and flea markets—while the appeal gambit seems to work best with enthusiasts who aren't under time pressure—such as antiques or collectibles dealers who have established stores or regular booths.

Let's see how Lowell and Susan leveled the playing field and negotiated the purchase of their armoire. Susan found an excellent selection of armoires at a nearby antiques dealer. The one that best met her needs was, not coincidentally, the one with the lowest price: $1,000. She found the owner of the shop, complimented her on the beautiful wares, and asked about antiques in general and armoires in particular. Susan listened with true fascination as the dealer explained how to tell the age of a piece and recounted each piece's history—or, as she called it, provenance. Susan said she could see the armoire was clearly worth what the dealer was asking, if not more, but that she couldn't afford it. Susan said she really loved the piece and was wondering if there was any way the dealer could help her. The dealer asked Susan how much she could afford. Susan apologetically said all she could spend was $700. The dealer responded that she really couldn't let the piece go for less than $900. Susan said she understood and would need to think about it, implying she needed to speak with her husband.

One month later, Susan returned to the antiques shop, this time with Lowell. The dealer recognized Susan and told her the armoire was still unsold. Susan brought Lowell over to see the piece and asked the dealer if she could once again explain its provenance and point out its important characteristics. The dealer did so and Lowell now listened attentively. Lowell stated his love of the item and respect for the dealer's price. He and Susan whispered a few words to each other and Susan then offered the dealer $750, saying that was really all they could afford. The dealer said she couldn't drop below $850. Susan and Lowell dejectedly started to leave the shop. As they were opening the door to go, the dealer called them back in. She said that since Susan and Lowell so obviously loved the piece she had changed her mind and would let them have it for $750.

## Arguing Over Aesthetics
## Buying Subjectively Priced Items

- If you're filling a need, buy an item for the best price.
- If you're filling a want, buy *this* item for the best price.
- If you're buying to meet a need the purchase is extremely negotiable.
- Negotiate with either the creator or the owner of an object.
- Is the time and effort it'll take worth a 20 percent savings?
- Demonstrate that you appreciate the seller's artistry or taste.
- Voice no objection to its stated value.
- With enthusiasts plead poverty and appeal for help.
- With artisans leave a bid and use time pressure.

# 10

# SHAVING SHINGLES

## Hiring Professionals and Service Providers

*"Between the amateur and the professional . . . there is a difference not only in degree but in kind. The skillful man is, within the function of his skill, a different integration, a different nervous and muscular and psychological organization. . . . A tennis player or a watchmaker or an airplane pilot is an automatism but he is also criticism and wisdom."*

—BERNARD DE VOTO

Margaret and Linda had finally decided to have the home of their dreams built on the rural property they'd purchased years earlier. But they knew they'd need help. First, since they wanted this home to be special, they'd need to hire an architect to design it. And second, since theirs was a nontraditional relationship, they'd need to make sure their individual 50 percent shares in the home would pass to the survivor when one of them died. That meant they'd need a lawyer to draft their wills.

## THE SERVICE USER'S SELF-EXAMINATION

In hiring a professional or service provider, just as in every other negotiation, the first step in the process is for you to analyze your needs and weigh your options, by getting to know yourself. That's accomplished by answering three questions: "What do I want?" "Is it worth my time?" "Is it important to me?"

### *WHAT DO I WANT?—SETTING SPECIFIC GOALS*

You can't successfully negotiate fees with a professional or a service provider until you're absolutely sure of what type of professional you need. By that I don't mean whether you need an accountant or a lawyer. Rather, you need to decide what type of accountant or attorney you need.

Within every profession there are various grades of practitioners who can be categorized by their experience, specialties, skills, and any number of other differences. I like to categorize professionals by the type of relationship I need to develop with them. I divide all professionals and service providers into three types of practitioners: supplicants, partners, and advisers.

A "supplicant" is a professional or service provider who does exactly what you tell him to do. You're looking strictly for competence, standard work requiring no creativity. A "partner" is a professional or service provider who works with you, adding his expertise to your package of skills. You're looking to him to provide a specific, often technical, skill you lack. An "adviser" is a professional or service provider who provides counsel. You're looking to him for wisdom or artistry. You want him to take charge of the situation and, basically, tell you what to do.

Let me explain the differences using accountants as an example. If all you need is an accountant to prepare your tax returns, you're looking for a supplicant. If you need an accountant to set up a bookkeeping system and keep your financial records during the year, you're looking for a partner. But if you need an accountant to counsel you on what legal form your business should take, you're looking for an adviser.

By determining what type of practitioner you need you can establish your goals and narrow down your choices to the right group of candidates. If you need a supplicant, your goal should be to find the least expensive, competent person. You can then choose from among a group of young general practitioners whose fees are relatively low. If you need a partner, your goal should be to find the person who'll do the best job for the money. In this instance you can choose from among young specialists and experienced generalists. If you need an adviser, your goal should be to find the best . . . period. That means you'll be choosing from the ranks of experienced specialists.

### IS IT WORTH MY TIME?— DECIDING IF IT'S READILY NEGOTIABLE

How readily negotiable a professional's or service provider's fee is depends, once again, on what type of individual you're looking for.

A supplicant's fee isn't readily negotiable. Generally, these types of practitioners are offering affordable competence. Since they're competing primarily on price they've probably calculated their fee very carefully. The differences between competitors' fees, therefore, will have more to do with their own overhead than anything else. When that's the case there's very little room to negotiate.

An adviser's fee probably isn't readily negotiable either. He knows his wisdom or artistry carries a certain value. Theoretically, the only way he can lower his fee is to cut back on his efforts. And if he's a good professional he won't be willing to do that. (You may, however, be able to negotiate things other than his fee.)

The most readily negotiable professional is the partner. That's because you've got the widest range of potential candidates for this job. You can select from young practitioners looking for an opportunity as well as from experienced practitioners looking for some easy money. The former are reaching up to you while the latter are reaching down. That leaves them both with room to negotiate their fees.

## IS IT IMPORTANT TO ME?—MAKING SURE IT'S WORTH DOING

When it comes to negotiating with professionals and service providers this step takes on a slightly different meaning. Your concern here isn't how much time it will take to negotiate and whether the potential savings will be worth the time invested. Instead, the main issue is will you be somehow hurting yourself by negotiating services.

Let me explain. Most professionals and service providers take pride in their work. Whether they're brain surgeons or auto mechanics they see themselves as highly skilled individuals. They want you, their customer, client, or patient, to respect their skills. By negotiating fees and services you may, in some instances, give your opponent the sense that you don't respect him. That could result in his doing a less than outstanding job for you.

Let's say you own a 1968 Triumph TR-6 sports car. Like most English sports cars it's temperamental. And since it's starting to get up there in years it's becoming even more so. You seek out a mechanic who specializes in English sports cars and bring the car in for work. You explain the problems you've been having and then start to negotiate the fee. The mechanic may be willing to negotiate, but he also may be taken aback by your lack of respect for his skills. After all, he's a Triumph specialist, an artist, not just a grease monkey. How dare you imply he isn't worth the fee he quoted. If he doesn't need your work he may tell you where you can park your TR-6. If he does need the work he may accept "the insult" but say to himself: "Since he's paying less than my standard fee, he's going to get less than my standard effort." As a result, you've succeeded in negotiating but you might have failed to get the job done correctly.

The answer, I believe, is that it's not worth negotiating custom work that relies heavily on the dedication of the professional or service provider. In other words, don't bother negotiating with advisers. Think about it. Would you attempt to negotiate the fee of a brain surgeon about to perform a delicate operation on you? Of course not. You'd be afraid of alienating him. The same holds true for any other professional or service provider you're using for his wisdom in addition to his skill and competence.

So where does that leave you? I've told you that neither supplicants nor advisers are readily negotiable and that it's also not worth negotiating with advisers since you risk their doing less than their best. That means the only professionals and service providers who are both readily negotiable and worth negotiating with are partners.

Let's see what Margaret and Linda learned in their self-examination. When it came to the architect, Margaret and Linda knew they wanted more than just a competent job (conforming to the local building code) since the aesthetics of the house were very important to them. At the same time they wanted their own feelings and ideas to be reflected in the design. From their conversations with others they learned that if they chose an experienced, name architect, they were more likely to get his vision than their own. That meant they were looking for a "partner." And since a partner relationship was both readily negotiable and worth negotiating, Margaret and Linda could move on to leveling the playing field.

Next, Margaret and Linda began thinking about their relationship with the attorney they'd need to hire to write their wills. While their relationship wasn't traditional, neither of their estates was very complex. Margaret and Linda had no children of their own. The only parent who was alive was Linda's mother. Both, however, had living siblings who, in turn, had children of their own. Margaret was close to her brother and sister, while Linda barely spoke to her sister. Margaret's and Linda's only fear was that if something happened to either of them, the dead partner's siblings might try to take ownership of 50 percent of the home. But their fears were allayed somewhat after they spoke to friends and did some preliminary research. An attorney friend of theirs told them it really was a simple matter that could be handled by any competent attorney—they didn't need a specialist. That meant they could look for a supplicant professional and base their decision on price. But that also meant the terms of the relationship would neither be readily negotiable nor worth negotiating. It would simply be a matter of getting recommendations, interviewing, and comparison shopping.

# LEVELING THE SERVICE USER'S PLAYING FIELD

The second step in hiring a professional or service provider is to get to know the opponent and to use that information to level the playing field. This is done by answering four questions: "What do I need to know?" "With whom should I negotiate?" "Are there any potentially disruptive side issues?" "What do I share with my opponent?"

## *WHAT DO I NEED TO KNOW?—*
## *GATHERING INFORMATION*

While the information-gathering process differs depending on what type of professional or service provider you need, there are some similarities. (For information about gathering information on service providers who aren't specifically addressed in this chapter, see chapter 11.)

First, before you can enter into a negotiation with an individual practitioner you need to have a clear idea of what the range of fees is for a particular profession and how those fees are determined. If you're going to be negotiating with a service provider—a plumber or auto mechanic, for example—ask your friends, co-workers, and neighbors about what they've paid for similar services. If you're going to be negotiating with a professional—an architect or attorney, for example—contact the national or regional organization that represents the profession and ask a source there about average fees for the services you require.

After you've got an idea of what the fees are and how they're determined, the next thing you need to do in gathering information is to ask the same source or sources for recommendations. Let me add a couple of notes of caution. When asking friends, co-workers, and neighbors for recommendations, make sure you're asking people who are in your economic bracket. Your boss, who makes twice your salary, wouldn't be as good a source for a lawyer as a co-worker who makes a salary similar to your own. When asking professional associations for recommendations be aware that most are loath to make subjective judgments about members. Your source at the local bar association, for example, won't want to offer a recommendation per se. Instead, he'll provide you with the names of two or three local lawyers who do the type of work you need. In addition, the association will only provide you with names of its members.

The third thing you need to do in gathering information is to speak directly with potential service providers or professionals. You'll be asking each about their experience, accreditation, and fee structure. You'll also be trying to get an idea of how organized and responsive each will be once hired. Look for someone whose place of business is well organized, whose staff seems well trained and caring, and who appears to respond well to clients. If you're looking for an accountant to organize your books, for example, you don't want to hire someone whose office looks like it has been hit by a tornado. Similarly, if you're looking for a physician, you don't necessarily want someone who's overweight or who smokes.

The fourth and final thing to do in gathering information about service providers and professionals is to obtain—and check—references. During your initial meeting with the candidate make sure to obtain the names of clients or customers who commissioned work similar to what you'll be having done. For example, if you're hiring a carpenter to install a skylight, ask for the names of others for whom he has installed skylights. That way you'll be comparing apples to apples. You'll also be compensating some-what for the natural tendency of people to provide you with the names of only "satisfied customers."

Once you've obtained the names, make it your business to actually contact them and ask about the professional or service provider. Try to ask yes-or-no rather than open-ended questions. References almost always hate to say bad things about someone they've hired unless their experience was absolutely horrible. And if that were the case you wouldn't have been given that name in the first place. But if you ask direct yes-or-no questions you can ferret out the information you need. For example, ask customers of the carpenters you're considering to install your skylight whether the work was done on time, if it came in for the price quoted, if the carpenter came back to fix any problems, and if the skylight leaks.

## WITH WHOM SHOULD I NEGOTIATE?— PUSHING THE UP BUTTON

Obviously, you should negotiate directly with professionals. In the case of service practitioners, you should negotiate with the individual who ei-ther manages or owns the company or business. Only he has the power to make binding agreements. For instance, if you're having your car re-paired you need to negotiate with the owner of the shop, not the individual mechanic.

## ARE THERE ANY POTENTIALLY DISRUPTIVE SIDE ISSUES?—ELIMINATING DISSONANCE

The primary element of dissonance you'll need to address in negotiating with service providers and professionals is any disparity in economic and social status between the two of you. As I mentioned earlier in the book, perceived status plays a large part in some negotiations, particularly those involving service providers and professionals. The dynamics of the relationship between you and your practitioner are such that, as the one paying the bills, you should automatically have a superior status economically. Whether you're dealing with an accountant or a psychiatrist, since you're the one paying for the service, you should be treated as a valued customer/client. He is working for you; you aren't working for him. At the same time, the practitioner has an obvious intellectual superiority: you're hiring him because he has a skill you lack and need.

The key to a successful negotiation, and a successful relationship, is to make sure neither side tries to turn its built-in, specific advantages into overall dominance. Even though you're the one paying the bills, you shouldn't hold that over the head of the practitioner. And even though you lack the skill of the practitioner, he shouldn't hold that over your head. However, it happens all the time. You may know nothing about automobiles, but you think because you're paying the mechanic he's beneath you. A doctor, since he knows a great deal more about medicine than you, treats you as his inferior.

In order to combat these tendencies you need to do everything possible to emphasize that you and the practitioner are equal in all things except for the financial and technical advantages that are built into your relationship. The way to do this is through your dress and attitude. When negotiating with service providers and professionals your goal should be to dress like them. Whether it means upgrading or downgrading your garb, you should make every effort to look like your opponent. That means wearing casual work clothes when meeting with an auto mechanic or carpenter, and wearing a business suit when meeting with an attorney or physician. This will eliminate the subconscious judgment that takes place when two parties meet.

But changing your appearance isn't the only way to eliminate any disparity in status. Unless you complement your dress with an attitude of equality your costume change will be meaningless. Your attitude should be one of two equal parties meeting for business. You both have something the other needs. You need work done on your car, for example, and the mechanic needs cars to work on. Regardless of what social status you assign to your opponent's profession you should respect it. After all, you can't do it. But this respect shouldn't turn you into an unquestioning supplicant yourself. In other words, feel free to ask questions but don't act like you already know the answers.

One way to physically demonstrate this attitude is to mirror your opponent's language. Quite often people subconsciously use language to indicate their superiority. Your auto mechanic may call you Mrs. Smith but you insist on calling him Bob. Your doctor, on the other hand, calls you by your first name while you address him as Dr. Jones. Although it may feel uncomfortable at first, mimic the way your opponent addresses you. Very quickly the other side will get the message and either be grateful for the respect or will cut out the condescension.

If you find your opponent is unwilling to treat you as an equal, find someone else. You cannot negotiate with a service provider or professional who treats your lack of knowledge with contempt. Regardless of how technically well-qualified he is, such an individual will do terrible work. If he isn't able to treat you as an equal he'll be unresponsive to your needs.

### WHAT DO I SHARE WITH MY OPPONENT?— FINDING AND DEMONSTRATING COMMON GROUND

Once you've eliminated the dissonance surrounding your negotiation you can move on to establishing common ground. All this entails is a direct statement of what should have become clear while you were establishing your equality. Directly say to your opponent, "I respect your skill and ability and expect that you, in return, will respect my wants and needs."

## INSIDER TIPS FOR SERVICE USERS

The third and final step in hiring a professional or service provider is to know the situation. That's accomplished by applying the lessons learned by those who are experienced with this particular situation. Not only am I a professional, I frequently help my clients hire other professionals. In addition, I've interviewed hundreds of different service providers and professionals for this book. All this has led me to develop three insider tips.

First, when dealing with a hungry young practitioner, you could imply you'll be able to bring him other business in exchange for a lower fee.

Second, when dealing with an experienced and established practitioner, you could leave his fee alone but negotiate a reduction in up-front deposits.

And third, you could reduce some of the practitioner's responsibilities and ask for fee reductions in response.

### IMPLY THAT YOU'LL BRING OTHER BUSINESS IN EXCHANGE FOR A LOWER FEE

A practitioner who has just gone into business needs customers more than he needs to maintain his fees. You can use his need to establish a client base to your advantage. During your discussions with him, imply that you may be able to bring him additional business. This needs to be done subtly. For example, you could say: "A lot of my friends are in the same situation as I am and are also looking for someone to help." Or, if you're a member of an organization, you could say, "Down at the lodge we've all been talking about how hard it is to find a good doctor/lawyer/mechanic." The idea is to plant the seed that you're in touch with a group of potential customers who'll be very open to your recommendations. There's no need for you to offer a quid pro quo (a lower fee in exchange for recommendations). If at some other point in the conversation you've had a frank discussion of fees the practitioner will be able to make the connection unaided.

## LEAVE THE FEE ALONE, BUT NEGOTIATE A REDUCTION IN DEPOSITS

If you're negotiating with an experienced and established practitioner, your power to offer recommendations is nice but not important enough to justify cutting his fee. However, you can turn his being established into a tool. Explain to him that you certainly don't question his fee; however, you're concerned about costs. Ask if you can lower the amount of money he requested as a down payment. If he's an established practitioner he has less of a need for this down payment than a young practitioner. Typically, a down payment is used to either pay for supplies or to cover initial expenses. It's important for a newcomer, since he may not have sufficient capital to cover initial expenses or he may not have enough of a past history with his suppliers to obtain supplies on credit. An established practitioner should have both. He looks on the down payment as a way of keeping on top of you. He wants to make sure he has at least some of your money before he begins to spend his own. If you agree to pay the standard fee, you're justified in getting something, like a lowered down payment, in return.

## REDUCE RESPONSIBILITIES AND ASK FOR A FEE REDUCTION IN RESPONSE

The third insider tip for negotiating with a service provider or professional is to reduce his responsibilities and in return receive a price reduction. Most often, services involve a bundle of different tasks. For instance, an accountant may create a financial procedure for a business, supervise the implementation of the procedure, audit the finances quarterly, and prepare the yearly tax returns. Not all of these, however, need be done by the same person. If you ask an accountant to simply set up a financial procedure and then prepare the yearly tax return, you'll be able to negotiate a lower fee.

Let's look at another example. If you've got a problem with your car there are actually two distinct services you need. First, you need someone to diagnose the problem. Second, you need someone to fix the problem. Very often, the best person to diagnose a problem isn't the best person to fix it, and vice versa. A transmission shop, for example, is liable to diagnose every problem as being transmission-related. And a service station mechanic, who rarely works on transmissions, may not know how to repair them. One way to both lower your costs and perhaps in the process obtain better service would be to split the job. Pay a service station mechanic an hourly fee to diagnose the problem; then pay the transmission shop a set price to repair it.

Let's go back to Margaret and Linda. They asked all their friends and co-workers for recommendations of architects. Once they'd compiled a list of three names, they began doing some general research about architects. They learned there were two ways architects charged for their services: some charged a fee equal to 15 percent of the cost of the entire project, while others charged an hourly fee. Hourly fees, they discovered, ran from $55 to $150. They also learned the fee included design, the drafting of a full set of plans, and job supervision. They were somewhat uneasy with the idea of paying a percentage, so they decided to insist on an hourly fee. Since during their self-examination they'd decided on a young architect, they assumed they'd be able to find someone at the lower end of the fee range. In addition, since they had a friend who was a local general contractor, they felt they wouldn't need any job supervision.

Margaret and Linda met with all three candidates, making sure to dress as if they were attending a business meeting. During each interview they asked the candidate about his experience and fees, and obtained references. They also made sure to observe each candidate's office environment and staff. In their discussions they stressed that they were interested in developing a partnership with the architect; they didn't want to stifle the architect's creativity but wanted some input. Margaret and Linda did their best to mimic the language of the architects, and found they were comfortable communicating on a first-name basis with one particular candidate. Probably not coincidentally, this was the candidate they also felt was most open to working with them. After checking out all the candidate's references their gut reaction was confirmed. They made an appointment to meet again with their chosen practitioner.

Once again, Margaret and Linda dressed in business suits. In their previous meeting they'd learned that while their opponent generally charged 15 percent, he'd be willing to work on an hourly basis, billing $75 per hour. Margaret began the meeting with the architect by stating that the primary reason they had selected him was that they respected his skill and creativity and felt that he, in turn, respected their needs and wants. She went on to mention that many of their friends had purchased land in the same area and all of them were afraid they wouldn't be able to find architects who actually took the clients' feelings and ideas into account. Next, Linda explained they'd be using a friend as their general contractor and didn't think they'd need job supervision. She stressed that while they wanted the best home they could buy, their finances were limited. She asked if it was possible for him to lower his hourly fee since he wouldn't be supervising the job. He agreed to cut his price to $65 per hour.

## Shaving Shingles
## Hiring Professionals and
## Service Providers

- For supplicants, find the least expensive competent person.
- For partners, find the best for the money.
- For advisers find the best . . . period.
- Know the range of fees and how they are determined.
- Ask economic peers for recommendations.
- Interview each candidate.
- Obtain and question references.
- Emphasize equality.
- Imply that you'll be able to bring additional business.
- Reduce up-front deposits and/or responsibilities.

# 11

# MORE NUMBER NEGOTIATIONS

## A Guide to Thirty-four Other Possible Opponents

It would be impossible for me to go over every possible numbers negotiation in the kind of detail used in the prior chapters. But since my goal is to make you a total negotiator I can't leave you completely on your own when it comes to other situations. That's why I've decided to close each section of this book that deals with a specific type of negotiation with a chapter that offers brief capsule guides for a host of other possible negotiations. In keeping with the total negotiator approach, each of these capsule guides is built around the three main steps in total negotiating: know yourself, know your opponent, and know the situation. And as in earlier chapters, I provide insider tips for each situation—based on my personal and professional experience as well as on research conducted for this book—so you won't need to rely on experience. In this chapter, which covers additional number negotiations, I've focused on the particular individuals you may need to negotiate with, rather than particular transactions, in order to cover as much ground as possible.

## ACCOUNTANTS AND FINANCIAL PLANNERS

### KNOW YOURSELF

- *What do I want?* Your goal should be looking for either a reduction in the fee or a broadening of services without an increase in fee.
- *Is it worth my time?* It's readily negotiable, especially if you're able to work with younger, independent professionals, eager to establish their practices.

- *Is it important to me?* As long as you won't receive a reduction in quality, it's worth negotiating since it will take little time or effort.

## KNOW YOUR OPPONENT

- *What do I need to know?* Learn the going rate for services in your area by asking friends and other professionals.
- *With whom should I negotiate?* Negotiate with the professional directly, not a secretary, deputy, or bookkeeper.
- *Are there any potentially disruptive side issues?* Never attack the fee as being too high or the services as not being worth their cost. Instead, stress that your appeal is based on affordability.
- *What do I share with my opponent?* The common ground is the natural meeting of interests in a mercantile transaction: both parties want the transaction to be completed.

## KNOW THE SITUATION

- Insider Tip: Insist on an hourly fee rather than a percentage or flat charge, with a budget based on an approximation of the total hours that will be involved.
- Insider Tip: Demonstrate how well organized you are and explain that the professional won't need to spend any time at all getting your numbers and figures together.
- Insider Tip: If you can't get a fee reduction for yourself, ask the professional to provide services to other members of your family (whose needs are simpler) at a reduced rate.

# ANIMAL BREEDERS

## KNOW YOURSELF

- *What do I want?* Your goal should be to buy the best animal you can for the least possible money.
- *Is it worth my time?* It's readily negotiable since it's essential for most breeders to sell their total "inventory" as soon as possible—they don't want to keep the animals themselves.
- *Is it important to me?* It's worth negotiating since value in this instance is totally subjective. There are little or no costs of production—value is in the eyes of the beholder.

### KNOW YOUR OPPONENT

- *What do I need to know?* Study the characteristics of the animal breed in question so you're an informed shopper. Check the reputation of the breeder with local clubs and associations and compare prices among breeders.
- *With whom should I negotiate?* Negotiate with a breeder who still has a large inventory. Someone whose animal just had twelve offspring will be more negotiable than someone with a remaining inventory of only two.
- *Are there any potentially disruptive side issues?* Don't approach it as the purchase of a commodity—that's not how the breeder sees it. State that your requests for price reductions are based on affordability, not on the value of the animal.
- *What do I share with my opponent?* Firm up the natural common ground present in a mercantile transaction between buyer and seller by stating and showing that you'll treat the animal as well as the breeder would.

### KNOW THE SITUATION

- Insider Tip: State your willingness to accept an animal that isn't "show quality." This gives the breeder a way to lower the price and still save face.
- Insider Tip: Try to present the transaction as a trade-off—what you can't offer in dollars to the breeder you'll offer in love and care to the animal.

## ARTISTIC SUBCONTRACTORS

These are building professionals—such as faux marble painters, stencilers, mosaic tile designers, and fireplace masons—who look on what they do as an art form rather than just a craft.

### KNOW YOURSELF

- *What do I want?* Your goal should be to bring the fee more in line with one charged by a quality craftsperson rather than one charged by an artist.
- *Is it worth my time?* It's readily negotiable; since the markup is entirely subjective there's lots of room for movement.

- *Is it important to me?* It's worth negotiating since it's possible to get large discounts simply by pressing for them.

### KNOW YOUR OPPONENT

- *What do I need to know?* Ask other professionals to give you an estimate of the time involved. Have your architect or general contractor check on the individual's credit and financial status.
- *With whom should I negotiate?* Negotiate with the contractor directly, not a family member, agent, or general contractor. Someone who is hungry for work will be more willing to negotiate than someone whose schedule is very busy.
- *Are there any potentially disruptive side issues?* Play to the subcontractor's ego by treating him or her as an artist. Then base your request for a price reduction on affordability, not on the value of his or her services or product.
- *What do I share with my opponent?* Firm up the natural common ground present in a mercantile transaction between buyer and seller by overstating your appreciation of the artistry of whatever it is he or she does.

### KNOW THE SITUATION

- Insider Tip: Offer the subcontractor a sizable role in the planning process. He or she may be willing to trade dollars for artistic fulfillment and satisfaction.
- Insider Tip: Say you're willing to let the subcontractor work whenever it's convenient for him or her. The ability to work at night or on weekends, when they normally wouldn't be earning money, may lead them to accept a lesser fee.

# ATTORNEYS

### KNOW YOURSELF

- *What do I want?* Your goals should be either a reduction in the fee or a broadening of services without an increase in fee.
- *Is it worth my time?* It's readily negotiable, especially with younger, independent professionals eager to establish their practices.

- *Is it important to me?* It's worth negotiating as long as you won't receive a reduction in quality; it's also worth negotiating since it will take little time or effort.

## KNOW YOUR OPPONENT

- *What do I need to know?* Learn the going rate for services in your area by asking friends and other professionals.
- *With whom should I negotiate?* Negotiate with the professional directly, not a paralegal, office manager, or bookkeeper.
- *Are there any potentially disruptive side issues?* Never attack the fee as being too high or the services as not being worth their cost. Instead, stress that your appeal is based on affordability.
- *What do I share with my opponent?* The common ground is the natural meeting of interests in a mercantile transaction: both parties want the transaction to be completed.

## KNOW THE SITUATION

- Insider Tip: Ask the attorney to farm out as much work as possible to the paralegal staff. This could cut hourly charges in half.
- Insider Tip: Set a budget based on an approximation of the total hours that will be involved.
- Insider Tip: If you can't get a fee reduction for yourself, ask the professional to provide services to other members of your family (whose needs are simpler) at a reduced rate.

# BUSINESS CONSULTANTS

## KNOW YOURSELF

- *What do I want?* Your goal should be either a reduction in the fee or a broadening of services without an increase in fee.
- *Is it worth my time?* It's readily negotiable, especially with independent part-timers or semiretired individuals who aren't burdened by overhead or who aren't looking to build up a practice.
- *Is it important to me?* It's worth negotiating as long as you won't receive a reduction in quality; it's also worth negotiating since it will take little time or effort.

### KNOW YOUR OPPONENT

- *What do I need to know?* Learn the going rate for services in your area by asking other business owners.
- *With whom should I negotiate?* Negotiate with the professional directly, not a secretary, deputy, or bookkeeper.
- *Are there any potentially disruptive side issues?* Never attack the fee as being too high or the services as not being worth their cost. Instead, stress that your appeal is based on affordability.
- *What do I share with my opponent?* Firm up the natural common ground present in a mercantile transaction between buyer and seller by implying that you'll be a steady customer if you're satisfied.

### KNOW THE SITUATION

- Insider Tip: Suggest some form of combined cash-and-barter payment. If both parties are service providers who could benefit from each others' skills, it makes sense to pay cash for each other's costs and barter the profit portion of the fees.

## CARPENTERS

### KNOW YOURSELF

- *What do I want?* Your goal should be to pay market rates, but in exchange to receive speedy work and timely completion of the project.
- *Is it worth my time?* It's readily negotiable if the contractor is hungry for work. That means the slower the season, the more open to negotiation the carpenter will be.
- *Is it important to me?* It's worth negotiating since, if you don't, you'll have no insurance that the job will be done speedily and in a timely manner, and that guarantees that the costs will be higher than anticipated.

### KNOW YOUR OPPONENT

- *What do I need to know?* Research the going rate for carpentry services from other professionals and investigate the carpenter's reputation, track record, and financial stability.

- *With whom should I negotiate?* Negotiate with the carpenter directly, not an agent or general contractor.
- *Are there any potentially disruptive side issues?* Don't attack the appropriateness of fee, but instead go after the carpenter's ability to finish the job on time and within the estimate.
- *What do I share with my opponent?* The common ground is the natural meeting of interests in a mercantile transaction: both parties want the transaction to be completed.

### *KNOW THE SITUATION*

- Insider Tip: Make sure you're negotiating with the right type of contractor for the work in question. There are two types of carpentry jobs: rough and finish. The easiest way to differentiate them is that rough work isn't visible and finish work is. Rough carpenters may provide lower bids on finish work simply because they're looking to shift specialties. Ambition is all well and good, but you don't want to be a guinea pig. On the other hand, finish carpenters may overcharge on rough work since they don't want to bother with it.

## CATERING HALLS

### *KNOW YOURSELF*

- *What do I want?* Your goal should be to get the highest quality hall and services for the least money, not to get more for the same money.
- *Is it worth my time?* It's readily negotiable if you're willing to book off days (weekdays rather than weekends) in off-seasons (winter and fall rather than spring and summer).
- *Is it important to me?* It's worth negotiating since you can save up to 50 percent.

### *KNOW YOUR OPPONENT*

- *What do I need to know?* Learn the going rate for hall rentals and catering services by comparison shopping.
- *With whom should I negotiate?* Negotiate with the manager directly rather than a salesperson who has little authority.
- *Are there any potentially disruptive side issues?* There's no disso-

nance in this negotiation—it's strictly the sale of a commodity.
- *What do I share with my opponent?* The common ground is the natural meeting of interests in a mercantile transaction: both parties want the transaction to be completed.

### KNOW THE SITUATION

- Insider Tip: Don't use the house photographer, florist, or band. Catering halls use these allegedly independent contractors to increase their profits.
- Insider Tip: Avoid frills such as printed matchbooks and napkins—they carry tremendous markups.
- Insider Tip: Watch out for inflated overtime fees.
- Insider Tip: Wait as long as you possibly can before booking. Catering halls are like airlines in that they're willing to cut their price dramatically if it means getting something rather than nothing. Of course, you must be flexible about days and dates.

## CONSUMER ELECTRONICS AND APPLIANCE SALESPEOPLE

### KNOW YOURSELF

- *What do I want?* Your goal should be to buy a specific product that you've already selected for the lowest price possible.
- *Is it worth my time?* Big ticket items are almost always readily negotiable. And these particular items are even more so since there is varied pricing among different types of retail outlets and the products themselves become obsolete quickly.
- *Is it important to me?* It's worth negotiating since you could save from 20 to 40 percent.

### KNOW YOUR OPPONENT

- *What do I need to know?* Analyze your needs and wants, thoroughly research the market, and determine exactly what particular product best fits your needs and budget.
- *With whom should I negotiate?* Negotiate first with the salesperson, but in order to get the best deal possible you'll need to deal with a manager.

- *Are there any potentially disruptive side issues?* Stress that you're a bona fide buyer, not a shopper, and that you're ready, willing, and able to make the purchase on this particular day.
- *What do I share with my opponent?* The common ground is the natural meeting of interest in a mercantile transaction: both parties want the transaction to be completed.

### KNOW THE SITUATION

- Insider Tip: You can often get a final price concession by asking for a discontinued or factory-reconditioned model. This gives the salesperson or manager an excuse to lower the price without losing face.
- Insider Tip: Research when new models will be coming out and time your purchase so you may be able to take advantage of informal clearance sales.

## CUSTOM TAILORS AND DRESSMAKERS

### KNOW YOURSELF

- *What do I want?* Your goal should be either to get better quality materials for the same price or to get additional fittings for the same price.
- *Is it worth my time?* It's readily negotiable in the summer, which is the slow season.
- *Is it important to me?* It's worth negotiation if getting the best quality and the best-fitting clothing you possibly can is important to you.

### KNOW YOUR OPPONENT

- *What do I need to know?* Learn everything you can about fabric quality by speaking with the experienced salespeople at high-quality clothing stores. Research the price range for the kind of clothing you're looking to have made.
- *With whom should I negotiate?* Negotiate directly with the tailor or dressmaker.
- *Are there any potentially disruptive side issues?* Don't attack the value of the services provided or the skill of the individual. Instead, base the negotiation on affordability.

- *What do I share with my opponent?* The common ground is the natural meeting of interests in a mercantile transaction: both parties want the transaction to be completed.

## KNOW THE SITUATION

- Insider Tip: Steer clear of custom tailors or dressmakers who have retail-style locations—their prices will be higher to pay for the increased overhead.
- Insider Tip: The bulk of the individual's labor and cost is involved in producing the first garment, since he or she needs to take precise measurements and transfer them to a pattern. By making a multiple purchase from the start, or implying that you'll become a regular buyer, you allow these initial costs to be spread out over more than one garment.

# DENTISTS AND DOCTORS

## KNOW YOURSELF

- *What do I want?* If the work is purely cosmetic in nature your goal should be to obtain a lower cost without a decrease in the quality of services. If the work is medically necessary your goal should be to get extended payment terms.
- *Is it worth my time?* Medical and dental procedures that are cosmetic in nature are readily negotiable since they aren't needed to maintain good health. The payment terms of fees for procedures that are medically necessary are readily negotiable if you stage the negotiation after the work has been completed.
- *Is it important to me?* It's worth negotiating since you could save from 25 to 40 percent off the cost of big ticket cosmetic medical or dental work, and you can obtain no interest terms on medically necessary services with little difficulty.

## KNOW YOUR OPPONENT

- *What do I need to know?* Get at least two opinions as to the extent of any cosmetic work and research the range of prices in the market.
- *With whom should I negotiate?* You need to negotiate with the dentist directly if you're negotiating the fee of cosmetic work. If you're

looking to negotiate terms, deal with the billing clerk or office manager rather than the professional.

- *Are there any potentially disruptive side issues?* Don't question the validity of fees for cosmetic work, but make sure both you and the doctor or dentist are in agreement that the procedure is purely cosmetic and that he or she understands that your decision will be based on affordability. When negotiating terms, stress your intention to pay the bill in its entirety through regular and prompt monthly payments.
- *What do I share with my opponent?* Once you've eliminated the dissonance you've established the natural common ground present in a mercantile transaction.

### KNOW THE SITUATION

- Insider Tip: Fees for cosmetic medical and dental services are very location-sensitive. Look for a qualified doctor or dentist who isn't located in an upscale area.
- Insider Tip: If you're a well-known individual or your professional success is tied to your appearance you may be able to imply that you'll be a walking billboard advertising the doctor's or dentist's skills.
- Insider Tip: If the doctor or dentist balks at reducing the fee, ask for a recommendation to another practitioner who's "almost as good" but who's in your price range. That presents the doctor or dentist with a clear-cut choice and provides an opportunity for him to reconsider.
- Insider Tip: Whenever you receive a prescription ask if there's a low-cost generic equivalent.

## FUNERAL DIRECTORS

### KNOW YOURSELF

- *What do I want?* Your goal should be to get the lowest price you can while still maintaining the dignity of the deceased.
- *Is it worth my time?* It's readily negotiable if you eliminate feelings of guilt and take charge of the process.
- *Is it important to me?* It's worth negotiating since you could save

as much as 50 percent off the cost of a funeral—costs can run upward of $5,000.

## KNOW YOUR OPPONENT

- *What do I need to know?* Comparison shop for prices. Funeral homes are required by federal law to provide itemized price quotes to you over the telephone.
- *With whom should I negotiate?* You should be able to negotiate with a funeral director, but if possible, try to negotiate with the owner of the funeral home.
- *Are there any potentially disruptive side issues?* Put any feelings of personal guilt aside—and instantly and vociferously object to any attempts by the funeral director to inflict guilt—and approach this as something you're doing for the estate, not the deceased.
- *What do I share with my opponent?* The common ground is *not* respect for the deceased, though that's what the funeral director may suggest. Once the dissonance is removed this is a mercantile transaction and should be treated as such.

## KNOW THE SITUATION

- Insider Tip: Rather than having a traditional funeral service, opt for either immediate burial or direct cremation followed by a memorial service without the body present. This reduces the need for the most costly services (those surrounding public presentation of the body) and offers an opportunity to focus on the life of the individual rather than his or her death.

# GARDENERS AND LANDSCAPERS

## KNOW YOURSELF

- *What do I want?* Your goal should be competent yard care, not artistry, for the lowest possible price.
- *Is it worth my time?* It's readily negotiable since this is one of the most competitive fields around, with everyone from professionals to high school students fighting for the work.
- *Is it important to me?* It's worth negotiating for inexpensive garden

care if you see your yard as a place for the kids to play. If you see it as an artistic statement, it's probably not worth negotiating.

## KNOW YOUR OPPONENT

- *What do I need to know?* Comparison shop for prices. Ask friends and neighbors for recommendations.
- *With whom should I negotiate?* The gardeners who will be most open to negotiation are those who solicit you—that means they need the work—or those who are already working on your street—proximity lowers their overhead and speeds up the job.
- *Are there any potentially disruptive side issues?* There's no obvious dissonance in this negotiation.
- *What do I share with my opponent?* The common ground is the natural meeting of interests in a mercantile transaction: both parties want the transaction to be completed.

## KNOW THE SITUATION

- Insider Tip: When dealing with professionals, solicit bids in the dead of the winter when the gardener has nothing to do and is beginning to worry about next year's business.
- Insider Tip: Insist that every bid from a professional contain an hourly fee, an estimate of total hours, and an explanation of what will be done during those hours.
- Insider Tip: If you're negotiating with a nonprofessional, insist on a job or project price rather than an hourly rate since you can't rely on his estimate of how long a job will take.

# HOTELS AND MOTELS

## KNOW YOURSELF

- *What do I want?* Your goal should be to either get a discounted room rate or to get a better room for the same money.
- *Is it worth my time?* It's readily negotiable any time the sun is down and there's a vacancy. For the hotel, an empty room is a total loss. It's better for them to get something for the room rather than nothing.
- *Is it important to me?* It's always worth negotiating hotel rooms

since it takes little time and there's no downside. If you don't succeed you'll simply pay what you would have paid if you didn't try.

## KNOW YOUR OPPONENT

- *What do I need to know?* All you need to learn is if the hotel has a vacancy.
- *With whom should I negotiate?* Negotiate with a manager if possible rather than a desk clerk, who probably has very little authority.
- *Are there any potentially disruptive side issues?* There's no dissonance in this negotiation—it's strictly the sale of a commodity.
- *What do I share with my opponent?* The common ground is the natural meeting of interests in a mercantile transaction: both parties want the transaction to be completed.

## KNOW THE SITUATION

- Insider Tip: Ask what discounts are available. You may belong to an organization whose members receive a discounted rate. You may even be able to join the hotel's own "saver" club on the spot for a fee that's lower than the amount you'll be saving on the room.
- Insider Tip: If you work for a mid- to large-size company, ask for the corporate rate whether or not your firm has previously done business with the hotel or its parent chain.
- Insider Tip: Ask the manager for the standard room rate, then inquire what floor the room in question is on. Offer to take a room on a lower floor if the rate is lower as well.
- Insider Tip: Offer to check out early—by 8:00 A.M.—or do anything else you can think of to provide the manager with an opportunity to lower the standard price.

# HOUSEPAINTERS

## KNOW YOURSELF

- *What do I want?* Your goal should be to obtain competent and neat work for the lowest price possible.
- *Is it worth my time?* As with every craftsperson, housepainters are readily negotiable if they need the work. The more desperate they are for a job, the more negotiable they'll be. They'll also be more

open to negotiation in their off-season, which is winter, when they can only do inside work.

- *Is it important to me?* It's worth negotiating since it's possible to save as much as 25 percent off the cost of a painting project.

## KNOW YOUR OPPONENT

- *What do I need to know?* Read *Consumer Reports* to learn about the quality and durability of various brands of paint. Then research the painter's background, reputation, and financial solvency.
- *With whom should I negotiate?* Negotiate with the painter himself or herself, and look for someone who is eager for the work.
- *Are there any potentially disruptive side issues?* There's no dissonance in this negotiation.
- *What do I share with my opponent?* The common ground is the natural meeting of interests in a mercantile transaction: both parties want the transaction to be completed.

## KNOW THE SITUATION

- Insider Tip: Make sure when you're comparing bids that they're actually comparable: each should be based on the same brand and amount of paint.
- Insider Tip: Say you're willing to let the painter work whenever it's convenient for him or her. The ability to work at night or on weekends, when they normally wouldn't be earning money, may lead them to lower their price.

# LAND SELLERS

## KNOW YOURSELF

- *What do I want?* If you're buying an isolated piece of land your goal should be to get it for as low a price as possible. If you're buying one lot out of a multilot parcel, your goal should be to obtain the best terms possible. That's because since land sale prices are recorded, every time a multilot seller makes a sale it sets a precedent for subsequent sales.
- *Is it worth my time?* Real estate is readily negotiable since it's al-

ways priced at the top end of a value range in anticipation of a negotiation.

- *Is it important to me?* It's not only worth negotiating the purchase of land because of the possible benefits, it's mandatory. The list price is automatically inflated, forcing you to negotiate it down to a fair level.

## KNOW YOUR OPPONENT

- *What do I need to know?* Research previous sales in the area. Look for any possible environmental problems. Investigate water, electrical, and utility access. Find out how long the current owner has owned the lot, how long it has been on the market, and whether or not there have been any other offers or aborted deals.
- *With whom should I negotiate?* Negotiate with the owner rather than a broker if at all possible.
- *Are there any potentially disruptive side issues?* The current owner is afraid of selling too cheaply and of having the deal fall through. You can eliminate those fears by stating that the land is being bought for your own use and by taking on the appearance of a cash buyer.
- *What do I share with my opponent?* The common ground here is your willingness to pay a fair price in exchange for good terms, or to pay cash in exchange for a low price.

## KNOW THE SITUATION

- Insider Tip: In exchange for paying the multiple-lot seller's price, ask for a long-term contract, perhaps one that requires only half the price up front, with the rest coming due when you're ready to build.
- Insider Tip: Alternatively, you could ask the multiple-lot seller to make some improvement to the property, such as digging a well, building an access road, or having electricity brought to the site, in exchange for your paying the price.
- Insider Tip: When negotiating the price of a single-lot seller down, back up your reduced offers with reasons, such as the need to make particular improvements to the land.

## NEW CAR SALESPEOPLE

### *KNOW YOURSELF*

- *What do I want?* Your goal should be to buy a specific car, which you've already selected, for the lowest price possible.
- *Is it worth my time?* New car prices are always negotiable since they're set with negotiation in mind and since there is tremendous competition among sellers of the same product.
- *Is it important to me?* New car prices are so high that it's worth negotiating. Even if you receive only a small percentage decrease in price, the number will probably be higher than whatever you could have earned in the time it took.

### *KNOW YOUR OPPONENT*

- *What do I need to know?* Analyze your needs and wants, thoroughly research the market, and determine exactly what particular product best fits your needs and budget. Learn the dealer's price from *Consumer Reports.*
- *With whom should I negotiate?* Negotiate first with the salesperson, but in order to get the best deal possible you'll need to deal with a manager.
- *Are there any potentially disruptive side issues?* Stress that you're a bona fide buyer, not a shopper, and that you're ready, willing, and able to close the deal on this particular day.
- *What do I share with my opponent?* The common ground is the natural meeting of interests in a mercantile transaction: both parties want the transaction to be completed.

### *KNOW THE SITUATION*

- Insider Tip: Consider shopping for a car by telephone. Call each area dealer of the car you're interested in, explain to the salesperson that you know the dealer cost and your sole concern is getting the best price. Be direct and even a little impatient. If a salesperson won't give you a price quote, hang up. After you've received quotes, call back the nearest dealer, tell the manager what your lowest price quote was, say you'd like to buy the car locally, and give the manager a chance to meet the price. If he or she does, buy it there. If he or she doesn't, buy it from whoever gave you the best price.

# PLUMBERS AND ELECTRICIANS

## *KNOW YOURSELF*

- *What do I want?* Your goal should be to pay market rates, but in exchange to receive speedy work and timely completion of the project.
- *Is it worth my time?* It's readily negotiable if the contractor is hungry for work. That means the slower the season, the more open to negotiation the plumber or electrician will be.
- *Is it important to me?* It's worth negotiating since if you don't, you'll have no insurance the job will be done speedily and in a timely manner. If you don't negotiate, the costs will be higher than anticipated.

## *KNOW YOUR OPPONENT*

- *What do I need to know?* Research the going rate for plumbing or electrical services from other professionals and investigate the contractor's reputation, track record, and financial stability.
- *With whom should I negotiate?* Negotiate with the contractor directly, not an agent or general contractor.
- *Are there any potentially disruptive side issues?* Don't attack the appropriateness of the fee, but instead go after the contractor's ability to finish the job on time and within the estimate.
- *What do I share with my opponent?* The common ground is the natural meeting of interests in a mercantile transaction: both parties want the transaction to be completed.

## *KNOW THE SITUATION*

- Insider Tip: Insist these contractors work on an hourly, rather than a per-fixture, fee.
- Insider Tip: The formula used for charging for materials (often cost plus 10 percent) should be spelled out in your contract.
- Insider Tip: Avoid paying an extra fee for a "helper." They're often unnecessary and are only there to pad the bill.

# PRIVATE NURSES, HOUSE CLEANERS, AND WINDOW WASHERS

### KNOW YOURSELF

- *What do I want?* Your goal should be competent work for the lowest possible price.
- *Is it worth my time?* It's readily negotiable since these are some of the most competitive fields around, with everyone from professionals to part-timers fighting for the work.
- *Is it important to me?* It's worth negotiating since it's possible to save up to 50 percent off the cost of these services.

### KNOW YOUR OPPONENT

- *What do I need to know?* Comparison shop for prices and ask friends and neighbors for recommendations.
- *With whom should I negotiate?* Negotiate with the service provider directly, not an agent or representative.
- *Are there any potentially disruptive side issues?* There's no obvious dissonance in this negotiation.
- *What do I share with my opponent?* The common ground is the natural meeting of interests in a mercantile transaction: both parties want the transaction to be completed.

### KNOW THE SITUATION

- Insider Tip: These service providers generally work for agencies that take a percentage of the fees in exchange for lining up jobs. The best way to negotiate fees with these individuals is to first work with an agency until you find someone you like. Then subtly ask them if they ever work privately. In effect you're offering them a chance to avoid paying a commission in return for a lower fee. Generally the economics work out well for both parties.

# PRIVATE USED-CAR SELLERS

### KNOW YOURSELF

- *What do I want?* Your goal should be to pay the low end of market value—wholesale book value.

- *Is it worth my time?* It's readily negotiable since this is one of the transactions where negotiation is assumed and items are priced accordingly.
- *Is it important to me?* It's worth negotiating since room for a price reduction has been added to the asking price—you must negotiate if you want to obtain a fair price.

## KNOW YOUR OPPONENT

- *What do I need to know?* Find out the wholesale book value of the automobile in question.
- *With whom should I negotiate?* Make sure you deal with the true decision maker. A teenager may be "selling" the car, but his or her parent may actually be the one with decision-making power.
- *Are there any potentially disruptive side issues?* The seller's fear is that the sale will take a long period of time—it costs money to sell a car privately—and might fall through. You can remove this by being a bona fide cash buyer. Your fear is that the car may have mechanical problems. This can be removed by having it examined by a mechanic.
- *What do I share with my opponent?* The common ground is the natural meeting of interests in a mercantile transaction: both parties want the transaction to be completed.

## KNOW THE SITUATION

- Insider Tip: When you're buying a used car from a private individual you've less protection than when you buy from a dealer. The dealer is in business and will still be there tomorrow . . . you hope. In addition, local regulations may require the dealer to disclose problems and offer at least a limited warranty. The private seller simply marks the bill of sale "as is" and you've no recourse if anything goes wrong. Use this lack of protection as leverage. Explain to the seller that you need to offer less than the book value of the car because of this lack of protection.
- Insider Tip: Agree to buy at book value, but insist that the deal is contingent on the car's being examined by your mechanic. If the mechanic finds problems, reduce your price by the amount it will take to resolve them satisfactorily.

# PSYCHOTHERAPISTS

## KNOW YOURSELF

- *What do I want?* Your goal should be a reduction in the fee without a decrease in the quality of services.
- *Is it worth my time?* It's readily negotiable, especially with younger, independent professionals eager to establish their practices. Therapists also have smaller educational and business loans to pay off than doctors and lawyers and so are more apt to be flexible with their fees. Many therapists feel guilty about the issue of money to begin with and are eager to get beyond it.
- *Is it important to me?* It's worth negotiating as long as you won't receive a reduction in quality.

## KNOW YOUR OPPONENT

- *What do I need to know?* Learn the going rate for services in your area by asking friends and other professionals.
- *With whom should I negotiate?* Negotiate with the therapist directly, not a secretary, deputy, or bookkeeper.
- *Are there any potentially disruptive side issues?* Never attack the fee as being too high or the services as not being worth their cost. Instead, stress that your appeal is based on affordability.
- *What do I share with my opponent?* There's no need for you to work at establishing common ground with a therapist; that's his or her job.

## KNOW THE SITUATION

- Insider Tip: If you have insurance coverage, ask that the fee at least be reduced to the ''reasonable and customary'' fee of your insurer.
- Insider Tip: If you don't have insurance coverage and the therapist balks at reducing the fee, ask for a recommendation to another therapist who's ''almost as good'' but who's in your price range. That may generate guilt in the therapist. It certainly will offer a clear-cut choice, providing an opportunity for the therapist to reconsider.
- Insider Tip: Whatever the hourly fee is, insist that you, not the therapist, decide how often you'll be coming for sessions. The frequency of visits should be determined by your financial comfort level, not by a therapist's desire to generate steady income.

- Insider Tip: Ask if the fee is lower for off hours. Some therapists charge less for sessions held during normal business hours.

# ROOFING CONTRACTORS

### *KNOW YOURSELF*

- *What do I want?* Your goal should be to obtain competent and neat work for the lowest price possible.
- *Is it worth my time?* As with every craftsperson, roofers are readily negotiable if they need the work. The more desperate they are for a job, the more negotiable they'll be. They'll also be more open to negotiation in their off-season, which is winter.
- *Is it important to me?* It's worth negotiating since it's possible to save as much as 25 percent off the cost of a roofing project.

### *KNOW YOUR OPPONENT*

- *What do I need to know?* Pay a home inspector to draw up a simple specification sheet for the project. Research the reputation and financial solvency of the roofer.
- *With whom should I negotiate?* Roofing specialists charge much lower fees than contractors who aren't specialists. That's because every craftsman hates roofing work. It's hard, hot, and dangerous. Contractors who don't specialize in roofing will often inflate their fees simply to avoid the work.
- *Are there any potentially disruptive side issues?* There's no dissonance in this negotiation.
- *What do I share with my opponent?* The common ground is the natural meeting of interests in a mercantile transaction: both parties want the transaction to be completed.

### *KNOW THE SITUATION*

- Insider Tip: Make sure when you're comparing bids that they're actually comparable: each should be based on the same amount of work and the same quality shingle.

# TENANTS

### *KNOW YOURSELF*

- *What do I want?* Your goal should be to maximize your security while obtaining a market rent.

- *Is it worth my time?* As a landlord it's your decision as to whether the terms of the lease are readily negotiable.
- *Is it important to me?* It's worth negotiating if you need a tenant and the individual in question appears to offer little or no risk.

## KNOW YOUR OPPONENT

- *What do I need to know?* Look into the prospective tenant's references for proof of the personal and financial integrity that will make it worth negotiating.
- *With whom should I negotiate?* Make sure you're negotiating with the person who will actually be living in the home or apartment full-time.
- *Are there any potentially disruptive side issues?* Simply by being willing to negotiate you dispel many of the fears the prospective tenant may have. Your fears can only be removed by gathering information on the prospective tenant's character.
- *What do I share with my opponent?* The common ground is the natural meeting of interests in a mercantile transaction: both parties want the transaction to be completed.

## KNOW THE SITUATION

- Insider Tip: Begin the negotiation with the least important issues. You'll be able to make minor concessions early on, letting the tenant feel victorious, and then hold your ground when important matters arise. Of course, tenants who have read the appropriate chapter in this book will try to do the reverse. In response to their entreaties to take up rent first you should respond with something like: "The integrity of my lease is the most important matter to me, and that's why I want to address it first." Another technique would be to say: "I think we should discuss the less important items first so we can build up some level of trust before we go on to tackle the major issues." And if neither of these work you can always fall back on a statement such as: "You know, most landlords won't even discuss these matters with a tenant. I think I'm being very open-minded and fair with you. The least you can do in return is allow me to pick the order in which we address items."
- Insider Tip: Go along with most requests to clean up the language and clauses in leases since they're, for the most part, horribly one-sided. Similarly, expanded tenant rights are fine so long as you retain veto power. However, when it comes to security I suggest you stand

firm. Insist on the cash rather than a third-party guarantee, but offer to pay interest as a compromise gesture.

- Insider Tip: When negotiating rent, avoid outright reductions but consider graduated payments. However, in exchange for graduated payments, increase your average annual yield. Explain that this is necessary to make up for the interest you'll be losing in the early years of the lease.

## USED BOOK STORES AND JUNK SHOPS

### *KNOW YOURSELF*

- *What do I want?* Your goal should be to obtain an item at the price you're willing to pay for it.
- *Is it worth my time?* Purchases in these types of shops are readily negotiable since pricing is entirely subjective. Sellers often have obtained items for next to nothing and have priced them at a level appropriate for only a wealthy collector—that provides lots of room for negotiation.
- *Is it important to me?* If negotiating turns you on, or if it could result in substantial savings, then it's worth it.

### *KNOW YOUR OPPONENT*

- *What do I need to know?* The only information you need is what the item is worth to you.
- *With whom should I negotiate?* Make sure you're negotiating with the owner. Only the person who bought the item and then put a price tag on it knows how much room there is for negotiation.
- *Are there any potentially disruptive side issues?* Don't present the negotiation as a criticism of the price. Instead, frame it as a question of your ability to afford the item.
- *What do I share with my opponent?* Try to establish your mutual love of the item as the common ground, but you may need to fall back on the common ground in any mercantile transaction: that both parties want the transaction to be completed.

### *KNOW THE SITUATION*

- Insider Tip: Try to inject some real world capitalism into what is essentially a fantasy world by placing a bid on an item and by making sure to place a deadline on your offer—otherwise you're simply an eternal insurance policy for the seller. When a seller is pressured to choose between making an actual sale or sticking to a fantasy price he or she might opt to sell the item. This works particularly well if you place a bid on a large number of items—let's say, a collection of twelve books—because that adds to the allure of making the sale.

# WEDDING VENDORS

### KNOW YOURSELF

- *What do I want?* Your goal should be to obtain dignified quality work for the lowest price possible.
- *Is it worth my time?* It's readily negotiable since there's a huge range in the fees charged by vendors such as florists, musicians, deejays, photographers, and videographers. All the fees are highly subjective. And there are many service providers competing for each assignment.
- *Is it important to me?* It's worth negotiating since it's possible to save up to 25 percent off the price with no decrease in quality or quantity.

### KNOW YOUR OPPONENT

- *What do I need to know?* Comparison shop to get an idea of the price range, and then look into the vendor's references for proof of professional integrity and quality.
- *With whom should I negotiate?* Make sure you're negotiating with the person who'll actually be performing the services, not someone who'll be farming out the work.
- *Are there any potentially disruptive side issues?* Deflect all efforts to inject emotion into the negotiation. Insist that this is a mercantile transaction and that you're interested in receiving the vendor's best price.
- *What do I share with my opponent?* If you successfully remove the dissonance, the common ground will be the natural meeting of interests in a mercantile transaction.

### KNOW THE SITUATION

- Insider Tip: When negotiating with bandleaders, try to reduce the number of musicians in the orchestra by instead opting for individuals who play more than one instrument.

- Insider Tip: When negotiating with floral designers, avoid those who have retail locations—you'll be paying extra for their higher overhead.
- Insider Tip: When negotiating with photographers, insist on keeping the proofs and make sure the contract contains a provision for a no-charge studio photo session if something goes wrong.

# PERSUADING PEOPLE

## Negotiating Actions

*"Only reason can convince us of those three fundamental truths without a recognition of which there can be no effective liberty: that what we believe is not necessarily true; that what we like is not necessarily good; and that all questions are open."*

—CLIVE BELL

Persuasive negotiations are dialogues in which one party wishes to obtain another party's agreement on a proposed course of action. Primarily, these involve discussions between two individuals about something one of them would like the other to do or not do.

One of the most obvious examples is when one spouse expresses to the other a desire to have a child. While that's clearly a dramatic situation, at its basis it's not unlike any one of a hundred other instances when one spouse suggests something to the other. It can be as inconsequential as going out to dinner, as exciting as deciding where to go on vacation, or as potentially divisive as asking to take an aged parent into the home. While most persuasive negotiations take place between individuals who have a close and ongoing relationship—such as parents, spouses, friends, lovers, partners, and family members—they can also take place between acquaintances or perfect strangers. A student asking a teacher to reconsider a grade and a driver asking a police officer to refrain from writing a speeding ticket are also engaging in persuasive negotiations.

Clearly it would be impossible to cover here all the persuasive negotiations you'll face in your life, since the possible scenarios are limitless. In selecting which persuasive negotiations to highlight in the full-length chapters and concluding capsule chapter in this part, I've tried to cover what I think are the most important, common, and/or educational situations

**153**

you'll face. My hope is that these examples will both address your most pressing needs and serve as guides in those persuasive negotiations I didn't have the space to cover.

Just to make sure you're prepared for any situation that's not covered, let me just go over a few generalities I've discovered over the years about persuasive negotiations. Remember, these are axioms, not rules; they're things to remember and think about when you're going through the three steps.

> ### Do everything you can to depolarize persuasive negotiations.

One fundamental truth about all persuasive negotiations is that you should do everything possible to depolarize the situation. By their very nature persuasive negotiations tend to put people on opposite sides of the proverbial fence. Once that happens a host of other elements—such as ego, pride, power, and fear—tend to cloud the actual issue under discussion. How you depolarize the negotiation depends on who you're negotiating with.

> ### When dealing with authority figures, mitigate results instead of appealing decisions.

Another important truth is that if you're trying to persuade an authority figure, you should refrain from questioning his or her authority over you or the actual decision. Calling into question an authority figure's judgment is often perceived—consciously or subconsciously—as an attack on his intelligence, ethics, and/or power. That can only lead to trouble. Instead, accept whatever decision has been rendered but do everything possible to mitigate the results of that decision. In other words, rather than negotiating the judgment, negotiate the punishment.

When dealing with peers, get them to
work with you toward a mutual goal.

When trying to persuade a peer to take a particular course of action, don't cast the negotiation as two parties warring over two separate goals. That tends to turn the negotiation into a battle of egos or an argument over who's right and who's wrong. Frame the negotiation as an attempt by two partners to find a common goal that benefits both and meets both parties' needs.

# 12

# PLEADING YOUR CASE

## Talking Your Way out of a Speeding Ticket

*"When constabulary duty's to be done,*
*The policeman's lot is not a happy one."*

—SIR WILLIAM SCHWENCK GILBERT

It had been a long day for Michelle. Her afternoon meeting downtown ran longer than she expected, and she was running late. She needed to be home by 6:30 in order to take Mitch Jr. to his Little League game. Since she'd missed little Mitch's last two games because of business, she had promised her son and herself she wouldn't miss this one. With that thought in mind, as she entered the expressway she pressed down a little harder on the accelerator of her car and picked up the pace. She was doing a steady seventy miles per hour when she rounded a bend to find a state police car sitting in the center median with its radar gun pointed straight at her.

As soon as she suspected she might be pulled over, Michelle began mentally preparing for a potential negotiation with a police officer. This is one negotiation where preparation is especially important since the actual negotiation will be very brief. (It's also one that offers you very little time to prepare—that's why I decided to include it in this book. Realistically, unless you think about this negotiation before it actually happens, you'll never be able to succeed.)

## THE SPEEDER'S SELF-EXAMINATION

In talking your way out of a speeding ticket, just as in every other negotiation, the first step in the process is to analyze your needs and weigh your options by getting to know yourself. That's accomplished by answering three questions: "What do I want?" "Is it worth my time?" "Is it important to me?"

### WHAT DO I WANT?—SETTING SPECIFIC GOALS

The obvious goal when you're pulled over for speeding by a policeman is to avoid a ticket. Whether or not you rely on your car to do business, you probably can't afford to lose your driving privileges. And even if you're not in imminent danger of that happening right now, a speeding ticket would make license suspension or even revocation that much more possible down the road. Besides, a speeding ticket will both cost you money and increase your insurance premiums dramatically.

What's not so obvious is that avoiding a ticket isn't a specific enough goal. You have been caught breaking a law, a law the police officer has sworn to uphold. There's no question of your guilt. Why then would the police officer let you get off without a ticket? Your goal should be to not get a *speeding ticket* in particular, since it's one of the most potentially damaging traffic violations.

### IS IT WORTH MY TIME?— DECIDING IF IT'S READILY NEGOTIABLE

Speeding tickets are negotiable. A police officer has a great deal of discretion when it comes to traffic stops. He can choose to write a ticket for any number of offenses, or he can choose to let someone go with a warning. The choice is his. However, if the officer takes the time to clock you, follow you, and pull you over, he's unlikely to let you off with just a warning—unless you're another police officer or a friend or relative of another police officer. He has invested time and effort and so wants something to show for it . . . something that will show his superiors he's doing his job. That means you'll have a better chance of getting the police officer to write you up for a lesser offense than you would of getting him to let you off without any ticket at all.

### IS IT IMPORTANT TO ME?—MAKING SURE IT'S WORTH DOING

Negotiating a speeding ticket isn't time-consuming and has very little potential risk: you're already about to get the ticket. On the other hand the potential rewards of a successful negotiation are great. First, you won't need to pay the sizable fine most speeding tickets entail. Second, your driving record won't have a black mark on it, which would increase your chances of potentially losing your driving privileges. Third, you'll save yourself an increase in your auto insurance premium. And fourth, if you're already in danger of losing your driving privileges, negotiating could save your license and, possibly, your job. My advice, then, is to always negotiate speeding tickets.

Let's see what Michelle came up with in her self-examination. As soon as she passed the police car, Michelle's mind shifted into gear. She told herself her goal was to avoid getting a speeding ticket. She knew that speeding tickets were readily negotiable. Finally, since she knew that negotiating wouldn't take any more time than not negotiating, and that her insurance premiums would soar if she was issued a speeding ticket, she decided it was worth trying to negotiate. Since this self-examination took all of about ten seconds, Michelle was able to quickly move on to level the playing field.

## LEVELING THE SPEEDING TICKET PLAYING FIELD

The second step in talking your way out of a speeding ticket is to get to know the opponent and to use that information to level the playing field. This is done by answering four questions: "What do I need to know?" "With whom should I negotiate?" "Are there any potentially disruptive side issues?" "What do I share with my opponent?"

### WHAT DO I NEED TO KNOW?— GATHERING INFORMATION

When you're about to be pulled over for a speeding ticket, you don't have much chance to do formal research or investigation, or to infiltrate the other side. All you've got the time to do is analyze what you already know about the other side—in this case, a police officer. Police officers are by the nature of their profession conservative. They're authority figures who are trained to intimidate. Being respected is more important to them than being liked. But on the other hand, they're constantly in danger, and, while they hate to admit it, are constantly afraid.

### WITH WHOM SHOULD I NEGOTIATE?— PUSHING THE UP BUTTON

While a judge clearly has the power to reduce charges or even throw tickets out of court, you're still better off negotiating with the officer himself. In most cases, the only people who win when a case goes to court are the lawyers. And even if you'll be representing yourself, the odds are you'll lose. Police officers are expert witnesses, and only an expert inter-rogator—such as an attorney—will be able to discredit them. While you may need to fall back on the court option eventually, your first and best choice is to negotiate directly with the police officer.

While I'm on the subject of fighting tickets in court, let me give another bit of advice: never imply or state that you'll be "seeing the officer in court." That will just about cinch you'll lose. You see, the single most effective way to fight a traffic ticket in court is to show the judge that the police officer doesn't clearly remember all the details of the incident. If you let the officer know, directly or indirectly, that you'll be fighting the ticket, you're going to stand out in his mind. He's going to sit in that car and make extensive notes about the incident. If you don't give a sign you'll be fighting it, he'll file you away with the hundreds of others he stopped that month, and when asked about it three months later, won't remember anything that isn't written down on the ticket.

### ARE THERE ANY POTENTIALLY DISRUPTIVE SIDE ISSUES?—ELIMINATING DISSONANCE

A police officer's fear that this routine traffic stop could turn into a high-speed chase or a physical confrontation—perhaps even a shooting—is the primary dissonance you need to eliminate before you can actually begin to negotiate. It is to be hoped that your appearance, and that of your vehicle, won't be offensive to the officer's conservative nature (no Guns 'n' Roses decal) or lead him to believe you could be dangerous (no gun rack). But unless you're in the habit of speeding, you won't have thought about how your garb and vehicle will be perceived by a police officer until it's too late to change them. That means your only way to make the officer feel at ease is your actions.

The best way to eliminate an officer's fear is to drive and then pull over in the least threatening manner. As soon as you think you've been caught speeding, slow down to the speed limit. That will make it easier for the officer to catch up to you. If he's forced to drive like a maniac to catch you, putting himself and others at risk, he's going to be in no mood to negotiate with you. Don't slam on your breaks, however. You've already been caught so there's no reason for you to react impulsively. Ease off the accelerator so your speed drops, and if you're not already there, move over to the right lane in as safe a manner as is possible.

When you see the police car in your rearview mirror, begin looking for a place to pull over. Look for the widest possible shoulder area without waiting too long to pull off the road. And when you find a good spot, pull as far to the right as is possible. The police officer will want to park his car closer to the road than yours so it provides him with some protection from oncoming traffic when he's standing next to your door. By making this easier you'll have eliminated his fear of being hit by oncoming traffic.

Once you've pulled off the road and the police officer has parked behind you, remain in the car. Sit calmly with both hands visibly on the steering wheel. If you look agitated and your hands aren't visible, the police officer thinks you may be dangerous and might have some type of weapon. Wait for the officer to come to you. It may take a few moments since the officer will be calling your license plate number in to his dispatcher to find out if the vehicle has been involved in any crimes. Don't turn around impatiently. Sometimes this computer search can take a few minutes, and your fidgeting will only make the officer nervous and/or suspicious.

Once he's checked your license plate, the officer will exit his car and approach yours. He's going to be watching you carefully for any signs of potential danger, so keep your hands on the steering wheel. Don't reach for your license and registration, even though you know he'll be asking you for them when he gets to your door. You may only be reaching for your wallet in the glove compartment, but the officer thinks you might be reaching for a gun. Besides, you're going to use the time it takes to find your paperwork to negotiate.

Don't ask the officer why you've been pulled over. If you were going faster than the speed limit the answer is obvious to both of you. And asking only demonstrates to the officer that you're either unaware of the rules of the road, a wise guy, or you think he's stupid—none of which is good. When the officer asks for your paperwork, tell him where it is before you reach for it. That will explain why you're opening the glove compartment or the console between the seats, or reaching into your pocket, briefcase, purse, or coat—once again, eliminating some fear. (If you must open something to get your paperwork, leave it open until the paperwork is returned by the officer. This subtly demonstrates you've nothing to hide.)

Don't call the officer ''sir.'' That's a word used only by those in the military or those showing phony respect. If he's a state policeman, call him ''trooper.'' If he's from the sheriff's department call him ''deputy.'' And if he's from the police department, or you're not sure what his affiliation is, call him ''officer.'' Treat female officers no differently than you would male officers. Do everything possible to demonstrate you truly respect him or her.

## WHAT DO I SHARE WITH MY OPPONENT?—
## FINDING AND DEMONSTRATING COMMON GROUND

What common ground do you have with a police officer? If you're willing to accept the fact that you've broken the law by speeding and deserve some punishment, you're on common ground with the police officer. The catch is that your punishment need not be receiving a speeding ticket.

# INSIDER TIPS FOR SPEEDERS

The third and final step in talking your way out of a speeding ticket is to know the situation. That's accomplished by applying the lessons learned by those who are experienced with this particular situation. There are lots of alleged experts in this situation, but I decided to go to the true experts: police officers. I spoke with law enforcement officers who, off the record, offered me the following insider tip.

Police officers have heard every excuse for speeding in the world, from having to go to the bathroom to having to hurry home to a sick relative. Unless such an excuse is true, the officer will know you're lying. And he'll also know you think he's stupid. This knowledge will translate into a speeding ticket with your name on it. Instead of trying to come up with some excuse, the best insider tip is to admit your guilt, ask for leniency, and offer a proposed lesser punishment.

While you're searching for your license and registration, admit to the officer that you know you were speeding. Instead of giving a reason for it, ask the officer if he can possibly write you up for a lesser offense, such as an equipment violation or failure to obey a traffic control device. Explain that a speeding ticket will boost your insurance to a level you can't afford or will get you into trouble with your boss, or whatever reason you have for not wanting to get the ticket. Basically, you're throwing yourself on his mercy. But surprisingly, police officers are often quite merciful.

Both you and the officer know that nearly everyone drives faster than the speed limit. You just happened to be unlucky enough to get caught. The officer will find your honesty refreshing and will relate to your reasons for not wanting to get a ticket. He too must pay exorbitant insurance premiums and has an unreasonable boss. You've also shown an understanding of his position. He's supposed to enforce the law that you've just broken, so letting you go without any punishment is difficult for him. And whether or not there's actually a quota, he also needs to demonstrate to his superiors that he's doing something out there on patrol. Now you're just a regular guy, like him, who's asking for a favor. And if you've also eliminated his fear and shown him respect, your chances of being written up for a lesser offense than speeding are excellent.

One last word of warning: some officers ask drivers, "Do you know how fast you were going?" They generally do this for one of two reasons: either they're not sure yours was the car they clocked on their radar gun or they want to test your honesty. Unfortunately, however you answer this leading question you're screwed. If you honestly answer with a speed above the limit, the officer, who may not have known if you were the speeder he was after, can feel justified in giving you a ticket. If you say you were going slower than you were, the officer knows you're a liar and won't even consider letting you off for less than the maximum offense. What's the solution? Throw the ball back into his court. Say, "I'm sorry, Officer, but I must not have been paying attention. How fast was I going?"

Let's see how Michelle leveled the playing field and negotiated her speeding ticket. Once she realized she'd been caught speeding she eased off the accelerator and, when she had a chance, pulled into the right lane of the expressway. When she saw the police car, with lights flashing and siren blaring, pull up behind her, she found a good spot to pull off the road onto the shoulder. She pulled as far over as possible and sat with her hands on the steering wheel. When the police officer came up to her door, Michelle could see he was a state trooper. He asked her for her license and registration. Michelle said, "My license is in my wallet, which is in the purse next to me on the front seat, Trooper, and the registration is in the glove compartment." As she reached for her wallet, Michelle said, "I realize I was speeding, Trooper, but I'd really appreciate it if you could write me up for something less than speeding." Then, as she reached for her registration, she added, "I don't know if I can afford the higher insurance premiums, and I really need to drive for my job." The trooper, relaxed due to Michelle's actions, and pleasantly surprised by her honesty and directness, wrote her up for a lesser offense instead.

## Pleading Your Case
## Talking Your Way out of
## a Speeding Ticket

- Try to avoid getting a *speeding* ticket, not to avoid getting *any* ticket.
- It's better to negotiate with the officer than to go to court.
- Minimize or eliminate the officer's fears.
- Show respect without appearing phony.
- Don't lie.
- Admit guilt but ask for a lesser punishment.

# 13

# AVOIDING BLOOD FEUDS

## Persuading a Family Member

*"No people are ever as divided as those of the same blood...."*

—MAVIS GALLANT

As soon as she hung up the telephone Jennifer knew she needed to sit down and have a talk with her husband, Neil. The telephone call had been from a friend of hers who told her about a job opening at a well-known glossy magazine. It was an excellent opportunity, the kind Jennifer had been dreaming of for over a year. Her friend had a contact at the magazine and could insure that Jennifer would be put on "the short list" for the job. But there were two problems. The first was that the magazine was located in the Midwest, and she and Neil lived on the East Coast. The second, and more important, problem was that Neil was very happy in his job as a newspaper reporter and didn't want to move.

## THE FAMILY NEGOTIATOR'S SELF-EXAMINATION

When negotiating with a family member, just as in every other negotiation, the first step in the process is to analyze your needs and weigh your options by getting to know yourself. That's accomplished by answering three questions: "What do I want?" "Is it worth my time?" "Is it important to me?"

### WHAT DO I WANT?—SETTING SPECIFIC GOALS

You negotiate with your family more than with anyone else. From the time you are born you're negotiating with siblings and parents. Even before you can speak you're using your limited communication skills to negotiate. And as you grow older you engage in uncounted negotiations with your immediate family over everything from whether you can stay up past your bedtime to who your own children will be named after. Upon leaving your parents' home the number of negotiations doesn't decline; instead, the opponent becomes your spouse or lover. And eventually, if you have children, they become opponents, bringing the entire process full circle.

With all this experience at negotiating with family members you'd think we'd all be experts at it. In fact, the reverse is true. We are at our worst in our negotiations with family members—whether parents, siblings, mates, or children. Rather than learning from our past mistakes we seem destined to repeat them . . . endlessly. We reflexively fall into the same patterns of behavior, patterns established in the early stages of our relationships. The result is that rather than actually negotiating we fight and resolve nothing. There are no solutions, just survivors.

I'd like to suggest that the primary reason for this is that we take the wrong approach to family negotiations, one that we would never consciously take when negotiating with individuals outside of our family. When negotiating with non–family members we're usually dealing with short-term issues. Sure, they may be incredibly important, but they're not forever. We simply want to achieve our goal. However, when we're dealing with family members we are often confronting long-term issues. Even if the specific issue being negotiated is short-term, the ramifications are long-term, since there will be a continuing relationship between the two parties for a long time after the negotiation. How long? Well, in most cases, for as long as both parties are alive. I think that consciously or subconsciously we are aware of this when we're negotiating with our family. That leads us to up the ante. It's generally not enough to simply achieve a goal. The other side has to be converted to our opinion as well. After all, we say to ourselves, the other person is a family member and, therefore, should feel the same way we do.

This is the great mistake at the core of almost all our negotiations with family members: that rather than looking to achieve our goal we look to change the other party. We're not just looking to successfully persuade in the one instance being negotiated; we're looking to persuade the other party *forever*. For better or worse, we cannot change our parents, our children, or our mate. He is who he is whether or not we think that's the way he should be. Nothing we do or say will change that. And, in fact, trying to change him will lead to nothing but trouble. That's because everyone, from the young child to the older adult, wants to control his or her own life and own environment. Trying to change someone will lead to continuous conflict in a never-ending battle for control. Since one side refuses to give up control and the other side refuses to stop trying to take control, both end up as losers.

What's the answer? I believe it's essential that when negotiating with family members we concentrate on achieving mutually acceptable goals, preferably those that benefit both parties. Rather than looking to convince the other side that you're right and that he should agree with you, the secret is to set up the negotiation so that both of you work together toward a mutually acceptable goal. As I'll explain later in this chapter, by developing a mutually acceptable goal you'll be establishing common ground separate from your family ties, making it much more likely you'll succeed.

Let me give you an example. You and your mate are planning a vacation. You love lying on the beach all day long. Your mate, on the other hand, gets a sunburn from a reading lamp. His love is sightseeing. For the past two years the two of you have had fights about this. Your goal has been to change him so he'll want to lie on the beach next to you. His goal has been to change you so you'll want to spend the day browsing through museums. Rather than actually negotiating, the two of you decided to compromise, electing to assume control of vacation plans on alternate years. As a result, two years ago you were miserable on the vacation—a trip to Chicago to tour all the museums—and your mate was angry that you were miserable. The next year, your mate was miserable on the vacation—a trip to the Virgin Islands—and you were angry that he was miserable.

Rather than approaching this negotiation as a chance to get your own way by getting him to change, or to find a compromise that makes neither side happy, your goal should be to come up with a mutually acceptable solution that meets both of your needs. For instance, the two of you could go to an area that has both culture and a beach. That way you could lie on the beach and your mate could take in the culture.

### IS IT WORTH MY TIME?— DECIDING IF IT'S READILY NEGOTIABLE

Family issues are always readily negotiable. The problem is that we tend to view them not as negotiations but as fights, debates, lectures, or judgments. In other words, rather than seeing them as opportunities for both sides to express their views and for the two parties to jointly come up with a solution, we see them as battlegrounds on which the two parties struggle for control and power. With such an approach it's no wonder the tone and language degenerates and nothing is really solved other than one party's asserting his will over the other.

In a negotiation no one party should have, or attempt to gain, control. That means in a negotiable situation you shouldn't try to get your way by using your power to control your elderly parent's life or your mate's life. I'm not suggesting there won't be family fights. Of course there will be. But if everyone is inculcated in the techniques of negotiation those fights can be put aside and turned into negotiations, with both parties working together to reach a solution.

There's no denying that negotiating with family is difficult. In fact, I think it's the hardest type of negotiation covered in this book. That's because there are so many other issues—primarily emotional and psychological—floating around the negotiation, and because your opponent is someone you'll be dealing with for the rest of your, or his, lifetime. Done well, family negotiations will probably take longer and require more preparation than any others. If you accept the idea that you can't control others, and are willing to consciously try to achieve mutually acceptable solutions to problems, then all family issues will be readily negotiable.

## IS IT IMPORTANT TO ME?—
## MAKING SURE IT'S WORTH NEGOTIATING

If you love and respect the person you have a problem with, the issue is always worth negotiating. A successful negotiation will result in a closer, more secure, more loving relationship, and that's worth any amount of effort.

On the other hand, I believe there are certain issues that transcend negotiation. You shouldn't negotiate health, safety, legal, moral, or conduct matters with those you're responsible for, whether they're minor children or elderly adults. If your three-year-old child runs across the street without looking you don't negotiate. You punish her and tell her never to do it again. If your elderly parent with Alzheimer's refuses to eat, you take control; you don't negotiate.

Let's see what Jennifer learned during her self-examination. She realized that her goal shouldn't be to convince Neil to give up his job and leave the East Coast. Instead, it should be to mutually come up with a solution that met both their needs. They needed to figure out a way in which she would be able to improve her career without Neil's being forced to sacrifice his. Jennifer knew that as long as she didn't try to turn the negotiation into a battle of opposing needs, and was willing to think in terms of what was good for both of them, the problem was negotiable. She knew from her conversations with her friend that there was no way she could take the job and stay east, so there was no point in negotiating the issue with the magazine. Clearly this was worth negotiating: she and Neil were happily married and wanted to stay that way. She very much wanted to improve her career, and Neil very much wanted to maintain his.

## LEVELING THE FAMILY PLAYING FIELD

The second step in negotiating with family is to get to know the opponent and to use that information to level the playing field. While you obviously *know* your opponent in this case, since he or she is a family member, that doesn't mean you *know* them in a negotiating context. You still need to answer four questions: "What do I need to know?" "With whom should I negotiate?" "Are there any potentially disruptive side issues?" "What do I share with my opponent?"

### *WHAT DO I NEED TO KNOW?—*
### *GATHERING INFORMATION*

In family negotiations there's a tendency to react reflexively. That often results in conflict rather than a solution. One secret to avoiding conflict and encouraging a successful negotiation is to think and plan prior to entering into a dialogue. Don't look on such preparation as somehow being improper or manipulative when dealing with family. You're not trying to undermine or overpower your loved one. You're simply trying to rationally examine the situation and come up with mutually acceptable solutions to the problem.

If the situation requires outside analysis to clarify the problem, do some research. For example, if you suspect your parent is having financial problems, find out about his income and expenses. If you think your child may be having trouble in school, speak to his teacher or guidance counselor. Try to come up with some rational and effective solutions to the problem. Perhaps there are some community services your aging parent could make use of to ease the financial strain. Maybe there are tutorial or extra help programs your child could take advantage of.

After you've completed your research, move on to observation and investigation. You're not spying on your loved one, you're simply trying to gather the facts. If you suspect your parent isn't doing well, pay a brief surprise visit to him if possible. Take a look around his home. Are there physical signs that he's having problems? If you think your child is having problems in school, ask him about his classes, take a look at his home-work. Don't go about this in an underhanded manner, but do try to be subtle.

After you've done your research, observation, and investigation, try to analyze what you've found out. Look on this analysis as an attempt to answer the other side's possible arguments and difficulties.

Put yourself in his place. Since the other party isn't preparing for this negotiation as you are, he'll probably react instinctively. That could mean he'll deny there's a problem. Or he may assume there's no solution. The instinctive reaction of a family member will be to polarize the situation. That's not because he wants to argue with you but because he automatically sees issues in terms of control. Whether it's your mate, your child, your sibling, or your parent, the other side in a family negotiation will automatically make the mistake you tried to avoid in setting your goal: he'll paint the discussion as a battle rather than a negotiation.

Your goal is to have enough information at your command to be able to answer the other three questions involved in "knowing" your opponent.

### WITH WHOM SHOULD I NEGOTIATE?—
### PUSHING THE UP BUTTON

In most cases it's clear who you should be negotiating with. If you and your mate are planning a vacation, the two of you should negotiate with each other. If your mother is driving you crazy, you need to negotiate with her. If your child is having problems in school, you need to negotiate with him. However, in some cases, your real opponent may not be obvious.

Let's use the most common example of misdirected negotiating: in-laws. For example, you and your mother-in-law aren't getting along. She seems to be constantly criticizing you and comparing you unfavorably to your mate's prior partner or to her other children-in-law. You complain to your mate about it and he reflexively rises to his mother's defense. What have you done wrong? Your mistake was to try to negotiate your mother-in-law's behavior with your mate. That places him in the impos-sible situation of having to choose between his mate and his mother. Instead, regardless of how frightening the prospect, you should have ne-gotiated your problem with your mother-in-law's behavior directly with your mother-in-law. Of course, it may be wise to precede this negotiation with another one in which you negotiate your problem with your mate's behavior directly with him.

Once again, it's an issue of misplaced control. You may assume that your mate can somehow control or change his mother's behavior. He can't do that any more than you can change his behavior. The story is the same if you replace mother-in-law with stepchild, or sibling, or anyone. The answer to the question "Who should I be negotiating with?" is the person with whom you have the problem. Only through dealing directly with him and trying to find a mutually acceptable solution will the problem ever be resolved.

## ARE THERE ANY POTENTIALLY DISRUPTIVE SIDE ISSUES?—ELIMINATING DISSONANCE

There are generally three types of dissonance that interfere with successful negotiations between family members: external pressures, special language, and past history.

By external pressures I mean all the things that go on outside of the family—such as work, pastimes, friendships, and school—and the actual physical environment in which the discussion is taking place. In order to eliminate such dissonance you need to time your negotiation very carefully and make sure it takes place in the right location.

Children provide excellent examples of both poor and good timing. When they're very young, they can hardly wait for a parent to come home before they launch into a negotiation. The stereotypical situation is when a child runs over to a parent who has just walked in the door after a long day at work and brings up what, to the child, is an issue that cannot wait to be addressed. The parent, exhausted and worn down by the day's labors, just wants to be left alone for a few moments so he can wind down. If he doesn't think before he acts, he'll respond curtly, perhaps even angrily, to the child's approach, trying to assert control and get the matter over with. A potential negotiation has become a conflict. After a few years, the child begins to learn about timing. He realizes there are good and bad times to approach a parent. Let's say he wants a new bicycle. He doesn't just ask for it, particularly if the parent isn't in a good mood. He waits and bides his time until he sees his parent is receptive. Perhaps he waits until he shows his parent a good report card.

We need to take a lesson from children. Negotiations should only take place when the other party isn't under pressure from external factors. He shouldn't be in the middle of a term paper, about to go to the doctor, doing the taxes, paying the bills, or worrying about work. He should be as relaxed as possible and have time to engage in a dialogue. Just as an aside, my favorite time to negotiate with family is on Sunday morning or afternoon. I think Saturdays are good for recovering from whatever has gone on during the week. By Sunday evening, everyone is thinking about the upcoming week, preparing for what's going to happen. The time in between is, at least for my family, the most leisurely and relaxed part of the week and, therefore, the best time to negotiate.

I don't think there's a best place to negotiate. However, there are bad places to negotiate depending on what issue you'll be addressing. A bad location can force the parties to focus on problems, not solutions, and lead to the place's becoming associated with conflict rather than communication. Location can even lead to polarization. For example, every psychotherapist in the world agrees that a couple shouldn't negotiate sexual issues in a bedroom. Siblings obviously shouldn't argue about care of an aging parent in the parent's hospital room or debate how an estate should be divided over a parent's grave. Parents shouldn't negotiate with children about their eating habits in the kitchen or at a restaurant, and they shouldn't discuss fear of swimming at the pool. The answer is to avoid what, for lack of a better phrase, I call "the scene of the crime." Instead, negotiations should take place in a neutral setting that offers few distractions.

Don't make the mistake of trying to manipulate negotiations so they take place in locations with positive associations. For example, discussing something with a spouse in the same restaurant where you proposed. Such manipulation may well work, just as the child's asking a parent for a bicycle after showing a good report card might work. However, it's not really negotiating. Manipulation is simply a way of augmenting your power in a conflict. You're just trying to exert control by using additional weapons. Believe me, it will come back to haunt you eventually. When the other side realizes he has been manipulated he'll resent it. And a repeating pattern of manipulation and resentment may become the norm. Remember your goal. You're not trying to beat the other person—he's your loved one. You're not trying to change him—you can't. You're simply trying to reach a mutually acceptable solution to a problem.

The reflexive response of the other party in a negotiation with a family member will be to defend his control over his own life. You probably have helped generate this reflex in the past by stating a gripe in language that polarizes. In order to eliminate this dissonance you must do everything possible to indicate that you're not looking to take control. The best way to do that is to use mutual rather than special language. Let me give you some examples. Instead of saying "I'm angry with you," say "We need to talk about something." Rather than saying "I think you should . . ." say "Here are my thoughts" and then ask, "What are yours?" Everything should be presented as "we," not "you" and "I." And that goes for negotiations with your sibling or parent as well as for those with your mate.

In addition to using mutual language, you can help eliminate dissonance and show you're not trying to assert power by avoiding interruptions and refraining from ridicule. Similarly, don't use terms such as *emotional* or *logical* to characterize positions or actions. Human beings are not computers. Emotion must, and should, play a role in our negotiations with family. Similarly, we are thinking creatures. While it need not be the only factor in a decision, logic should be a big part of our negotiations. By characterizing someone as logical or emotional you're, in effect, criticizing him or her for not having enough of the opposite trait. And criticism is seen as a play for power and control.

The single biggest element of dissonance in a negotiation between family members is past history. I'm continually amazed by the ability of family members who are fighting to recall every slight they've ever suffered at the hand of the other. Don't get me wrong. I'm not saying such slights aren't important. And I'm not belittling the obvious and real trauma of emotional and psychological (let alone physical and sexual) abuse. While I have some problems with labels such as ''dysfunctional families'' and goals such as the healing of ''inner children'' becoming the basis of an entire social movement, the concepts clearly have some merit. But when it comes to negotiating with a family member, bringing up every resentment and disappointment from the near and distant past is an obstacle to achieving success. Just as you shouldn't try to control the other party, and should encourage him not to try to control you, so you should put your past difficulties with the other party behind you and encourage him to forgive you for past mistakes.

I know that's a tall order. The temptation to let your brother have it for the time he stomped on your Barbie Dream House, or to get a dig in on your mother for when she blamed you for the 1965 East Coast blackout, or to let your spouse know you haven't forgotten the time he bought you a blender for your anniversary, is very strong. And if the hurts and resentments are based on more important matters than the ones I've jokingly used as examples, then the need to express anger is even more powerful. I'm not a psychotherapist. I can't help you work out your feelings about your loved ones. But I am an expert negotiator, and I can help you successfully negotiate. If you insist on using your past history you'll fail to reach a mutually satisfying solution and will be establishing or encouraging a pattern that will sabotage all your future negotiations with this person.

Just as it's extremely difficult to put your own feelings aside, it's tough for the other party to bury the hatchet. You can't expect to accomplish this with a simple apology preceding a negotiation. Not only won't the other party have had time to actually put the past behind them, but your apology will ring false. It will appear to be nothing more than an effort to manipulate, even when actually it's an honest effort to promote a successful dialogue. So begin making amends as far in advance of the actual negotiation as possible. And do it with as much subtlety as you can. The further in advance of the negotiation the amends are made, the more genuine they will be perceived as being. And by the way, do stick with your new attitudes and behaviors after you've gotten what you want.

If you know your mother is upset because you don't see her as often as in the past, and you'll need to negotiate her assistance in your purchase of a home, try to make amends. Tell her you realize you haven't been spending enough time with her and explain why. Say you've decided to make a conscious effort to spend time with her and demonstrate your changed ways. Only after both acknowledging past wrongs and demonstrating a new attitude should you enter into the negotiation. Since it hasn't taken place directly in advance of a negotiation it won't be seen as a ploy, and since there will be some evidence to back up your new behavior, it's likely your mother would be able to "forgive" the past.

Obviously, there are some instances when such subtlety won't be possible or sufficient. Perhaps there's an emergency and you've had no chance to plant the seeds ahead of time. Or maybe the hurt is so deep that regardless of what you do it won't be completely healed by the time you have to negotiate. In those instances all you can do is ask the other party to try to put the past behind them. Say, "Based on our past, I wouldn't be coming to you for this unless it was terribly important to me. I hope you can put all that behind us because I really need your help right now." He may be able to, or he may not. But simply by making the request you increase the chances of a successful negotiation.

## WHAT DO I SHARE WITH MY OPPONENT?— FINDING AND DEMONSTRATING COMMON GROUND

One of the biggest traps of negotiating with family members is to assume that the common ground between the two parties is their relationship. In other words, asking someone to do something for you simply because of who you are to each other. The stereotype is the mother asking the son to "do it for me." This is nothing more than using guilt as a weapon. It's just a variation on asserting control. There's no automatic entitlement that comes with family relationships or marriage. Assuming there is leads to ill feelings and anger rather than mutual satisfaction.

The actual common ground in this negotiation is the goal you came up with in your analysis of what you want, since you should have developed one that was mutually beneficial. In the vacation example both of you want to have an enjoyable and relaxing vacation. It's important that this common ground be stated directly and early in the negotiation. With all the past history between the two parties there's a great deal of anxiety about exactly what the agenda really is in a family negotiation. Don't skirt around an issue. Address it directly. If you're afraid your mother isn't able to pay her bills anymore, don't hint at it in an attempt to be diplomatic. You're engaging in a negotiation with a family member, not a foreign power. Simply say, "We need to talk about the money situation."

# INSIDER TIPS FOR FAMILY NEGOTIATORS

The third and final step in negotiating with family members is to know the situation. That's accomplished by applying the lessons learned by those who are experienced with this particular situation. While I have extensive experience as child, sibling, spouse, parent, in-law, and, as of late, grandparent, I thought I'd better reach out to experts with a less personal involvement in these negotiations. That's why I interviewed family therapists for this chapter. They offered me five wonderful insider tips. The first two are ways to increase your chances of success. The rest are innovative techniques for breaking impasses.

## OFFER A MENU OF CHOICES

Consider offering alternatives rather than a single option. By giving the other party a choice, you offer him control, which, as I've said many times in this chapter, is what he's most afraid you're trying to take away from him. Rather than trying to talk your young daughter into getting dressed up to go to Grandma's, or to wear a particular outfit, you should offer her a choice of outfits and let her select the one she'd like to wear.

## EXPAND THE OPTIONS AVAILABLE

Focus on how you can expand the options available to both parties rather than concentrating on how to narrow the gap between you. Let's go back to the vacation debate example I used earlier in this chapter, in which one mate wanted to lie on the beach and the other wanted to go sightseeing. Expanding this negotiation would consist of considering other types of vacations and other types of locations in an effort to find a solution that satisfies both parties' needs.

Sometimes all your best efforts may go for naught and you end up at an impasse in your negotiation with your family member. In that case, you may want to try one of these three insider tips.

## *GIVE A VETO*

Sometimes all that's required is for the other party to know that he will never lose control of a situation. Tell him that at any time he can tell you to stop doing whatever it is the two of you agreed to do.

## *ASSUME PERSONAL RESPONSIBILITY*

At times people are paralyzed by the fear of making a mistake or being held responsible. If you directly state that if anything goes wrong you'll accept the responsibility, your family member may be able to move forward.

## *BRING IN A THIRD PARTY*

Many times the past history between the two parties is so involved, or the reason for the paralysis is so powerful, that only an outsider can help get the process moving. Suggest that the two of you bring in an unbiased third party to offer advice. That person's opinion need not be binding, but it may be enough to get your opponent going again.

Let's see how Jennifer leveled the playing field and negotiated with her husband, Neil. Jennifer knew that Neil's objection to relocating would be based on his career. She decided to find out what career opportunities there might be for Neil in the area they'd be moving to. She discovered there were five daily newspapers within an hour of the city where the magazine was located, all of which were comparable to the paper Neil worked for now. She calculated how much their income would increase with her new job and how much their cost of living would decrease. She also began to compile a list of possible solutions to the problem of her taking a job in the Midwest. She knew Neil was upset that she hadn't been able to spend as much time at home with him as he'd like, so she made a conscious effort to come home early and stay out of the office on weekends. She told him she was sorry she'd been spending so much time at the office and was trying to change it.

Two weeks later she sat down with Neil on a Sunday morning and said, "There's something we need to talk about." Using mutual language Jennifer told Neil about the potential job. She stressed that her goal was for the two of them to see if they could come up with some mutually acceptable solutions in case she did find a good job out of town. Jennifer stressed that this discussion wasn't necessarily about this particular job. She decided to use the expansion gambit and said that she had some ideas that might help spark him to come up with ideas. She said that Neil might be able to get an even better job in the place they relocated to. She said that since her income would probably be going up substantially, Neil might be able to have the opportunity to go back to college for his master's degree. At that point Neil came up with an idea of his own. Rather than going back to college he could use this as an opportunity to go into business for himself as a free-lance writer, something he had always wanted to do but never had the chance to try before. They had discovered a solution that answered both of their needs. Four months later Jennifer was hard at work in her new job in the Midwest and Neil was launching his free-lance career.

## Avoiding Blood Feuds
## Persuading a Family Member

- Look for a mutually acceptable and beneficial goal.
- Don't try to convince the other side you're right.
- Negotiate directly with the person with whom you have the problem.
- Pick the right time and location.
- Use language that frames the problem in mutual terms.
- Apologize for, forgive, and forget, past problems.
- Offer alternatives rather than a single option.
- Focus on how you can expand the options available.

# 14

# STANDING UP FOR YOUR KID

## Appealing an Educator's Disciplinary Action

*"The true teacher defends his pupils against his own personal influence. He inspires self-trust. He guides their eyes from himself to the spirit that quickens him. He will have no discipline."*

—AMOS BRONSON ALCOTT

Cally was surprised when the principal of her son Nolan's school called to tell her Nolan had cut school for a day and as a result would be suspended for two days. Fifteen-year-old Nolan had always been a good student. Even after Cally and her husband divorced two years ago, Nolan had kept up his grades and behavior. But whatever it was, it was clear something had happened. When Nolan came home that afternoon, Cally had a talk with him. After some hemming and hawing he finally admitted he had cut school, but quickly added it was the first time. When she asked him why he had cut school Nolan eventually admitted that he and his girlfriend had a fight the night before and he didn't want to see her. Cally knew Nolan deserved to be punished, but she thought a two-day suspension was too severe. She decided to speak with the principal.

## THE CHILD-DEFENDING PARENT'S SELF-EXAMINATION

When negotiating with an educator, just as in every other negotiation, the first step in the process is to analyze your needs and weigh your options by getting to know yourself. That's accomplished by answering three questions: "What do I want?" "Is it worth my time?" "Is it important to me?"

## *WHAT DO I WANT?—SETTING SPECIFIC GOALS*

When a child is disciplined by an educator most parents instinctively rush to their offspring's defense. That's wonderful, but it's not always done for the right reason.

There's a growing trend in America for parents to hold schools responsible for the teaching of manners and behavior as well as school subjects. There are any number of theories as to why this perception has taken root: parental guilt over not being able to spend enough time with the child due to work demands; the proliferation of single-parent households; the baby boom generation's desire to be more of a friend than a parent to its children; anger over increased school taxes and escalating teacher salaries; the projecting of anger that otherwise would be self-directed. Whatever the reason or reasons for this perception, it has led to the creation of an adversarial relationship between educators and parents.

A parent is told his child has been disciplined by an educator and his immediate response is to take his child's side in the dispute and attempt to get the educator to change the decision. The parent's goal becomes getting a decision overturned or tempered, regardless of whether it's justified or not. Often, the parent's anger over the situation becomes focused on the educator. Rather than blaming the child, or himself, the parent blames the teacher. He says "The teacher wasn't doing his job" or "The principal reacted too harshly." While in some cases that may be true, bringing this adversarial relationship into the negotiation does nothing but make both sides—parent and educator—take extreme positions, and it doesn't help the all-important third party—the child.

Instead of trying to have a disciplinary decision overturned, parents should have as their goal *doing what's best for their child*. Parents should focus on discovering if there's an underlying cause to the problem behavior, and remedying the situation. If you do this you're not taking the school's side and you're not taking your child's side in an argument of facts. You're simply looking out for the long-term interests of your child. The phrase *long-term* is important. It may be in the child's short-term interest to have a suspension overruled since then he'll be able to play in the big game, or go to the upcoming dance . . . or even get into the college he wants. But it may not be in his long-term interest, since if there's an underlying problem that goes unaddressed the outward symptom of it— his behavior—will simply reappear, perhaps in a potentially more destructive form, down the road.

I believe your goal in negotiating a disciplinary decision with an educator should be to do whatever, in your judgment, is in the long-term interest of your child.

## IS IT WORTH MY TIME?—
## DECIDING IF IT'S READILY NEGOTIABLE

Educators are very interesting negotiation opponents. Their openness toward negotiating a disciplinary decision depends, to a large degree, on what type of problem sparked the discipline and the past behavioral record of your child.

If the problem was one dealing with subjective school policy—grading, or how many cuts it takes to merit a suspension, for example—educators can be very flexible. That's because of their psychological training. Educators see themselves as being, in part, social workers. Educators have enough insight into children to realize that poor behavior is often a manifestation of an underlying issue that needs to be addressed. In such cases educators are more than willing to give kids second, third—even fourth—chances, especially if the child has been a "good citizen."

However, if the problem is a black-and-white issue based on an objective school policy—such as cheating on a test or buying a term paper, for instance, or an illegal act involving alcohol, drugs, or vandalism—educators are very inflexible. That's because of their need to draw an unequivocal line in the sand on some issues to maintain discipline and standards. Educators see violations of objective rules as situations that require quick and severe justice according to a predetermined list of punishments. The only negotiating space available in such instances is what action the school will take after the punishment has been completed.

In addition, educators seek to reinforce good behavior as well as punish bad behavior. If your child has a clean record and has never had a behavioral problem before, an educator is more likely to be flexible in meting out punishment. The rationale is that by showing "mercy" the educator is rewarding the past good behavior rather than simply punishing the apparently aberrant bad behavior.

## IS IT IMPORTANT TO ME?—
## MAKING SURE IT'S WORTH NEGOTIATING

A disciplinary decision by an educator is, I believe, always worthy of negotiating. It's not a matter of how this particular decision will affect your child's grade point average, or social life, or sports career, or even chances to get into a particular college. What's at stake is your child's long-term relationship to authority, which in the final analysis is a lot more important. A child needs to learn he must take responsibility for his behavior, that if he does something wrong he must pay the consequences. And no less importantly, a child needs to learn that if he has been wronged, there are ways to seek redress, that there's justice and mercy as well as retribution.

My advice is to always negotiate educational disciplinary decisions. That doesn't mean you'll always be able, or even want, to have them changed. It simply means that you'll be making sure your child's long-term interests are being protected.

Let's look at the results of Cally's self-examination. She realized that while instinctively she wanted to go in and fight for Nolan's suspension to be overturned, her goal actually should be to do what was in Nolan's long-term best interest. And she knew that probably meant he would need to suffer some type of punishment. Cally also realized that since the problem—cutting school—was a subjective school policy, and that Nolan's previous record was clean, the punishment would be readily negotiable. Finally, Cally realized it was important for her to become involved in the situation. If nothing else it would help her show Nolan that while he should pay for his mistakes, she believed the punishment should also fit the crime, and she would stand up for that belief. Cally's next step was to level the playing field.

## LEVELING THE SCHOOL DISCIPLINE PLAYING FIELD

The second step in appealing an educator's disciplinary action is to get to know the opponent and to use that information to level the playing field. You do that by answering the same four questions but, in this negotiation, in a slightly different order than in others: "With whom should I negotiate?" "What do I need to know?" "Are there any potentially disruptive side issues?" "What do I share with my opponent?"

### WITH WHOM SHOULD I NEGOTIATE?— PUSHING THE UP BUTTON

This is one instance when the immediate parties to a situation shouldn't necessarily be the individuals conducting the negotiation. Rather than a student, or his parent, negotiating with a teacher, in most instances this process should begin with a parent negotiating with an administrator.

Once there's been a problem or an incident between a student and teacher, both sides are immediately polarized. If brought together, the two immediate parties often argue over the facts of the case or the past history between them, rather than the underlying issue. And if you as a parent enter into a negotiation with a teacher, you're likely to be forced into either accepting the teacher's position, and in the process denying your child, or accepting your child's position, and in the process calling the teacher's honesty and judgment into question. That's clearly a no-win situation.

The educational bureaucracy understands this and provides an outside, presumably unbiased, party: an administrator. The administrator's role is to resolve the superficial problem, identify any underlying cause, and seek to make sure the problem doesn't reoccur. A good administrator is no more on the side of the teacher than he is on the side of the student. The administrator's mission is to do what is best for the school and the student. That makes him an excellent party to negotiate with.

## WHAT DO I NEED TO KNOW?— GATHERING INFORMATION

Your information gathering in this negotiation should be concentrated on two areas: the facts of the incident and the school's official policy.

Begin by sitting down with your child and trying to get to the bottom of what happened. Explain to him that he has already been punished by the school, and unless he tells you exactly what happened you won't be able to help him. This questioning may not be easy, and it certainly won't be quick, but it is important.

One way of making the process easier is, whenever possible, to ask questions that can be answered with either a yes or a no. For example: Rather than asking for the names of other students who cheated, simply ask whether others cheated; rather than asking about the student's feelings toward the teacher, ask if he has ever felt the teacher singled him out before this incident. Bear in mind that you're unlikely to get the full story from your child. There will probably be some gaps that you'll be able to fill in only by speaking with the administrator.

Once you've learned everything you can from your child, contact the school. Ask to speak to the principal's office. Don't be surprised, however, if you're directed to either an assistant principal or some other administrator. In many schools, principals don't directly handle disciplinary matters—they feel they must remain above the fray, so to speak. Instead, a particular administrator is designated as the "discipline" person. Tell the administrator that while you're interested in speaking with him about the matter as soon as possible, you were interested in getting some information from him first. Ask him for the school's formal policy regarding your child's situation. Ask if there are any specific procedures you need to follow or should be aware of. Once you've gotten your information, ask if you could have a preliminary meeting between just you and the administrator. That's also your first step in eliminating dissonance.

## ARE THERE ANY POTENTIALLY DISRUPTIVE SIDE ISSUES?—ELIMINATING DISSONANCE

There are two primary causes of dissonance in this type of negotiation: animosity between the immediate parties and parental anger at the school as an institution.

You can eliminate the former by not having either your child or a teacher present at the initial meeting. As I mentioned earlier, when the immediate parties to a dispute or problem get together there's often an instinctive polarization that takes place. The negotiation, rather than focusing on how best to resolve the situation, becomes a matter of *who's right and who's wrong* or *who's lying and who's telling the truth.* The antagonism between the two immediate parties often forces the other two parties—the parent and the administrator—to take sides. You see your child being accused and you rise to his defense. The administrator sees his teacher being attacked and rises to his defense. It's natural but counterproductive.

For you to be able to discuss your child's past and present behavior openly, and for the administrator to be able to honestly discuss the teacher's or school's response, you'll both need to be free from the pressure to take sides. At some point it will probably be necessary to have all the parties together, but that need not take place until after you and the administrator have had a chance to speak alone.

And when you begin that one-on-one conversation you can eliminate the other primary cause of dissonance in the negotiation. The administrator is anticipating that this meeting, and in fact the entire process, will turn into an adversarial situation. He's afraid you're going to blame the school for your child's behavior. It's the same psychological reflex that causes people to blame the victim of a crime. A parent doesn't want to accept that his child could have done this alone, or that the parent could bear some responsibility. The rationalization becomes: it must be the teacher's or school's fault.

Instead of blaming the school or the teacher, begin your dialogue with the administrator by directly saying something like: "I don't blame the school for this. I think there's an underlying problem that caused this behavior, and I'd really like your help in figuring out what the problem is and how we can deal with it." This is a remarkably powerful statement. It not only keeps the situation from becoming adversarial, but in fact enlists the administrator as an ally in your cause. You've not only eliminated dissonance, in the process you've gained tremendous power.

Of course, if you honestly believe the situation *is* the teacher's fault you'll need to bring that to the administrator's attention. Rather than presenting it as an adversarial situation, however, frame it in mutual terms. Say, "I think that Mr. Smith and Jimmy might just have a personality conflict and perhaps that's the cause of the problem."

### WHAT DO I SHARE WITH MY OPPONENT?— FINDING AND DEMONSTRATING COMMON GROUND

Whichever of these statements you use, it should immediately be followed with a statement of what you see as the common ground in the negotiation. Since your goal should be to do whatever is in your child's long-term best interest, and the administrator's goal should be to do whatever is in the school's and the child's best interest, the obvious common ground is your child's best interest. For example, you could say: "If my child has done something wrong he must take responsibility for it. What I'm really interested in is getting to the cause of the problem and doing whatever we can to make sure it doesn't happen again. My concern is doing what's best for my child." Such a statement demonstrates that you understand the administrator must protect the school's best interests by issuing some type of punishment. However, you're asking that in return for your acceptance of that, the administrator should also keep the best interests of your child in mind.

## INSIDER TIPS FOR APPEALING EDUCATIONAL DISCIPLINARY DECISIONS

The third and final step in appealing educational disciplinary decisions is to know the situation. That's accomplished by applying the lessons learned by those who are experienced with this particular situation. While I've spoken to educators on behalf of my own children, I sought out experts on this situation: primary and secondary school administrators. The educators I spoke with offered two insider tips: one for situations when the punishment is flexible and your child has a clean record, and another for situations when the punishment isn't flexible and/or if your child has a history of behavioral problems.

### SHOW THE PUNISHMENT TO BE EXCESSIVE OR COUNTERPRODUCTIVE

If the punishment is flexible, and the behavior was out of character, you should try to demonstrate that the school's response is either excessive or counterproductive. For example, if a child has missed a week of school due to illness and then earns a suspension for cutting class, it would be counterproductive to force him to miss even more school.

If in explaining that your child has had no previous problems you feel the administrator isn't familiar with your child's record you should refer him to a guidance counselor or teacher who could vouch for your child. These character witnesses could have a great deal of impact on an administrator's decision—especially if they attest to the child's past history but don't try to pressure the administrator. If a coach, for example, comes to the assistant principal and attempts to pressure the administrator to amend the suspension so the child can play in the big game, it's apt to backfire.

## ACCEPT THE PUNISHMENT BUT MITIGATE SUBSEQUENT ACTIONS

If the problem is one that offers the administrator no flexibility, or if your child has had a history of bad behavior, the only thing that might work is to accept the mandate punishment but negotiate what the school's subsequent response will be. If, for example, a child has had repeated problems with a particular teacher and the final incident results in a one-week suspension, you should begin by acknowledging the validity of the punishment. However, you can move on to note that obviously there's an underlying problem that needs to be addressed: the relationship between your child and the teacher. You can suggest that when your child returns from the suspension he be transferred into another class, or that he at least receive a guarantee there will be no repercussions for past actions.

Now let's see how Cally handled her negotiation with the school over Nolan's two-day suspension. Since she had already learned from Nolan that he had indeed cut school and that he had done so because of a fight with his girlfriend, Cally could move on to gather information from the school. She knew she should first negotiate with an administrator directly, rather than involve Nolan right away. She called the principal and was referred to Nolan's grade level administrator, an assistant principal. He explained to Cally that policy stipulated a two-day suspension for a first cutting-school offense. Cally asked for an appointment to meet the administrator to discuss the matter and for the punishment to be delayed until after the meeting.

When she sat down with the administrator the next morning she began by saying that both she and Nolan realized he had made a mistake and deserved to be punished. She added that she in no way blamed the school for the problem, and explained what she had learned from Nolan about the fight with his girlfriend. Cally then said that she did, however, think that a two-day suspension was too severe a punishment, especially for someone who had no previous discipline problems. She also thought it wrong to force Nolan to miss more school as a punishment for missing school in the first place. Couldn't there be a more equitable and appropriate punishment, she asked.

The administrator admitted he didn't know Nolan well, adding that perhaps that proved he had a clean record. Cally suggested the administrator contact Nolan's guidance counselor and his English teacher. The administrator also conceded that it was ironic to use out-of-school suspension as a punishment for cutting school. He said that he'd look into the matter and speak to her later that day. That afternoon he telephoned Cally. He said Nolan's guidance counselor and English teacher had indeed backed up her statement that he had never been in trouble. The administrator said that in reconsidering the matter he had decided to have Nolan serve detention before and after school for two days, rather than be suspended out of school.

## Standing Up for Your Kid Appealing an Educator's Disciplinary Action

- Do what's in the long-term interests of your child.
- Punishments based on subjective policies are readily negotiable.
- Punishments for academic violations or illegal acts aren't readily negotiable.
- Approach administrators first.
- State that you don't hold the school responsible.
- Say that you understand wrongdoing must be punished.
- Add that you think the punishment shouldn't be excessive or counterproductive.
- If the administrator has no flexibility, negotiate the school's subsequent response.

# 15

# LEANING ON LENDERS

## Appealing a Credit Rejection

*"The rich ruleth over the poor, and the borrower is servant to the lender."*

—THE BIBLE

Jay was tired of living in a bare apartment. He had moved in two months before, just after getting his first job after graduating from college. The studio apartment initially looked small, but now that Jay's few belongings were inside it, it looked cavernous. His audio/video system, which had gone a long way to filling up his dorm room, filled only one corner of his apartment. And his mattress, which he'd had to squeeze into the dorm, looked tiny lying on the bare floor of the apartment. He was getting depressed using his mattress for a chair and dining room table as well as for sleeping. It was clearly time to buy furniture. Unfortunately, Jay had no savings. He was trying to put some money away, but until he did, he'd be living from paycheck to paycheck. That meant if he wanted to buy furniture now he'd need to get a credit card.

Throughout his four years of college Jay scrupulously avoided all the approaches of credit card companies and took a certain obstinate pride in his refusal to give in to plastic. But now that he was waking up next to empty cartons of Chinese takeout, he was ready to swallow his pride and apply for a credit card. He went down to his local bank, found an application, went home, filled it out, mailed it in, and figured he'd have his card in a month. Two weeks later he received notice that he'd been rejected. Jay had a choice—he could try going for variety by sitting on the floor now and then, or he could negotiate. He chose the latter.

# THE REJECTED BORROWER'S
# SELF-EXAMINATION

In appealing a credit rejection, as in every negotiation, the first step in the process is for the individual who has been rejected to analyze needs and weigh options; to know himself or herself. That's accomplished by asking three questions: "What do I want?" "Is it worth my time?" "Is it important to me?"

## *WHAT DO I WANT?—SETTING A SPECIFIC GOAL*

When negotiating with lenders it's essential to pinpoint exactly what your goal is. Are you looking for a specific amount of money? Or are you simply looking to qualify for a loan, with the amount being secondary? It's essential to differentiate between the two goals early on, since the tactics for each situation are different. Generally, if you're shopping for a loan for a specific purpose—to buy a home or car, or to do home renovations—your primary concern is the amount of money. If, on the other hand, you're simply looking to obtain a line of credit or to obtain the maximum loan you possibly can, your primary goal is to qualify.

## *IS IT WORTH MY TIME?—*
## *DECIDING IF IT'S READILY NEGOTIABLE*

Despite what you may have been led to believe, almost every loan rejection is readily negotiable. Lenders are required by law to give you a reason for a rejection and to provide an appeals process. Loans are rejected for one of three reasons: you're judged to not have a sufficient stream of income to make the monthly payments; your past credit history doesn't demonstrate a strong enough willingness to pay on time or completely; or the collateral or item that's to secure the loan—the house or car you are buying—isn't of sufficient value to merit a loan of the size you're requesting.

Rejections for the first two reasons—ability to pay and willingness to pay—are entirely subjective judgments and are readily negotiable. Rejections for the third reason—insufficient collateral or too high a loan-to-value ratio—are negotiable, but only by professionals who know how to work with and around lenders' rules.

If you are rejected because your income is too low or you've a questionable credit history you can readily negotiate. But before you start you need to do some attitude adjustment.

Most people believe lending rejections aren't negotiable because they look on them as decisions. Loan rejections are actually judgments, not decisions. And these judgments are based only on the limited amount of information that has been provided. Despite the fact that this chapter is located in the persuasive negotiations section, your mission isn't to persuade the lender that he was wrong in rejecting your credit application. Your mission is to accept the lender's judgment but point out that it was not based on all the facts. In other words, you're not asking the lender to change his mind but to reexamine the issue in light of new evidence . . . evidence I'll suggest later in this chapter.

## IS IT IMPORTANT TO ME?— ## MAKING SURE IT'S WORTH NEGOTIATING

Even though it'll be time-consuming it's always worth negotiating a lender's rejection. Generally, lenders don't reject for reasons peculiar to their own way of doing business. Competing lenders have similar systems. In other words, if your application for a $100,000 thirty-year mortgage was rejected by one bank due to your credit history, other banks will probably reject your application for the same reason. If Visa has turned you down for a $1,000 credit line, MasterCard probably will as well. That means wherever you go you're likely to face the same rejection. You're going to need to clear this hurdle at some point, so you might as well do it now.

Deciding not to even try to clear the hurdle—not to even enter into the world of credit—is a mistake as well. Though the excessive personal, business, and government borrowing of the Reagan era has been justifiably criticized, credit remains a valuable tool. It's the only way most Americans will ever be able to buy their own home. It could be the only way you'll be able to buy the kind of transportation you need. And finally, credit allows you to leverage against your future. Through credit you can go to Paris while you're still young enough to climb the Eiffel Tower. While that may be an extravagant example, the message is clear: credit lets you do today what otherwise you'd need to wait for. I'm not suggesting you give up on the idea of saving for a goal. I'm simply saying there's a time for saving and a time for borrowing. (Personally, I believe you should save for things you *want* and borrow for things you *need*.)

Let's see how Jay's self-examination went. While he did have a particular goal in mind—buying furniture—Jay didn't have a set amount he was looking for. That meant his goal was simply to obtain credit. Despite his anger, he kept telling himself the rejection wasn't the bank's irrevo-

cable decision. It was simply a judgment based on the facts provided—
the answers on his application form. And Jay knew that a judgment on a
set of (limited) facts is readily negotiable. Finally, Jay understood he'd
probably have the same problem wherever he applied. He knew that obtaining credit was often a catch-22 situation. If he had credit he could
qualify for more, but since he had none, he didn't qualify. Since he was
going to need to make it over this hurdle at some point, Jay decided it
was worth negotiating the rejection.

## LEVELING THE CREDIT PLAYING FIELD

The second step in appealing a credit rejection is for you to get to know
your opponent and to use that information to level the playing field. This
is done by answering four questions: "What do I need to know?" "With
whom should I negotiate?" "Are there any potentially disruptive side
issues?" "What do I share with my opponent?"

### *WHAT DO I NEED TO KNOW?—*
### *GATHERING INFORMATION*

The single most important piece of information you'll need to obtain is
the reason you were rejected. This shouldn't be too difficult to find out
since lenders are legally required to provide a reason for a credit rejection.
A telephone call should get you all the information you need. If you're
told there's a problem with the value of your collateral or with the loan-
to-value ratio, you'll need to enlist the aid of a professional. But if you're
told the problem is you've insufficient income or there's a problem with
your credit history, then you can forge ahead.

Whether or not you're able to pay back a loan is a mathematical judgment that can only be refuted with different numbers. The lender will have
a formula that shows how much money you need to earn each month in
order to be able to meet a certain loan payment. They will factor other
loans you may have obtained into this analysis. If you either don't make
enough money to meet the payments or you've already taken out as much
credit as they think you can pay back comfortably, the lender will reject
you automatically. In order to combat this judgment you'll need to gather
information that shows you make more money or have fewer outstanding
debts than they think.

Your willingness to repay a loan is based on your credit history and
personal stability. Your credit history is contained in a document called a
credit bureau report. While these reports have languages all their own
they're basically a series of judgments by your various creditors as to how

you've been as a debtor. Each creditor categorizes you as paying on time, paying late, or not paying at all. Potential lenders look on this record of your past behavior as an indication of your future behavior. However, it's possible your credit bureau report contains outright mistakes. Or it could contain "errors in judgment."

Let's say you delayed paying a charge on your department store card because the television you purchased was broken. The department store might have characterized you as paying late. Perhaps your credit bureau report contains accurate but incomplete information. You may actually have paid a bill late, but what isn't shown in the report is that it was due to your being hospitalized for emergency surgery. Once you returned home you paid your bills promptly, but the characterization stands.

If there are any such marks on your credit bureau report you need to have them removed or add an explanation. Both can easily be done—and at no charge if you've recently been turned down for credit. If there's a mistake you simply inform the credit bureau of the error and ask them to either remove it or prove it—the burden of proof is on them. If you need to include an explanation, simply write a hundred-word statement and have the credit bureau add it to your file—by law they must. While you can bring mistakes and explanations to the attention of the lender who turned you down, their judgment won't change until the credit bureau report has been changed. That will mean waiting and reapplying at a later date.

The second element that's seen as proof of your willingness to pay back a loan is personal stability. To a lender, personal stability is exemplified by strength of character. However, there's no way that can be determined on an application. That's why they rely on lesser measures, such as how long you've lived in one place or how long you've worked at one job. I've already discussed one method of turning these inaccurate, potentially damaging measures to your advantage: supplementing your application. But if you've already been turned down after submitting an application you'll need to make a more concrete demonstration of personal stability. And that can only be done in person.

## WITH WHOM SHOULD I NEGOTIATE?—
## PUSHING THE UP BUTTON

The obvious answer to this question is: the person who made the negative judgement. But in negotiating with lenders finding that person gets very complicated. Most lending organizations have structures that simultaneously make the decision making—excuse me, judging—as simple as possible and insulate the judges from those they judge. So in order to negotiate you need to go beyond the original judge or to fight your way through red tape to actually find the judge.

In an attempt to speed up the process lenders use a system called scoring. Rather than actually sitting down to interview potential borrowers, or to examine their credentials on a case-by-case basis, they've drafted standardized applications. These applications are designed to reduce your personal and financial information to its most basic elements. (Have you ever noticed how little room there is to answer the questions on a credit card application? That's intentional.) Those basic elements are then given point totals. For example: Lenders believe that living in the same place for a long period of time, or working at the same job for a long period of time, indicates stability. That's why they ask if you've lived at the same address for five years or more or have worked at the same job for five years or more. If you have, they give you the top point total. If you haven't, they give you a lower score. In fact, the more places you've lived and the more jobs you've had in those five years, the lower your score.

A group of clerks are given the responsibility of scoring all the applications. Each day they're given a point score representing the minimum qualifying number for acceptance. The clerks have no discretion. They simply go through the application, scoring the answers and then accepting or rejecting it. Theirs is what I like to call a reflex judgment.

In order to insulate the actual judges—those deciding what the minimum acceptable score will be—from those being judged, lending organizations have set up "complaint" and "appeals" procedures. These are most often bureaucracies designed to diffuse tension, not reexamine judgments. Typically the people who staff these departments are trained in calming people down and explaining "company policy." They generally have no power. Like the scoring clerks, these individuals only make reflex judgments.

In order to negotiate you need to find someone who can make a reasoned rather than a reflex judgment; someone who can rationally examine facts presented outside the typical application format and then make an individual judgment based on those facts; or someone who can rationally listen to an appeal as a representation of facts, not as a complaint, and can respond with a judgment, not a reflex recitation of the company line.

The best way to obtain a reasoned judgment is to bypass the scoring system entirely. While it's not strictly a negotiating technique, I think this process is so important that I'll spend a little time telling you how to do it. Remember, the application has been set up to simplify information in order for clerks to be able to score answers. In order to get beyond the clerks you need to make your application complex. How do you do that? You don't let yourself be content to respond with short answers. In the little space the lender has provided to list all the jobs you've held in the past five years you write: "See Supplement A." Then, on a separate sheet of paper you proceed to turn what would be a negative—frequent job shifts—into a positive. Before giving the names and addresses of your employers you describe why you've shifted jobs so often. If your income has gone up dramatically with each move this needs to be explained. If frequent job shifts are common in your industry this needs to be pointed out. In other words, no answer should be left unexplained.

When an application comes in accompanied by five typed pages of supplements the scoring clerk has no idea of what to do. He can't simply score the answers since they don't fall into the prescribed pattern. Instead, he passes the application on to his superior. This person will see that this is a special case and either make a reasoned judgment himself, pass the application on to someone else to make a reasoned judgment, or try to sabotage your efforts by rejecting it out of hand. In any of the three cases you've won. In the first two you've gotten the reasoned judgment you're after. In the third case you've excellent grounds for an appeal to a higher authority . . . one outside the traditional channels.

If you've failed to make your application complex and have been victimized by scoring, or if your customized application has been rejected, the way to obtain a reasoned judgment is to "push the up button" and move up the corporate ladder. Work through proper channels, even though they're designed to derail you. But at each point when you reach a brick wall, ask to speak to the individual's superior. Don't do this nastily. Be gracious. Say you understand he can't do anything for you and offer your gratitude for all his help. Say you'll be telling his supervisor how well you've been treated. Just explain that you think yours is a special case and therefore in need of special attention. Generally, no one will be able to refuse such a nice request to go over his head. But once again, if he does, you've got grounds for a special out-of-channels appeal right to the top of the organization.

Eventually, if you persevere, you'll get to someone who has the power to make a reasoned judgment . . . in your favor. Keep looking for that person until you find him, or you can climb no farther.

## ARE THERE ANY POTENTIALLY DISRUPTIVE SIDE ISSUES?—ELIMINATING DISSONANCE

The dissonance in this negotiation is the lender's fear, as manifested in its rejection of your application, that you won't be able or willing to pay back a loan. Once you've found someone who seems receptive to at least hearing your case, ask to schedule a meeting. It's next to impossible to eliminate a lender's dissonance over the telephone or through the mail. You need to give this person a chance to look you and your personal finances up and down.

If he shows some hesitancy to schedule a meeting, plead for fairness. Say that your credit file is very important to you, that you really want to establish a relationship with his lending institution, that it's important for you to establish credit. Say whatever it takes to play on his heart strings. Above all, ask for his help in resolving your problem. People have an innate desire to respond to those who ask for help. Few of us feel secure enough to place ourselves in others' hands. We all know how much it takes for us to ask someone else for help, especially someone we don't know. Few people can resist such a request, especially after they or their institution has already turned you down once before. People are loath to turn someone down twice.

If possible, schedule your meeting for the first appointment after lunch. Most people in the financial world see lunch as an elaborate ritual. I know, I was a banker and a venture capitalist. This predilection for elaborate luncheon meals, often accompanied by a couple of drinks (still), led to my lingering hatred of lunch meetings. I'd go to bank luncheons that dragged on for hours and accomplished nothing. But no one would think of forgoing the lunch. It was part of the financial culture. When I returned from these luncheon meetings I must admit I was in a much better mood. I felt satisfied, perhaps even a little high. If potential borrowers came in after lunch I was much more likely to listen to them, to like them, and to lend to them. I even went back and analyzed my lending pattern to check to see if I was just imagining this. I wasn't. I clearly was more amenable to those who saw me after lunch than to those who saw me in the morning.

Dress for this meeting as you would for a job interview . . . if that job was with a bank. Forget about style, panache, and élan. Be as conservative as possible. That means blue or gray business suits, discreet cologne or perfume, no ostentatious jewelry, and sensible shoes. If you're going to be presenting numbers or new information, organize and type it. Consider drafting a memo summarizing your case and bringing a copy you can leave with the other party. Your deportment, dress, and demeanor should demonstrate that you consider this a serious business meeting.

When introduced shake hands firmly, looking the other party in the eye. Introduce yourself, using his name as well. For example: "I'm Stephen Pollan, Mr. Smith. It's a pleasure to meet you." Sit only when invited to. When seated, keep your back straight and keep both your feet flat on the floor. Lean forward from the waist when listening or making a point. I know this sounds like I'm turning you into a marine, but believe me, it works. Proving yourself to be of good character is more than half the battle. And a satisfied, slightly groggy lender likes nothing more than lending money to a marine.

## WHAT DO I SHARE WITH MY OPPONENT?— FINDING AND DEMONSTRATING COMMON GROUND

You see, lenders want to lend you money. I know you don't feel that way, particularly after you've been rejected. But the only way a lender makes the money to pay for those magnificent offices, expensive suits, and elaborate lunches is to lend money and charge interest. His natural reticence and initial rejection of you are simply products of a misunderstanding brought on by the impersonal nature of lending today. What you need to do is bring him back to the good old days when lending was done face to face—and to remind him of the common ground that exists between you.

What do you have in common with a lender? First, you both respect the power of money. But second, and most important, you both want to make a loan. Granted, the loan that results from this meeting, the loan that meets your common needs, may not be exactly the same as the one you first requested. But it will be approved. Early on in your meeting with the lender you need to come right out and tell the lender that you're willing to do whatever it takes for him to feel comfortable making the loan and that, just as important, you want to establish a relationship with his institution. If you do that you can come out of this meeting with a loan.

# INSIDER TIPS FOR REJECTED BORROWERS

The third and final step in appealing a credit rejection is to know the situation. That's accomplished by applying the lessons learned by those who are experienced with this particular situation. I've been a banker and a venture capitalist, and as an attorney I've represented literally hundreds of individuals and businesses who needed to have lending judgments reversed. I've also written articles in books on credit and have lectured on the topic at more than one hundred major universities. All that experience, as well as research I conducted for this book, leads me to offer you the following four insider tips.

## ELIMINATING DISSONANCE WILL OVERTURN CHARACTER-BASED REJECTIONS

If you've successfully eliminated the dissonance surrounding the negotiation during your meeting, your character should no longer be an issue.

The lender will be so impressed with you as an individual that he'll be willing to do whatever it takes to make a loan. The only obstacles left will be insufficient income or a poor credit bureau report.

### IF THE EXACT AMOUNT ISN'T IMPORTANT, ASK FOR LESS

If you were rejected due to insufficient income, and the exact amount you receive *isn't* your primary concern, ask the lender if the judgment would be different if the loan were for less money. The requirements for borrowing are understandably keyed to the amount being borrowed. You need show less of an income, and probably need to have less of a sterling credit bureau report, if you borrow less money. By asking for less you offer the lender an opportunity to custom-fit the loan amount to your creditworthiness.

### IF THE EXACT AMOUNT IS IMPORTANT, ASK FOR MORE TIME

If you were rejected due to insufficient income, and the exact amount you receive *is* important, ask the lender if the judgment would be different if the loan term were lengthened. Most lenders gauge creditworthiness on a monthly scale. By asking for a longer loan term you effectively lower your monthly payment while increasing the amount of interest income the bank will generate from the loan. You'd be surprised at the number of instances when someone can turn a rejection into an acceptance simply by shifting from a three-year loan to a five-year loan.

By offering such suggestions to the lender you give him an opportunity to use his discretion and make the loan you originally requested. Many times there's actually a range of acceptable scores. The lender, impressed by your character and new documentation, may be moved to completely overturn the prior judgment. However, in all honesty, it's more likely he'll use the opportunity created by your suggestion to slip you into a loan program for which you clearly qualify.

### IF YOUR CREDIT IS THE PROBLEM, BRING IN A GUARANTOR

Rejections based on credit reports are a little bit more difficult to overcome. As I mentioned earlier, even if the judgment was based on a mistaken credit report there's little the lender can do until the credit report itself is changed. If you've done a good job of eliminating dissonance the lender will want to work with you. But your credit report will have tied his hands. The answer is to bring in some external security for him in the person of a guarantor or co-signer.

Basically, a guarantor or co-signer is someone who agrees to assume responsibility for the debt in case you default. This offers the lender a security blanket similar to the protection offered by collateral. The guarantor can be anyone who's willing to do it and whose credit is good: a parent, employer, friend, or relative. In some instances you can even become your own guarantor. If you have some savings that you weren't planning on using in the near future, ask the lender if that money can be kept on deposit as collateral for your loan. In effect, you're using your own money to guarantee your loan. This is called a passbook loan and it's a very effective way to establish credit. Of course, the catch is that if you had the savings you probably wouldn't need the loan. However, if what counts is establishing credit, this will do the trick.

Let's see how Jay leveled the playing field and negotiated with his bank. In order to gather information he called up the bank and asked why his credit card application was rejected. He was told he had insufficient income for the credit line he'd requested and he had no credit history to speak of.

Jay realized he'd made a mistake in simply filling out the application form without thinking. But rather than reapplying with a supplemented form, Jay decided to use his rejection as an opportunity to work his way up the bank's bureaucracy, pushing the up button until he reached someone who could make a reasoned rather than reflexive judgment.

Jay sat down and reexamined his application. First he looked at his income. When he took his job he had been told to expect a minimum of another $1,000 in bonuses. He had forgotten to include that in his application. In addition, he received $40 per month in interest income from a certificate of deposit his grandmother had put in his name. Finally, he received approximately $50 a month from his parents to help him cover his medical insurance costs. That was a total of another $2,080 a year he could add to his income.

Next, he looked back over his financial history to see if there were any examples he could use to establish a credit record. He remembered he'd had charge accounts with a bookstore and clothing store in college, which, while not credit lines, demonstrated his prompt payment history. In addition, he had been paying his own electric and telephone bills promptly for more than four years.

He typed up a memo outlining his new application information and telephoned the bank. He pushed the up button until he finally got through to the branch manager. He asked the branch manager for an appointment to discuss his credit card rejection, and while the manager wasn't enthusiastic about the situation, Jay's appeal to fairness got him an appointment the next afternoon.

Jay dressed in his dark blue interview suit and arrived five minutes early. He used all the job interviewing skills he'd learned in the past year to make a good impression. He presented the branch manager with his memo, outlining verbally what it contained. He then asked the branch manager if it was possible for him to qualify for a credit card with a lower credit line. He admitted he had no credit history, but appealed to the branch manager for help. He said that he wanted to establish a relationship with the bank, as demonstrated by his having had a checking account there for the past four years. He pointed out his exemplary history with the checking account, the book and clothing store accounts, and in paying his electric and telephone bills, while acknowledging that none of these had any bearing on his blank credit report. He finally asked the branch manager for help.

Jay said he needed someone to cut through the catch-22 and help him establish credit, and asked if the branch manager could somehow help him. The branch manager looked over Jay's memo and looked Jay over. The branch manager told Jay he'd need to speak to the district office but would recommend that the bank give Jay a credit card with a $500 credit line. The branch manager explained that while this was low, it could be increased once Jay had established a credit history with the bank. Jay thanked him profusely and went home. Two weeks later the card arrived in the mail.

## Leaning on Lenders
## Appealing a Credit Rejection

- Are you looking for a specific amount or any amount?
- Find someone who can make a reasoned judgment.
- Find out why you were rejected.
- Have a face-to-face meeting to demonstrate good character and provide information.
- State your willingness to do whatever it takes for the lender to feel comfortable.
- If rejected for insufficient income, and the amount *isn't* important, ask for less.
- If rejected for insufficient income, and the amount *is* important, extend the term.
- If rejected due to credit problems, bring in a guarantor or offer collateral.

# 16

# BARGAINING WITH BUREAUCRATS

## Negotiating with Institutions and Organizations

*"Bureaucrats are the only people in the world who can say absolutely nothing and mean it."*

—HUGH SIDNEY

Christine was upset that her insurance company was refusing to pay for her visit to the dermatologist and the prescription she had received. The form response from the insurer claimed that her treatment was for a preexisting condition and therefore wasn't covered. According to the insurance company's rule book, a preexisting condition was one that Christine would have been treated for within a year of having signed up with the insurer. But Christine hadn't been to the dermatologist for more than two years. Clearly, the insurer had made a mistake.

## THE BUREAUCRACY-BUSTER'S
## SELF-EXAMINATION

In trying to bargain with bureaucrats, as in every negotiation, the first step in the process is for you to analyze needs and weigh options, to know yourself. That's accomplished by asking three questions: "What do I want?" "Is it worth my time?" "Is it important to me?"

### *WHAT DO I WANT?—SETTING A SPECIFIC GOAL*

The reason most people get upset when dealing with bureaucracies— large multilevel organizations and institutions such as insurance companies, government agencies, corporations, and utilities—is that they don't understand how bureaucracies work. While you may actually be speaking with a human being who represents a bureaucracy, you really aren't dealing on a human-to-human level. That person, while a living breathing creature, is acting as a bureaucrat. And bureaucrats go by an entirely different set of rules than human beings. A human being looks at a problem and tries to find the best solution; a bureaucrat looks at a problem and tries to figure out which of the preassigned solutions—A, B, or C—is the proper response. Innovation and insight aren't part of the bureaucratic process. Everything must fit into strict parameters.

Let me give you just one example, since I'm sure you've plenty of your own. A good friend of mine had his New York State driver's license revoked many years ago for having received three speeding tickets within eighteen months. Since at the time he spent half of the year in Florida, he simply applied for a Florida license instead of reapplying for a New York license. Just last year he decided to sell his Florida home and stay in New York for the entire year. He realized that would mean he'd need a New York driver's license. He went to the Department of Motor Vehicles and filled out an application for a license. When he came across the question "Have you ever had a New York license before?" he honestly answered yes, explaining that his previous license had been revoked back in 1978. When he brought his application up to the clerk and she began to process it, she told him there was a problem. It seemed the computer had no record of his ever having had a New York license. As long as he answered the question honestly, she couldn't process his application. My friend asked her what he should do. All she said was that he couldn't lie, but if he told the truth she couldn't process the application. That's a classic example of "bureaucratese."

How do you get out of this hall of mirrors erected by bureaucracy? By establishing a simple goal for yourself and sticking with it: you just want to be treated like a human being by another human being. That means finding some way to get through, around, or past the bureaucratic red tape.

## IS IT WORTH MY TIME?—
## DECIDING IF IT'S READILY NEGOTIABLE

It's impossible to negotiate with a bureaucrat since he has no decision-making power. All a bureaucrat can do is respond according to an organization's prescribed pattern. It is possible to negotiate with a human being, however. The secret, then, to making your confrontation with bureaucracy readily negotiable is to find someone who can respond like a human rather than a bureaucrat. If you can find a person who has the power to listen and react independently of prescribed patterns—or, barring that, someone who can offer you a way around the prescribed patterns—then you'll be able to negotiate.

### IS IT IMPORTANT TO ME?—
### MAKING SURE IT'S WORTH NEGOTIATING

Whether or not it's worth going to all this trouble to get to someone to negotiate a bureaucratic decision depends on what you're negotiating. Obviously, if you're talking about a large sum of money or a very important matter then it's worth all the effort involved. But if it's only a small amount of money and an inconsequential matter it may not be worth all the trouble. I'm all for standing up for principles, but when it comes to banging your head against a bureaucratic wall I'd suggest you make sure the principles are awfully important to you.

Let's see how Christine's self-examination went. Her goal in negotiating with her insurance company was to get beyond the form rejection she'd received and find someone she could deal with on a human-to-human level. She knew that if she was able to do that her problem would be readily negotiable. Finally, Christine thought it was worth negotiating the problem. While this initial claim wasn't for a great deal of money—it was just $50—she was planning on visiting the dermatologist monthly for the next year. That meant it wouldn't be just $50 but would end up being $600.

## LEVELING THE BUREAUCRATIC
## PLAYING FIELD

The second step in negotiating with a bureaucracy is for you to get to know your opponent and to use that information to level the playing field. This is done by answering four questions: "What do I need to know?" "With whom should I negotiate?" "Are there any potentially disruptive side issues?" "What do I share with my opponent?"

### WHAT DO I NEED TO KNOW?—
### GATHERING INFORMATION

There are only two pieces of information you're likely to need to gather for this negotiation: the facts of the case in question and the rules of the bureaucracy. The former should be obvious. Just jot down the objective facts surrounding your problem. The latter, while not obvious, are easy to

obtain. Simply contact the bureaucracy and ask. Bureaucracies may not
be easy to negotiate with but they are efficient at providing information.

## WITH WHOM SHOULD I NEGOTIATE?—
## PUSHING THE UP BUTTON

Your selection of an opponent in this negotiation is more than half the
battle. How do you find a human being among the bureaucrats? By looking
and asking for help. There are two good techniques I encourage you to
use in your search for someone with discretionary power or who can give
you a way around the red tape. The first is the standard method of finding
the right person to negotiate with: pushing the up button. The second is
a technique I call "speaking hypothetically."

Pushing the up button, as I'm sure you know by now if you've been
reading this book carefully, refers to working your way up the bureaucratic
or organizational ladder. During each conversation you have with a bureaucrat get him to do as much as he possibly can for you within the limits
of his power. When he can do nothing further for you, ask to speak to his
supervisor—that's pushing the up button. In this manner you can work
your way from supervisor to supervisor, eventually reaching someone who
has discretionary power. I've had clients who successfully used this technique to get all the way to the chief executive of a company. The secret
to this technique is to remain on good terms with each individual. You're
not going over their heads because they're rude or because they've done
something wrong. You're pushing the up button because you've reached
the limit of their power. Make it your business to get the name of everyone
you speak with and thank each before moving on. Then, when you speak
to their superior, remark on how helpful the underling was, using his
name, and stress that he suggested you move up the ladder. Believe me,
you'll catch more flies with honey than with vinegar, even if they're bureaucratic flies. Eventually, if you keep pushing the up button, you'll reach
someone who has the power to act like a human being rather than a
bureaucrat.

The other technique to working your way to a human being is to speak
hypothetically. As soon as you reach a person in the bureaucracy who
sounds like she wants to be a human being but can't, or who at least
realizes that you're enmeshed in ridiculous bureaucratic red tape, you can
try to turn her into an adviser. In order to get her out of the bureaucratic
mold, ask her to "speak hypothetically." What this does is remove the
constraints to respond according to company or organizational policy.

Let me give you an example. Let's go back to my friend who was
having a problem at the Department of Motor Vehicles. If the clerk behind

the counter seemed to realize the lunacy of the situation and appeared sympathetic, my friend could have turned to her and said, "Speaking hypothetically, if you had a friend in my situation what would you advise him to do?" This offers the bureaucrat a chance to suggest a course of action outside the prescribed channels, but that would succeed nevertheless without violating anyone's position. For instance, the clerk could have told my friend, "Hypothetically, of course, if someone fills out the application in accord with the facts contained in the computer, then, according to the computer they aren't lying." In other words, the clerk could have told my friend to just lie on the application since the computer didn't have a record of his having had a license revoked. I'm not saying that's what the clerk told him, mind you, but she could have.

"Pushing the up button" is more involved and time-consuming than "speaking hypothetically," but it's guaranteed to work. If you go high enough you will eventually find someone who can help you. If you need to correct a mistake you'll need to push the up button. If you simply need to work your way around red tape, speaking hypothetically should be sufficient.

## ARE THERE ANY POTENTIALLY DISRUPTIVE SIDE ISSUES?—ELIMINATING DISSONANCE

The dissonance likely to surround your negotiation with a bureaucracy is the impersonality of the exchange. Remember that the bureaucrat has been trained to treat you not as a human being but as a particular situation for which there is an assigned response or set of responses. In order to eliminate this dissonance you need to present yourself as a human being and get him to be a human as well. This is done by remaining calm and by asking for, and then using, his name.

The worst thing you can do with a bureaucrat is get angry. Once you lose your temper the bureaucrat's response is to stonewall. If you're going to scream and yell the bureaucrat is going to require you to fill everything out in triplicate—it's the bureaucrat's way of getting revenge for the abuse you're dumping on him. Remember, he didn't create the red tape, he's just supposed to implement it. While he's a convenient target for your rage he doesn't necessarily deserve it.

The best thing you can do to a bureaucrat is ask him for his name and then use it repeatedly in your conversation. This is someone who is continually dehumanized by his employer and those he deals with in the general public. Remind him that he's a person and treat him like one, and you'll be surprised how accommodating he'll become. He may not be able to break the rules, but he'll be able to help you bypass them or get to someone else who can help.

### WHAT DO I SHARE WITH MY OPPONENT?— FINDING AND DEMONSTRATING COMMON GROUND

During each of your conversations with bureaucrats make sure you establish and state the common ground between the two of you: respect for the process. Rather than denigrating the bureaucracy, say you understand the need for an established process and in fact respect it. Like it or not, this is the situation you're in and you must work within the rules. Explain, however, that your circumstances are special and require special attention that the process might not normally provide. If you reject the value of the bureaucratic process you are, in effect, rejecting the people you'll be negotiating with. There's a reason for a bureaucracy to exist: it's the most efficient way to handle standard situations. However, it is inefficient at handling nonstandard situations. Bureaucrats are perhaps more aware of this than anyone else. Ironically, by showing your respect for the process and them, you open the way for your situation to be handled outside the process.

## INSIDER TIPS FOR DEALING WITH BUREAUCRACIES

The third and final step in negotiating with a bureaucracy is to know the situation. That's accomplished by applying the lessons learned by those who are experienced with this particular situation. While I've been handling bureaucratic negotiations for my clients for some years now, in the past four years, as CNBC's Answer Man, I've become a real expert at it. Every week viewers send me letters about their problems, most often with bureaucracies, and I help them. From my experience I've gleaned three insider tips for you:

First, you can do the bureaucrat's work for him.

Second, you can put it in writing.

And third, you can enlist the help of a powerful ally.

### DO THE BUREAUCRAT'S WORK FOR HIM

Bureaucrats, even those you've turned into human beings, don't want to do anything outside the scope of their job. If clearing up a matter requires doing some research, or digging up facts, or clarifying information, the bureaucrat won't be interested. The answer is to do his job for him. If you want the matter resolved you may need to do his job and then present him with all your findings.

## PUT IT IN WRITING

After you've done his job for him, the best way to present the information is in writing. Bureaucracies respond differently to written documents than to telephone conversations. In fact, different individuals or even departments may be involved. When you write a letter you're documenting your case and forcing the bureaucracy to formally respond to it. A telephone call can be forgotten; a letter, especially registered or certified letter, cannot be forgotten or ignored.

## ENLIST THE HELP OF A POWERFUL ALLY

When all else fails, or in an effort to expedite other efforts, bringing in an outside ally can help in negotiations with bureaucrats and bureaucracies. Such an effort works best if the outside ally has some pull with the bureaucracy. Let me give you some examples. If you're dealing with a government agency, have your elected representative intercede on your behalf. If you're dealing with an insurance company, consider using your broker or agent as an ally. Since your broker's commission depends on your continuing to pay premiums, it's in her interest to make sure you're satisfied. She may have inside contacts with an insurer that can be used to expedite matters.

Don't be afraid of using regulatory agencies as allies. The Better Business Bureau, the Federal Trade Commission, state and local consumer affairs commissions or departments, or state and local licensing authorities can all be used as potential allies in disputes with bureaucracies. For instance, a state utility board could help resolve a dispute with an electric company.

Allies can also be other interested parties. For instance, if you're negotiating with your co-op or condominium board about renovations you need done to your unit, have your neighbors come forward as allies. After all, it's their interests the board is supposed to be protecting. If they rise to your defense the board's objections may be made moot.

Let's see how Christine handled her negotiation with her insurance company. She began by calling the insurance company and making sure she understood both the reason for her claim's being rejected and the policy on preexisting conditions. Next, she double-checked her facts. It was clear the insurer had made a mistake. Christine realized that since her problem wasn't one of working around red tape but of correcting a mistake, she'd need to "push the up button" until she found someone with the power to help her. Christine began working her way up the bureaucratic ladder, pushing the up button until she found someone with the power to resolve her problem. Throughout all her conversations she was calm and friendly, and continually stated her respect for the process. After telling her story to three separate individuals, Christine finally found someone with the power to investigate the matter. This individual said he believed Christine but he needed proof in order to overturn the rejection. Christine promised to provide the proof he needed. She knew he couldn't be counted on to do the research involved so she went about it herself. She drove over to the dermatologist's office and asked the office staff to write up a letter stating exactly which dates she had visited. Christine then saw where the mistake had been made. It was obvious that someone in the insurance company had mistakenly recorded an August 1990 appointment as an August 1991 appointment.

When she got home Christine drafted a letter telling her story from beginning to end and including her belief as to where the mistake came from. She included a copy of the evidence she'd obtained from the dermatologist. She then sent one copy of this letter to the receptive bureaucrat she had spoken with previously and another copy to her insurance broker. On the copy she sent her broker she attached a note asking him to see if he could expedite matters. Four days later she received a call from the bureaucrat saying he had received her letter and had spoken with her broker. He said the insurance company had overturned its rejection and would be paying the claim. Three days later she received her check.

## Bargaining with Bureaucrats
## Negotiating with Institutions
## and Organizations

- Find someone who can respond like a human rather than a bureaucrat.
- Either "push the up button" or "speak hypothetically."
- Know the facts of the case in question and the rules of the bureaucracy.
- Remain calm.
- Ask for, and use, the other party's name.
- State your respect for the process.
- Do the bureaucrat's job for him and present your findings.
- Put your case in writing to force the bureaucracy to respond.
- Bring in an outside ally with influence over the bureaucracy.

# 17

# MORE PERSUASIVE NEGOTIATIONS

## A Guide to Nine Other Important Situations

Just as it was impossible for me to go over every possible number negotiation in great detail, so too it's impractical to go over each potential persuasive negotiation with the depth of the previous five chapters. But as I've repeatedly said, my goal is to make you a total negotiator. That means I can't just leave you completely on your own when it comes to these other persuasive situations. In this chapter you'll find brief capsule guides for nine other important persuasive negotiations. In keeping with the total negotiator approach, each of these capsule guides, like those in the earlier capsule chapter, is built around the three main steps in total negotiating: know yourself, know your opponent, and know the situation. And as in earlier chapters, I provide insider tips for each situation—based on my personal and professional experience, as well as research conducted for this book—so you won't need to rely on experience. In this chapter, rather than covering the particular individuals you may need to negotiate with, as I did in the capsule summaries of numbers negotiations, I've focused on specific situations.

## APPEALING A FAILING COURSE GRADE

### *KNOW YOURSELF*

- *What do I want?* Your goal should be to get an opportunity to do additional work to turn an overall course failure, not to overturn a decision.
- *Is it worth my time?* It's readily negotiable if you demonstrate sub-

stantial effort and provide proof that your knowledge of the material is satisfactory.

- *Is it important to me?* It's worth negotiating a failing course grade if you need that particular course to graduate or advance.

## KNOW YOUR OPPONENT

- *What do I need to know?* Learn the reason for the failing grade and come up with any potentially mitigating factors. Then, try to determine what additional work might be sufficient to merit a reconsideration.
- *With whom should I negotiate?* Negotiate directly with the teacher or professor who gave you the failing grade; it's his or her judgment you need to change.
- *Are there any potentially disruptive side issues?* Never attack a grade as being unfair, instead ask for a reconsideration based on new facts—the additional work you're going to do. Ask that any past problems between you and the professor or teacher be put aside.
- *What do I share with my opponent?* The common ground you need to create here is respect for the grading process. You demonstrate your respect for the process by showing a willingness to earn a passing grade.

## KNOW THE SITUATION

- Insider Tip: The secret to this negotiation is to impress on the teacher or professor the importance of your receiving a passing grade—perhaps you need this course to graduate on time—then to offer an extenuating reason for your failure—such as an illness in the family.

## BORDERLINE COLLEGE ADMISSIONS

### KNOW YOURSELF

- *What do I want?* Your goal should be to be accepted into a particular college or university.
- *Is it worth my time?* It's readily negotiable if you already meet the minimum standards of the institution.

- *Is it important to me?* It's worth negotiating if there is something particularly important about getting into this one institution. Otherwise, don't bother.

## KNOW YOUR OPPONENT

- *What do I need to know?* Through research and investigation learn which of your personal attributes or skills are attractive to the university. Do they need trumpet players? Are they looking for students from Montana?
- *With whom should I negotiate?* Negotiate directly with either the admissions officer who's handling your application or the dean of admissions if it's a small school.
- *Are there any potentially disruptive side issues?* Admissions officers are afraid of appearing to show favoritism or excessive flexibility to people outside the university community. You remove this dissonance by finding an ally who's already in the university community.
- *What do I share with my opponent?* The common ground in this negotiation is your need to be accepted into the school and the school's need for you.

## KNOW THE SITUATION

- Insider Tip: Everyone knows how a promising young athlete whose grades put her on the borderline can ask her prospective coach to put in a good word with Admissions. The coach, interested in maintaining the caliber of her program, becomes an advocate for the applicant. The same technique can be used for nonathletes. If your child is a borderline candidate for admission and has some special skill, there's no reason he can't get an advocate of his own. For example: If your son is a skilled saxophone player, why not have someone from the music department put in a good word; if your daughter is a talented writer, a creative writing professor can be enlisted to help.
- Insider Tip: Similarly, any connection you can establish with the college community can be used as an inside advocate. If your employer serves as a university trustee or your neighbor is an active alumnus, both could put in a good word—and they're likely to have some influence.

## COLLEGE-LEVEL DISCIPLINARY DECISIONS

### *KNOW YOURSELF*

- *What do I want?* Your goal should be to minimize the effects of a penalty, not to overturn a decision.
- *Is it worth my time?* It may be readily negotiable, depending on the nature of the transgression and any mitigating factors.
- *Is it important to me?* It clearly is worth negotiating, since in order to move to another school, either now or later, you'll need to clear up this blemish on your record.

### *KNOW YOUR OPPONENT*

- *What do I need to know?* Find out whether you've broken an objective rule or a subjective rule. If you've broken an objective rule— say, you've endangered the welfare of the college community, been involved in illegal acts, cheated on an exam, or perpetrated some form of abuse—it will be viewed more seriously than if you've broken a subjective rule—such as not maintaining a certain grade point average or missing a certain number of classes.
- *With whom should I negotiate?* Negotiate with the dean who is in charge of dispensing punishment for disciplinary infractions.
- *Are there any potentially disruptive side issues?* You can remove some of the dissonance surrounding your past behavior by either admitting culpability and/or enlisting the aid of an advocate, such as a university ombudsperson.
- *What do I share with my opponent?* The common ground you need to establish is respect for the university's rules and regulations. You show that you now have that respect by admitting your mistake and accepting the decision.

### *KNOW THE SITUATION*

- Insider Tip: The secret here is to offer mitigating evidence and ask for a reduced penalty or an easier readmission. For example, if there's a death in the family and your grade point average drops below the mandated level, it will be difficult for the school to waive its rules and keep you enrolled as a student. However, since it's a subjective rule, you can ask that the reason for the poor grades be noted and that it be considered when you apply for reinstatement in six months. While you won't receive a guarantee of readmission, you'll have maximized your chances.

## DOWNSIZING PARENTAL ASSETS

### KNOW YOURSELF

- *What do I want?* Your goal should be to insure that your parents qualify for Medicaid without having to dispose of all their assets.
- *Is it worth my time?* It's readily negotiable if you can demonstrate it's in their best interest.
- *Is it important to me?* It's worth negotiating if it's the only way they'll be able to pay for long-term nursing home care.

### KNOW YOUR OPPONENT

- *What do I need to know?* Consult with an elder care attorney and learn all you can about the rules of Medicaid eligibility. Then speak with your parents to get a grip on their financial situation.
- *With whom should I negotiate?* Make sure to speak to both parents, not just the one who has historically handled the finances, the one you have a better relationship with, or the one who's healthier. In addition, make sure siblings are present, or at least are advised of the situation.
- *Are there any potentially disruptive side issues?* Parents are afraid they're signing over control of their lives and will be left penniless. By having an elder law attorney speak with them, and by directly stating that your primary concern is with their being able to *maintain* control of their lives—albeit through placing assets in other people's names—you should be able to overcome those fears.
- *What do I share with my opponent?* The common ground is the mutual desire to see that your parents' assets aren't dissolved. It helps to state this directly and to openly put all past bad feelings behind you.

### KNOW THE SITUATION

- Insider Tip: If there's still hesitancy on the part of your parents despite all you've done, schedule a meeting in which they can speak to the elder law attorney alone, without you or any of your siblings present. At this meeting the attorney should be able to demonstrate that all their fears can be addressed and that he or she is their advocate, not yours.

## NEGOTIATING WITH CHILDREN

I don't believe you should negotiate with children. While there's nothing wrong with explaining the reason you are or aren't doing something, you know better than your child and you should be making the decisions. When the time comes for you to deal with your child as an adult, someone who's capable of making sound decisions and taking responsibility for his or her actions, then you can negotiate with them as you would any other family member. Until then, don't negotiate.

## REPRESENTING YOURSELF IN A LEGAL PROCEEDING

Whether you'll be facing off with a judge, a justice of the peace, a district attorney, or simply an attorney, you should be represented by a qualified member of the bar. Not only will you never be able to gather enough information to level the playing field, but since these professionals won't view you as a peer, you'll have little chance to establish any common ground. Of course, if the proceeding will be in small claims court, where neither party is entitled to legal representation, you must represent yourself. But in that situation, rather than treating it as a negotiation, simply present the facts as you know them and let the judge handle the rest.

## RESOLVING NEIGHBOR DISPUTES

### *KNOW YOURSELF*

- *What do I want?* Your goal should be to eliminate anything that is interfering with your use and enjoyment of your own property without turning the negotiation into a fight.
- *Is it worth my time?* The extent to which neighbor disputes are negotiable depends on how eager you and your neighbor both are to maintain good relations.
- *Is it important to me?* It's obviously worth negotiating something that's a major disruption to your enjoyment or use of your home.

But that determination must be weighed against the desire to maintain good relations in the face of opposition.

## KNOW YOUR OPPONENT

- *What do I need to know?* Confirm that your neighbor is in fact responsible for the problem you're having. Then try to determine if he or she has a good reason for doing whatever it is that's bothering you. Finally, try to find out if this will be a permanent situation or is just temporary.
- *With whom should I negotiate?* Negotiate with the owner of the property, whether in residence or not. In the final analysis it's the owner's responsibility.
- *Are there any potentially disruptive side issues?* Put any prior problems between you in the past, and then make sure you make it clear that you respect your neighbor's rights to free use of his or her own property.
- *What do I share with my opponent?* The common ground is your mutual desire to maintain good relations. The more you state this, the firmer it will be.

## KNOW THE SITUATION

- Insider Tip: Sometimes it helps to cite an outside source as the reason for your approaching a neighbor. For instance, if a barking dog is keeping you awake at night, explain that your boss is about to fire you for falling asleep on the job and ask your neighbor's help in keeping your job.

## SUPERVISOR'S SEXUAL HARASSMENT

### KNOW YOURSELF

- *What do I want?* Your goal should be to stop the offending behavior immediately and forever.
- *Is it worth my time?* It's readily negotiable now and will be even more so in the future, as the law and society at large continue to become better informed.

- *Is it important to me?* It's worth negotiating because unless you take action it will continue and it may even escalate.

### KNOW YOUR OPPONENT

- *What do I need to know?* You need not gather any information. You're the sole source of all the necessary facts.
- *With whom should I negotiate?* Negotiate with the perpetrator directly, not another employee or supervisor.
- *Are there any potentially disruptive side issues?* In this situation you're looking to remove your own dissonance—fear—and to instead instill it in the other party. You do that by having a totally uncompromising attitude. The more determined you are, the more likely you are to stop the offending behavior because you'll demonstrate that you'll let nothing stop you from pressing your case.
- *What do I share with my opponent?* Here you must point out common ground to the harasser. You do that by saying that you want to keep your job and you assume the harasser wants to keep his job as well. Then explain that unless the harasser stops whatever it is he is doing, he will, in fact, be in danger of losing his job.

### KNOW THE SITUATION

- Insider Tip: If you're afraid the confrontation may lead to a battle of wills ("It's your word against mine" or "They'll never believe you"), speak with another supervisor or with someone in the personnel department first. That way if the harasser makes one or both of these threats you can respond by informing him that you've already discussed the matter with higher-ups.
- Insider Tip: If a harasser ever responds to you by saying "There's nothing you can do to me," simply say that's not what your lawyer believes, and walk out the door.

## TAX AUDITS

Is it possible to negotiate with the IRS? Yes. Do I recommend that you do it yourself? No. The Internal Revenue Service has all the negative traits of a bureaucracy combined with extraordinary power. I think that negotiating with it is best left to professionals—tax attorneys, certified public accountants, or enrolled agents—who know the ins and outs of this most powerful of bureaucracies.

Let me give you an example of how complex and dangerous it can be to deal with the IRS. When you're told that your tax return will be audited you are often asked to bring along returns from other years. Theoretically you don't have to show the IRS other returns, since it's not supposed to be able to just fish for information. However, since it has asked you to bring them with you how do you deny its request? A professional can finesse this problem by saying the other returns were left back at his or her office.

In addition to this conundrum there are a myriad of other dilemmas. Should you appeal an auditor's decision to a supervisor? Should you bring up unused deductions in an effort to exchange them for disallowed deductions? I went through a TCMP audit once—that's the comprehensive line-by-line audit the IRS randomly puts a few tens of thousands of taxpayers through every four years. Even though I'm a professional negotiator, I didn't try to negotiate with the IRS on my own. I hired the best tax attorney/certified public accountant I could find to do it for me. I advise you to do the same.

# TWO-PART TUSSLES

## The Rules of Hybrid Negotiations

*"Put all your eggs in the one basket, and—WATCH THAT BASKET."*

—MARK TWAIN

The third type of negotiation is what I call the hybrid, a two-part negotiation with both persuasive and numeric elements. Typically these are complex negotiations in which one party must first persuade the other to adopt a course of action and then incrementally negotiate the details of that action.

Probably the best example of a hybrid negotiation is an employee approaching an employer for a pay increase. The employee must first convince the employer that an increase is merited, and then must negotiate the amount of that increase. As you'll see in this section, nearly every negotiation between employers and employees is a hybrid. That's because the employer has both decision-making and financial power over the employee. However, hybrid negotiations aren't limited to the workplace. Anytime you're discussing both actions and dollars, whether it's with your spouse, your parents, or your boss, you're engaging in a hybrid negotiation.

It would be impossible to cover all the hybrid negotiations you'll face in your life since the possible scenarios are limitless. In selecting which hybrid negotiations to highlight in the full-length chapters and concluding capsule chapter, I've tried to cover what I think are the most important, common, and/or educational situations you'll face. My hope is that these examples will both address your most pressing needs and serve as guides in those hybrid negotiations I didn't have the space to cover.

Just to make sure you're prepared for any situation that's not covered, let me just go over a few generalities I've discovered over the years about hybrid negotiations. Remember, these are axioms, not rules; they're things to remember and think about when you're going through the three steps.

> **Every hybrid negotiation requires persuading someone to act and quantifying the action.**

By their very nature hybrid negotiations require you to take two steps. First you must persuade the other party to take some type of action. Then you must negotiate the extent or the value of the action. For instance, when you're going on a job interview you must first convince the interviewer that you're right for the position and should be hired—that's the action. Then you and the interviewer must agree on what your starting salary should be—that's the extent—or, in this case, the value—of the action.

> **The more powerful your persuasive argument the more value you'll obtain for the action.**

The more persuasive you are in convincing the other party to take an action, the more you'll get as a result of that action. Let's go back to the example of asking for a raise: the better case you make for deserving a raise, the more of a raise you'll get.

> **The closer you link a proposed action to its proposed value the more likely you'll be to receive it.**

In hybrids you're asking the other party to make two concessions: first to concede that a particular action is required; and then to concede that the action has a particular value. It's tough to get people to make two concessions without your making one in between. In order to maximize your chances of getting this double concession you need to make the two appear to be one and the same to the other party. You can do that by linking the action and its value, saying something like "This is the action and this is what it costs." By implying that the value of the action isn't negotiable, you may be able to get the other party to accept it outright. Of course, this carries a risk: the other party may say no to the entire linked proposal.

> **If close linkage is dangerous, expand the discussion to include things other than dollars.**

If you're afraid that directly linking action and value could lead to a total rejection, then you need to broaden your horizons somewhat. When negotiating the value of an action think in terms other than money. This will give both parties room to make concessions and will lower the odds of an outright rejection. Let's look at the job interview again. If you link your abilities to a particular salary figure ("I deserve $75,000 and won't settle for a penny less"), you're giving the interviewer an opportunity to reject you outright regardless of your qualifications. Instead, by opening up the discussion of compensation to include benefits and perquisites as well as salary you provide lots of room for both parties to reach an agreement.

# 18

# BECOMING A HUMAN PROFIT CENTER

## Landing a Job and Negotiating Initial Salary

*" 'People don't look for kinds of work anymore, ma'am,' he answered impassively. 'They just look for work.' "*

—AYN RAND

Alex wasn't surprised when he lost his job as marketing director of the Oneonta Clock Company. He had taken part in most of the recent board meetings that outlined the company's precarious economic condition. He knew the owners were shopping the company around, looking for someone to bail them out. Then one day word came that OCC had been purchased by clock-making giant Longko Inc.

While most of the employees rejoiced at the news, Alex knew better. Most of the assembly line workers would probably keep their jobs, but administrators would eventually be let go since Longko already had people doing those jobs. That's why he immediately began updating his résumé and reactivating his network. Unfortunately, he couldn't find another position before he was let go from OCC. That was followed by three months of pounding the pavement looking for work. Then one day Alex received a telephone call from the personnel manager of the Ithaca Picture Frame Company. She was looking for a marketing person and had been intrigued by Alex's résumé. An appointment was scheduled.

## THE JOB HUNTER'S SELF-EXAMINATION

In finding a job, as in every negotiation, the first step in the process is for you to analyze needs and weigh options, to know yourself. That's accomplished by asking three questions: "What do I want?" "Is it worth my time?" "Is it important to me?"

## WHAT DO I WANT?—SETTING A SPECIFIC GOAL

For those who are out of work the goal is clear. Obviously they want a job. However, I think there should be more to the goal than that. If you and your family are in dire economic straits and your sole concern is to obtain a stream of income, regardless of its size, quality, or likelihood of permanence, then you're right, your goal should be to get a job . . . any job.

But if you're not in dire straits, if you're concerned with getting a good job that offers a chance for income growth and career advancement, if you're looking for a position you'll want to stay in for two years or more, then your goal needs to be different. You need to focus on getting the best job you can at the best salary possible.

I think one of the great mistakes made by job seekers is that they don't realize they're engaging in a hybrid negotiation. They see themselves as being in a persuasive negotiation, looking to convince the potential employer that they're the right man or woman for the job opening. If they achieve that they see themselves as successful. But that's only half the battle. In order to be truly successful in a job hunt you need to land a job that is economically rewarding. In addition to trying to persuade the potential employer that you're right for the job, you also need to negotiate the best salary/benefits package you can. In other words, you shouldn't accept a job, then negotiate salary. Instead you should persuade the other party to want to hire you, negotiate salary, and *then* accept the job.

The desperation and anxiety of the job seeker leads to a narrowing of goals. That may help you land a position but it almost always eventually leads to long-term disappointment in the job. That's why I advise those who aren't truly desperate to broaden rather than narrow their goals during the job hunt and include salary as being just as important as getting the job. (When I say "broaden," I don't mean your goal should be vague. It still must be specific—but it must contain two components, not just the narrow component of finding a job.) Let me explain.

However you look at the numbers, the factor that plays the most important role in determining your job income now and in the future is starting salary. Raises, regardless of their generosity, and promotions, however dramatic, never really result in large increases in salary. That's because pay increases are based on percentages.

Let's look at an example. Joe and Valerie are both hired as editorial assistants in a book publishing company. Joe negotiates a starting salary of $25,000. Valerie doesn't negotiate salary and accepts a starting salary of $20,000. Both are very good at their jobs and receive steady pay raises. The first year the raises are 5 percent. But since Joe started at a higher salary than Valerie his increase is actually higher: Joe's salary jumps to $26,250 and Valerie's to $21,000. The next year they both receive another 5 percent raise. Joe's pay increases to $27,562.50 while Valerie's increases to only $22,050. The original $5,000 difference between their salaries has now increased to more than $5,500. And as time goes on the gap will just keep on widening. If all other things are equal, the only way Valerie will ever catch up to Joe is to leave the company and get another job so she can receive a substantial, non-percentage-based, increase in salary.

(By the way, in this example I intentionally gave Valerie the lower salary. I believe women still receive lower pay for the same work because they start at lower salaries. Partly that's because of lingering gender stereotypes: the assumptions that a woman won't be the main income producer for a family; that she will leave the workplace and become a full-time parent; and that she is on a different career track than the man. But another reason is that I believe women are less likely to negotiate salary as part of the job-search process than men are. Don't get me wrong, I'm not trying to blame the victim. I think women are often more concerned with job fulfillment than salary, while men see salary as more important than job fulfillment. Employers are all too happy to pay as little as possible. The result: women make less money than men for the same work. That's one reason I believe it's especially important for women to become effective negotiators in the workplace.)

Your goal must be more than just "a job." In order to obtain long-term success and financial as well as emotional fulfillment, your goal needs to be: to land a good position at a good starting salary.

## *IS IT WORTH MY TIME?— DECIDING IF IT'S READILY NEGOTIABLE*

When an employer has an open position, he has a salary range in mind. If the position is an existing one that has just been vacated, the employer is probably looking to pay approximately what he was paying the last individual who held the job. Obviously, the employer would love to pay less, but he's probably also willing to pay more if he believes the new jobholder will contribute more to improving the company's bottom line. If the position being advertised is a new one, the employer probably has a figure budgeted for salary. Once again, the employer would love to pay less but is also willing to pay more if he believes it will result in an improved bottom line.

Clearly, one secret to making the second half of this process—the salary discussion—readily negotiable is to convince the prospective employer that you'll somehow contribute to an improvement in the company's bottom line, thereby justifying a salary in the higher end of the range he's willing to pay. The second secret is to convince the prospective employer of this *before* you ever discuss salary.

By the time you reach the salary part of the negotiation you want the prospective employer to see you as the answer to all his prayers. You will never be in as strong a negotiating position as you are just before you've accepted a position. At that moment you are all potential. The prospective employer sees only your positives. You've never made a mistake, had a failure, or suffered a setback that can be used against you.

If you wait until the salary discussion itself to make a case for your being able to improve the company's bottom line it'll be seen by the prospective employer as an obvious ploy to get more money. He will rise to what he sees as a negotiating challenge and will play hardball on salary. In other words, you want the prospective employer to be more afraid of losing you than you appear to be afraid of losing the job offer.

If you successfully portray yourself as having a potentially positive impact on the company's bottom line before you actually begin to discuss salary, the starting salary itself will be readily negotiable. I'll explain how to do just that later in the chapter.

### IS IT IMPORTANT TO ME?— MAKING SURE IT'S WORTH NEGOTIATING

In outlining why it's important for you to have a goal that combines a good salary with actually getting the position, I hope I've also clearly demonstrated why it's certainly worth negotiating your new job. But just to reiterate, let me stress that the secret to present and future financial satisfaction lies in an effective negotiation of your initial salary. If money is at all important to you it's worth turning your job interview into a hybrid negotiation.

Let's go back to Alex and his self-examination. Alex knew that, while he was currently unemployed and certainly needed a job, just getting a job wasn't a sufficient goal. In addition to simply wanting a job, he wanted a position that offered a future with a steadily increasing stream of income that would offer the financial resources necessary to improve his life. Alex understood that if he successfully portrayed himself as having a potentially positive impact on the Ithaca Picture Frame Company's bottom line, and did this before he actually began to discuss salary, his starting salary would be readily negotiable. Finally, Alex knew all this negotiating was well worth the effort to improve his present and future standard of living.

# LEVELING THE JOB-HUNTING PLAYING FIELD

The second step in landing a new job and negotiating initial salary is for you to get to know your opponent and to use that information to level the playing field. This is done by answering four questions: "What do I need to know?" "With whom should I negotiate?" "Are there any potentially disruptive side issues?" "What do I share with my opponent?"

## WHAT DO I NEED TO KNOW?— GATHERING INFORMATION

Most job seekers limit their information gathering to learning the desired qualifications for a position, the name of the person they'll be meeting with, and the time and location of their interview. That may be sufficient if your goal is simply to get a job, but if your goal is to get a good job and to negotiate a good initial salary it's not enough.

In order to be a successful negotiator in this situation you need to begin gathering information the moment you apply for a job and continue to do so up until you've been offered the position. Besides the obvious information about minimum requirements you should try to learn everything you can about the company or organization. What is its standing in its industry? What is its corporate culture? What are its long- and short-term goals? What are its immediate needs and what does it see as its eventual needs? You're not going to get this information from a classified ad or a headhunter, you're going to need to do some research.

If you'll be interviewing with a public company, get a copy of its most recent 10K and its annual report. If it's a private company, try to obtain its Dun & Bradstreet report. Your local library should be able to get you the information. While you're at the library go through magazine and newspaper indices to find any recent trade or consumer articles about the company. Read them. Find out which is the premier trade magazine in the field, telephone the editor, and pick his brain about the industry and company. Draw on your contacts and on your contacts' contacts. Reach out for help to anyone and everyone who knows about the industry and the company. You need to become as much of an expert on the company's past, present, and future as you can be in the time permitted.

During your meetings with individuals in the company, ask questions. Try to determine exactly what type of person the company is looking for. Obviously, you'll then try to demonstrate that you're that individual. Remember that the result of almost all successful negotiations is that mutual needs are satisfied. In the initial stages of this negotiation you should be just as, if not more, concerned with demonstrating how you fit the company's needs than with determining whether the company fits your needs.

You may not be able to directly use all of the information you've gathered in your negotiation, but that doesn't mean the effort will have been wasted. Everything you learn will help you hit the ground running if you do get the job. You'll know exactly what the standards for measuring success will be and you'll be able to address them. In addition, your background information will go a long way toward helping you determine exactly how you should go about eliminating the dissonance in the negotiation.

### WITH WHOM SHOULD I NEGOTIATE?— PUSHING THE UP BUTTON

When you're negotiating a job offer and initial salary you want to negotiate with the person who has the power to hire you and determine your salary. That's easy to figure out when you're dealing with a very small company or when the opening is for a low level position. But the larger the organization is, and the higher up the bureaucratic ladder the opening is, the more complex this question becomes.

Let's look at a series of openings in the same company, a national chain of record stores, and see how the complexity of the negotiation changes. If you're applying for a job as a salesperson in one of the stores, you'll be meeting with one person: the manager. If you're applying for a job as manager of that same store you'll be meeting with the personnel director and the regional manager. If you're applying for a job as regional manager you'll be meeting with the personnel director, the national sales manager, and the vice president of sales. And it would get even more complex if you went higher up the ladder.

Obviously, the more people you meet with the more difficult it is to figure out who is actually making the decisions. Let me give you a tip. Generally, the person who's immediately superior to the open position is the individual who actually makes the decision. If you're applying for the job of salesman, the store manager will make the decision. If you're applying for the store manager's job, the regional manager will make the decision. And if you're applying for the regional manager's job, the national sales manager will make the decision. In each case the decision maker is the person who will be supervising the new person and who will be held responsible for that person's actions. The decision, however, will be affected by input from the other individuals who are conducting interviews.

Aside from the actual decision maker, a job candidate forced into a complex hiring process will face two other types of interviewers I call "security guards" and "approvers." Security guards do the initial screening of candidates. Their job isn't to select but to reject. Their concern is with minimum standards in experience, technical skill, personality, appearance, attitude, and behavior. The security guard is the one who conducts the first round of interviews. If you pass his inspection you'll meet with the decision maker. But after the decision maker has met with you, you may be forced to meet with an approver. Approvers are typically the executives who supervise the decision makers. In effect, they're not so much evaluating your skills as they are judging their direct subordinate's decision-making ability. Potential peers may also serve as approvers. For example, all the other vice presidents in a company may meet with a prospective vice president just to make sure they can all get along. You can expect security guards to be the toughest, most probing interviewers, and approvers to be the easiest, most superficial questioners, with decision makers falling somewhere in between.

Since this book deals with negotiating, the information in this chapter will necessarily concentrate on the meeting with the decision maker. But before I put security guards and approvers aside let me offer a couple of words of advice. When you're meeting with a security guard your goal should be to prove you're qualified. If you do that you'll get past him. When meeting with an approver your goal should be to keep from alienating her. If you don't give her a reason to disapprove of you, she'll give her approval to the decision maker's selection.

## ARE THERE ANY POTENTIALLY DISRUPTIVE SIDE ISSUES?—ELIMINATING DISSONANCE

The major elements of dissonance in a job interview with a decision maker are her bottom line concern—can you do the job—and her biggest fear—will you cause trouble. If you can answer those two questions to the decision maker's satisfaction you'll be able to then move on and convince her you're the best person for the job and are deserving of a salary at the high end of the price range.

The question of whether or not you can do the job has, to a large part, been answered before you even walked in the door. Traditionally, résumés serve the purpose of weeding out unqualified candidates. If your résumé didn't demonstrate that you had the qualifications for the position you wouldn't have even been called for an interview. But just to make sure, most interviewers, particularly security guards, will double-check your qualifications. They may ask you about specific tasks and projects you handled in the past in an effort to confirm your skills and experience. If you're in a multiple interview situation, your ability to do the job is accepted as a given by the time you meet with a decision maker.

More important, both security guards and decision makers will be trying to make sure you won't be a destructive element. The best way to prove this is to demonstrate, through your garb, manner, and attitude, that you're a team player.

Volumes have been written about how you should dress and act in a job interview, so I won't bore you by repeating the traditional advice. It's all true, and it's important. Most candidates who are ruled out are rejected by interviewers within the first thirty seconds. That means the instant rejections are all based on appearance and manners. Let me just stress one point before moving on to discuss attitude. If through your information gathering you were able to discern a distinct corporate style, make sure your garb matches it. For example: If you're being interviewed by IBM, you'll probably come across best if your garb matches their particular corporate image: conservatism. For years there was a belief that you had to wear a white shirt if you worked for IBM. While I doubt decisions were ever solely based on the color of the applicants' shirts or blouses, I wouldn't doubt that, all other things being equal, the person who dressed more conservatively was hired. On the other hand, if you're being interviewed by Apple, which has a more entrepreneurial corporate culture, more stylish—or at least less conservative—garb might be appropriate.

There's a great deal of conflicting advice as to what kind of attitude you should project in a job interview. The reason for the different opinions is that, to a large extent, it varies from interviewer to interviewer. Some interviewers may look for respect for authority. Others may like a sense of humor. Still others may want to be impressed by your verbal skills. If you don't know the personality of the decision maker I suggest you just be yourself. Unless you're a professional actor you'll always come across best when acting naturally.

That said, there is one area where I'd suggest you do enhance your performance. In my experience the only surefire attitude that eliminates dissonance for every type of interviewer is enthusiasm. Regardless of whatever other personality traits an interviewer is looking for, he wants to hire someone who really wants this job. Enthusiasm is considered—correctly, I think—an indicator of hard work, confidence, and dedication. When it comes down to the wire and it's a choice between two equal candidates, the more enthusiastic one always wins out.

## ESTABLISH COMMON GROUND

The common ground you need to demonstrate in the job interview is love of the company. You demonstrate your love of the company by first saying you admire the organization, then by explaining why, and finally by stating your eagerness to be part of such a wonderful organization. You can assume that since your opponent has reached a level sufficient for her to be interviewing you for a job, she loves the company as well. After all, she's dedicated enough time and effort to get to a level where she's making managerial decisions. She'll be happy to welcome another enthusiast to the team. But even if she doesn't love the company, she won't hold your positive feelings against you—she'll feel that as an outsider you don't have all the facts. However, she'll be savvy enough to realize that your love of the company makes you an outstanding candidate.

## INSIDER TIPS FOR JOB HUNTERS

The third and final step in landing a job and negotiating initial salary is to know the situation. That's accomplished by applying the lessons learned by those who are experienced with this particular situation. Since the economic downturn of the late 1980s I've spent a great deal of my time advising clients about conducting job searches and negotiating initial salary. And in researching this book I spoke with personnel executives, headhunters, and career counselors. From my own experience and my research I've come up with four insider tips for you to absorb and use. I call them "adding value," "after you," "the mosaic," and "the final grab."

### SHOW HOW YOU'VE CUT EXPENSES AND/OR BOOSTED REVENUE

"Adding value" refers to the technique you should use to convince the decision maker that you're worth top dollar. In the final analysis, every business—and, therefore, every executive—cherishes two things above all else: cutting expenses and increasing revenue. If you want to get top dollar you'll need to show the decision maker you can help him do one or both of these things. The way to do that is to show that you've done it in the past. Throughout your interview you should stress instances where you saved your previous employers money (cut expenses), made your previous employers money (increased revenue), or best of all, saved your previous employers time. Saving time is actually the best accomplishment since it not only saves money but simultaneously offers the opportunity to make more money.

The secret in describing these previous accomplishments is to dwell on the results of your actions without getting too much into exactly what those actions were. While you don't want to act like you possess a magic formula, you also don't want to offer the decision maker an opportunity to say why your actions wouldn't work at his company. You don't even need to say you'll be able to replicate your past accomplishments; it will be understood. You want the decision maker to picture you cutting his sales department's budget in half while doubling it's productivity. If you're able to create that image in his mind, you'll have got yourself into the top end of his salary range; you'll have transformed yourself from qualified candidate to most desirable candidate; you'll have turned the negotiation around. Rather than you having to pursue the decision maker for a position, the decision maker will now be pursuing you to fill the position.

## TRY NOT TO BE THE FIRST TO STATE A SALARY NUMBER

When discussing salary it's essential that you not be the first person to mention a number. Let me explain. If you're the first to name a number the negotiation will be about decreasing it. On the other hand, if the potential employer is the first to name a number, the negotiation can be about increasing it. That's as dramatic a difference as you'll find anywhere in this book. And that's also why decision makers will try to press you to be the first to name a figure.

Typically an employer will cloak this negotiating gambit in a seemingly innocuous question such as "How much of a salary are you looking for?" Don't fall for the trap. Respond to such entreaties with equally innocuous responses, such as "I'm looking for a salary comparable to my experience and skills." And then turn the question around, in effect saying, "No thanks, after you." You should then ask the decision maker, "What salary were you willing to pay the person who takes this position?" Or you could try to add a little ego boost into the process by saying, "You're certainly a knowledgeable source," and then asking, "How much do *you* think my experience and skills are worth?" I'm sure you get the idea. It's sort of like the old comedy routine where two people are overly polite about who will go through a doorway first. One says, "After you." The other replies, "No, after you." And it continues on to ridiculous levels.

Obviously, if they do go first, you should try to push their number higher. Assume there's a 20 to 25 percent flexibility in the salary for the position—for example, from a low of $80,000 to a high of $120,000, with a midpoint of $100,000—and that your opponent's first offer is in the low end of that range. So, if you're offered $40,000 you should feel comfortable coming back with a counter offer closer to $50,000.

If they refuse to go first, don't allow this game of "after you" to go on too long. Just as in the comedy routine, it's easy for the dialogue to develop into conflict. If you're backed up against the wall to come up with a price, increase your current salary by 25 percent and state that you assume the standard benefits such as health insurance and paid vacations will also be included.

## INCLUDE THINGS OTHER THAN SALARY IN THE NEGOTIATION

When negotiating compensation it's important to realize there are things other than money that can be very valuable. Compensation is actually a mosaic of various elements. Would you like a nice office? A better title? A personal secretary or administrative assistant? A company car? Additional paid vacation? Tuition reimbursement? A clothing allowance? All of these things can and should become part of the negotiation. In many cases the decision maker will have an easier time coming up with these noncash items than in finding more cash. I don't believe there's anything wrong with trading cash for benefits as long as they are truly of "economic" benefit. I wouldn't make a cash concession in exchange for a better office, but I would for tuition reimbursement or a better title, for instance. Both of those benefits will not only help you in your current job, they'll boost you in the eyes of future employers as well.

Every time you make a concession, provide a reason for it. The best reasons to give are things such as "Since I really want to work here . . ." or "Because I think this is a fantastic opportunity . . . " or "Because I so want to be a part of this team . . . " These not only provide an explanation for your concession—which will indicate that you've a finite amount of negotiating space—but will also reinforce the message that you're the right person for the job.

## MAKE A FINAL GRAB FOR MORE

Finally, never accept a decision maker's offer without trying to get a little bit more out of her—in effect, making a "final grab." Believe it or not, this can be done very subtly. When you're tempted to accept the decision maker's offer, hesitate. Look her directly in the eye and ask, in a very even tone, "Is that the best you can do?" Don't break eye contact or say anything else until she responds. And then, regardless of her answer, say, "I'm excited about the position but I'd like to go home and think about everything we discussed." Then ask, "Would it be okay if I get back to you tomorrow morning?" This gives her yet another chance to up her offer—this time, in exchange for your immediate acceptance.

Let's see how Alex made out in his meetings with the Ithaca Picture Frame Company. As soon as the interview was set up he headed over to the local library to do some research on the company. He consulted trade publications and financial reports and checked for any magazine and news-paper articles that had been written about the company. When he returned home that afternoon he telephoned his business contacts to gather even more information. After dinner he sat down and read through all the ma-terial he'd found and notes he'd taken to get a sense of the company. He discovered that the Ithaca Picture Frame Company, while a major player in camera stores, wasn't doing well in gift shops—an industry he was very familiar with. Alex also learned that the Ithaca Picture Frame Com-pany's corporate culture stressed style and innovation—that led him to pick out a stylish tie and shirt to wear with his suit for the next day's interview.

Since he was being interviewed for the marketing manager's position, and since his initial meeting was with the personnel manager, Alex knew this first meeting was with a security guard. The person he'd really need to negotiate with was the marketing director, who would be his immediate superior. That individual would actually have the power to decide whether Alex was the best candidate and to determine what his starting salary would be. Alex knew, however, he'd first have to prove himself to the security guard before being able to sell himself to the decision maker.

Alex's initial interview with the personnel director went well. She seemed most concerned with going over his résumé and past experience. Throughout this meeting with the security guard Alex stressed his exten-sive experience and knowledge. He was soon passed on to the vice pres-ident of sales and marketing. In this interview with the woman who was clearly the decision maker, Alex stressed his proven ability to help a com-pany crack into the gift store market. He demonstrated enthusiasm and continually referred back to his past successes in cracking new markets while cutting costs. He directly stated that he was eager to become part of the Ithaca Picture Frame Company team and hoped they were eager to have him come on board.

Obviously they were, since the interviewer asked Alex how much of a salary he was looking for. Using the "after you" technique, Alex deflected her attempts to get him to be the first to name a price. Finally, she mentioned a salary of $50,000. Assuming there was at least a 20 percent range in salary, Alex responded by saying he was interested in a total compensation package of about $60,000. That seemed higher than the decision maker was willing to go, so Alex began broadening the discussion by mentioning that part of that $50,000 package could be use of a company car and that he'd like a clothing allowance. The decision maker offered Alex a salary of $53,000, a clothing allowance of $5,000, and a leased company car. Rather than responding right away, Alex asked if that was the best the company could do and waited for a reply. When told that it was, Alex said that he was excited about the possibility of working there but would like to think the matter over. He asked if it would be okay if he got back to her the next morning. She responded by raising her offer to $55,000 with the clothing allowance and car—if Alex would accept on the spot. He did.

## Becoming a Human Profit Center
## Landing a Job and Negotiating
## Initial Salary

- If in dire straits your goal should be to get a job . . . any job.
- Otherwise your goal should be to get the best job at the best salary possible.
- Negotiate with the person with the power to hire and determine salary.
- Résumés attest to technical abilities, while interviews demonstrate enthusiasm.
- State you want to be a part of the team.
- Demonstrate you've cut expenses, increased revenue, and/or saved time.
- Try not to be the first to mention a salary figure.
- Include benefits and nonfinancial compensation in your salary discussion.
- Directly ask the interviewer if his offer is the best he can do.
- Ask for a day to think about your answer.

# 19

# GOING TO BAT FOR YOURSELF

## Asking for a Raise

*"Your father used to say, 'Never give away your work. People don't value what they don't have to pay for.'"*

—NANCY HALE

After eight months as assistant manager of Truffles, a pub/restaurant, Connie thought it was time to ask for a raise. When she took the job the manager had told her that salary reviews were done every January. But since she was hired in November, her initial review was skipped. That meant if she waited for the next January review she'd have to go fourteen months without an increase. And since she was hired her job description had changed dramatically. While she still had the title of assistant manager, she had assumed almost total management of the dining room and kitchen staffs, the menu, and purchasing, freeing the manager up to pursue his specialties: upgrading the decor and invigorating the marketing. Connie thought that because of the change in her responsibilities it wasn't out of line to ask for an early review.

## THE RAISE SEEKER'S SELF-EXAMINATION

In asking for a raise, as in every negotiation, the first step in the process is for you to analyze needs and weigh options, to know yourself. That's accomplished by asking three questions: "What do I want?" "Is it worth my time?" "Is it important to me?"

### WHAT DO I WANT?—SETTING A SPECIFIC GOAL

Perhaps the most common and potentially damaging mistake made by most people who try to negotiate a salary increase is to begin the process with the wrong goal. For some reason—maybe effective employer prop-aganda—we tend to view the two potential outcomes of this negotiation as either (a) getting a raise, or (b) not getting a raise. Actually, it's rare that an individual who asks for a raise doesn't receive one, or at least the acknowledgment that one is called for, if not now, then at a later date. So the simple goal of getting "a raise" is not sufficient. The real goal of the negotiation should be to get a raise of a certain size. What's important is *how much* of a raise you get, not whether you get one or not.

Let me explain further. If you don't quantify how much of a raise you want, you allow the negotiation to center on whether or not you're de-serving of an increase and leave the second, and actually more important, part of the decision—how much of an increase—up to the discretion of the employer. That's why so many times people return disappointed from a raise discussion with their superior, even though they do come out with an increase. While they said their goal was "to get a raise," actually their goal was "to get a substantial raise"—without ever quite defining what *substantial* meant. All they're sure of is that whatever they got doesn't qualify as substantial. Your goal, therefore, should be to receive a pay raise of a specific percentage, or to increase your compensation to a spe-cific amount.

How much of a percentage, or how much of an increase, you ask for, of course, depends on your particular circumstances. The number should be based on an investigation of what others in the marketplace who are similarly successful and skilled are earning. You should be paid at least the market rate for your services.

One other note: keep inflation in mind. One reason almost everyone who asks for a raise receives one is that inflation causes the cost of living to go up. Employers are as aware of this as anyone. In an effort to *main-tain* employees' income level, they increase salaries to keep up with the increased cost of living. That's why, for instance, you may be told that the company will be giving a 5 percent increase across the board this year, or something to that effect. The 5 percent increase really isn't a raise—it's a cost-of-living adjustment. I maintain that in order to actually be happy with a raise you'll need to receive more than just a cost-of-living adjustment. That means your raise must be greater than the rate of infla-tion.

Don't make the mistake of limiting your request to dollars alone. There are a lot of other things that make up compensation, some of which might be easier for your employer to part with than cash. For example, you could ask for more vacation time, flexible working hours, a better title, an im-proved health or pension plan, equity in the company, tuition reimburse-ment, a company car, an automatic expense allowance, or a personal assistant. There's no limit to what you can ask for. Just make sure, however, that whatever you include in your compensation request has a definite monetary value and isn't just an ego boost.

## IS IT WORTH MY TIME?—
## DECIDING IF IT'S READILY NEGOTIABLE

The traditional cost-of-living raise often isn't negotiable. Companies present their salary decisions as part of a system. Employers generally say salaries are reviewed every January, or on the yearly anniversary of employment, and that they'll be increased based on some percentage selected by the organization. They present salary increases as being nonnegotiable.

But such systems are a smokescreen. They're designed to keep salary increases as infrequent and as insignificant as possible. Often they're simply a way of keeping up with the cost of living, cloaked in the mantle of a performance review. It borders on the immoral for an employer to say that your salary will be increased to keep up with inflation only if your performance was satisfactory. In effect they're saying that maintaining the status quo is sufficient reward for your efforts.

The secret to making your request for an increase negotiable is to present it as compensation for a change in facts, not as simply a periodic pay raise. In order to do that you need to demonstrate one or more of the following:

- that you've made more than your expected contribution to the success of the organization;
- that your responsibilities or job description has changed; or
- that there are some other special circumstances that merit an extraordinary rather than an ordinary increase in compensation.

If you can show your supervisor that one of these three has occurred, your raise request will be negotiable.

## IS IT IMPORTANT TO ME?—
## MAKING SURE IT'S WORTH NEGOTIATING

If you want to get more than just a cost-of-living increase then it's worth negotiating a pay raise. There are some nonfinancial benefits to it as well. You'll be demonstrating to your immediate supervisor and others in the hierarchy that you're an ambitious, driven individual who has the determination to get what you deserve. As long as you don't wield a knife and hack your way to the top, such ambition, drive, and determination will be seen as a positive factor. It can help single you out from your peers in an organization. Savvy employers are always looking for people in their organizations with leadership potential. These are the individuals who receive promotions, special assignments, and who are placed on the organization's "fast track."

Let's see how Connie's self-examination went. Connie realized her goal needed to be more than just getting a raise; she had to have a specific figure in mind. Otherwise she'd simply be put in the position of debating whether or not she was worthy of an increase. Connie also knew that in order to justify asking for a particular sum she needed to demonstrate that this was an extraordinary request. Her assumption of added responsibilities and her having been passed over when the last reviews were held gave her the ammunition she needed. Finally, Connie knew that her efforts were worth the risk and time involved. If she was ever going to move up financially and professionally she'd need to break out of the status quo of inflation-based raises.

## LEVELING THE RAISE PLAYING FIELD

The second step in asking for a raise is for you to get to know your opponent and to use that information to level the playing field. This is done by answering four questions: "What do I need to know?" "With whom should I negotiate?" "Are there any potentially disruptive side issues?" "What do I share with my opponent?"

### WHAT DO I NEED TO KNOW?—
### GATHERING INFORMATION

Since in order to be both negotiable and successful, raise requests must center on a specific number and be based on extraordinary circumstances, they need to have a strong underlying foundation of solid information. This information comes from three places: inside the organization, outside the organization, and inside yourself.

### Gathering Information Inside the Organization

Begin your information gathering by learning everything you can about the company's salary structure and policies. Are there guidelines for how much every tier of employees earns? Are there limits as to how much pay is increased at any one time? How strictly are such rules enforced? Are there any precedents for breaking the rules, and what are they? To find the answers to these questions you'll need to ask your peers and your supervisor. As long as you don't directly ask what someone else is earning you'll find most people are glad to offer advice. Seek out longtime employees. They tend to be the unofficial historians of an organization and will give you the facts rather than just the party line. Don't bother with Personnel; in this instance they'll simply give you the party line.

### Gathering Information Outside the Organization

Once you've finished your internal research, start looking outside the organization for information. Your goal is to determine exactly what your value is on the job market. Check with the Bureau of Labor Statistics. Speak to friends and acquaintances who work for competitors. Ask your contacts at the industry trade association. Research trade magazines and journals—most have annual salary surveys. Discreetly check help wanted ads for positions similar to yours. If need be, contact employment agencies and headhunters.

(If you stumble across an opening that interests you, don't hesitate to apply. One of the best ways to obtain a raise is to have another job offer. It's also a no-lose situation. If you do have another more lucrative offer and your current employer won't meet it, you can simply take the other job. However, don't use the threat of another job offer unless you actually have one—it's a bluff that's too easy to call.)

### Conducting a Personal Job Inventory

Once you've concluded your internal research on your company and your external research on your industry, you should move on to conduct what I call a "personal job inventory." Make an objective analysis of your contribution. Has your performance improved? Are you more productive or skilled than your peers? Have you been responsible for saving money, increasing revenue, or saving time? Have your job responsibilities increased since you were hired? Has your job description changed? Have you been a problem solver?

### *WITH WHOM SHOULD I NEGOTIATE?—*
### *PUSHING THE UP BUTTON*

In order to successfully negotiate an increase in compensation you need to negotiate with an individual who has the power to make salary decisions. Discovering who in your organization actually has such power, and getting to him, can be difficult, especially if you're in a small company.

Very often, a manager who doesn't have the power to make salary decisions may nevertheless position himself as the decision maker in order to maintain his authority. He will discourage you from going over his head to the true decision maker. He may say he has been given guidelines on how much raises will be and there's no room for appeal. While it carries some risk, I suggest you disregard his warnings and bypass him.

Since it's so difficult to determine exactly who has the power to grant a raise request, I advise you to automatically go to the highest member of the bureaucracy who has knowledge of your weekly, if not daily, activities. If you do this with the blessing of your immediate day-to-day supervisor, that's a plus. But if you don't receive such a blessing don't let it deter you. Presenting your request as extraordinary can be helpful here as well. It gives you a reason for going outside the normal channels and an excuse for going over your superior's head.

Does it risk endangering your relationship with your day-to-day supervisor? In a word, yes. However, that's a risk you may need to take if you're to move beyond the normal nonnegotiable cost-of-living increase. If you must go over your superior's head, do it gently. If you must present your request to a powerless person first, just for political purposes, do it. Look on it as a trial run, as a warm-up bout for the main event. Don't figuratively push him aside or step on him to get over his head. If your immediate supervisor doesn't have the power to give you justice then you're completely within your rights to appeal to a higher authority.

Before I get into telling you how to eliminate the dissonance affecting your opponent, I want to say a few words about the dissonance affecting you. It's fear. For many people, asking for a raise is a frightening process. Some are so fearful that they forego asking. They think that in asking for a raise they are asking that a judgment be made of them as a human being. They simply rely on their employer to initiate the discussion, rationalizing their inaction by saying it's demeaning to ask for a raise; their boss should know what they do and should gratefully come to them with an increase. Let's face it—that's ridiculous. No employer is going to, of his own free will, give an extraordinary pay increase. If you're going to move ahead you must rely on yourself. No one will do it for you, no matter how much he admires and appreciates your work.

My suggestion for eliminating the fear surrounding asking for a raise is to reexamine what your salary actually indicates. It is not, as many seem to feel, an indication of your value as a human being. Some of the most skilled, most brilliant, and most important people in the world don't receive high salaries. If you need evidence just look at what the president of the United States earns, or what a teacher educating our young earns. Salary is a purely economic judgment on the value of the tasks you're paid to perform—and perhaps a judgment on how well you're performing those tasks—or perhaps just a number based on company tradition and history. There are many stupid, horrible individuals earning large salaries for doing tasks that are morally bankrupt, that produce nothing of value to the world. And there are many brilliant, wonderful people earning meager salaries for doing tasks that are monumental in their moral import and who add immeasurably to our society. Salary often is an objective economic judgment completely separate from our worth as human beings. If you keep that in mind you'll find that many of your fears surrounding asking for a raise will vanish.

Now that you've eliminated your own mental dissonance you can move on to eliminate the dissonance affecting your opponent: the timing of your request and his fear of losing you.

Timing plays a tremendous role in all raise discussions. If a date for your next salary review was set during your last review, stick to it unless your previous raise was interim in nature, your job description has changed, or it will hurt your chances to wait. If a date was not set, try to time your request based on the general business cycle. For instance, it's better to ask for a raise before budgets are drawn up for the year, before an inventory is conducted, and before the selling season begins. But don't try to base your timing on the company's profits.

Obviously, when things are going well for a business the chances of getting a significant increase are better than when things are going poorly. But it can be very difficult and, in fact, counterproductive to try to tie your raise request to the company's overall economic health. You're an employee, not a partner. The response to someone who asks for a raise because the company is doing better is to ask them if they'll be willing to take a pay cut when the profits drop.

Pay similar attention to the weekly and daily cycles of business as well. I'd avoid Mondays, since they're almost always hectic. Your supervisor may not have the time to engage in a negotiation and may cut you short. I'd avoid Fridays as well. Your supervisor may not want to get into a discussion with you on a day when he wants to leave, or at least stop work, early. Mornings and late afternoons tend to be bad for the same reasons as Mondays and Fridays, respectively. That's why I'd advise you to set up the raise negotiation so it takes place either at midmorning or just after lunch on a Tuesday, Wednesday, or Thursday.

With time pressures addressed you can move on to addressing the other element of dissonance affecting your opponent: his fear that he'll lose you if he doesn't give you a satisfactory raise. Most people are so fearful of asking for a raise that they never think of the other side's fear. Assuming that your boss is rational—and that you're indeed good at your job, have taken on added responsibilities, and have saved money, increased revenues, or saved time, and are well liked—then he'll see you're clearly a valuable employee, one the company can ill afford to lose. It costs a great deal of time and money to replace someone, particularly someone who is good at his job. And there's a risk involved as well. After all, there's no guarantee your replacement will be as good as you. That's why intelligent employers will do everything possible to keep from losing you.

If he's irrational you shouldn't be working for him in the first place. Either push the up button to negotiate with someone who is rational or spend your time looking for another job rather than asking for a raise at this one.

In this negotiation we're not trying to eliminate this dissonance. In fact, we're going to try to exploit it. This can be done in two ways: first, by pointing out all of the contributions you make to the success of the company; and second, by demonstrating that you're strong and determined but not a troublemaker. Your information gathering will help with the first item, but it's your manners that need to address the second.

While a great deal has been written about how to act during an initial job interview, very little has been written about how to act when asking for a raise. Let me take care of that gap right now. Your attitude should be warm and caring but not overly friendly. The discussion should be businesslike, not personal. But since you've already got a relationship with this individual there's no need to maintain a forced distance. One way to achieve the proper tone is to always refer to the company, not the individual you're speaking with, as your employer. For instance, say "I think the company benefited from my work on the Johnson account" rather than "I think I helped you a great deal with my work on the Johnson account." Don't come in as an adversary with threats and demands—that's not how a model employee would do it. But don't feel guilty about asking for a raise either. This isn't a time for humility. Address the other party the same way you always have and dress the same way you usually do. Any special language or garb will only come off as an attempt to manipulate.

If you envision having trouble breaking the ice consider using this line: "I love my job, but I have a problem I need your help with." This simultaneously establishes you as a model employee while planting the seed of fear that they might lose you.

## WHAT DO I SHARE WITH MY OPPONENT?— FINDING AND DEMONSTRATING COMMON GROUND

At some point in your presentation you need to establish and state the common ground between you and your employer. I suggest that the common ground you want to stake out in this negotiation is the fact that you are indeed deserving of an increase. Once both sides can agree to that you can go on to negotiate how much of an increase.

You can establish this common ground by making some verbal assumptions. For instance, you can say things like: "I hope we both recognize that my work has been more than satisfactory." Or you can use lines such as: "You're probably aware that I've taken on a great deal more responsibility than was originally included in my job description" or "The company's numbers indicate that I've helped increase sales/cut costs/save time dramatically." The key phrases are "I hope we both recognize . . ." "You're probably aware that . . ." and "The company's numbers indicate . . ." By using such language you're directly stating that you're deserving of an increase and are daring the employer to dispute it. You're saying that your compensation no longer matches your contribution and therefore must be adjusted upward. If such statements go unchallenged (and if they're true, I can almost guarantee they'll be accepted), you'll have established common ground and will be ready to move on to your tactical gambits.

(If your actual achievements are debated, or if you're simply given a flat no to a pay increase, it's time to look for another job. If a person who has weekly contact with you and who's familiar with your work fails to recognize or reward your accomplishments you've no future in the company. If you're placed in this unfortunate position keep one thought in mind: the largest raises are received by those who find new jobs.)

## INSIDER TIPS FOR RAISE REQUESTS

The third and final step in asking for a raise is to know the situation. That's accomplished by applying the lessons learned by those who are experienced with this particular situation. I've been coaching my clients through raise requests for more than two decades, and in researching this book I've spoken with personnel executives and managers. This research has led me to realize that the best insider tips are actually responses to your opponent's possible objections. Assuming the other party accepts that you're deserving of an increase, he can have only three possible reasons for not meeting your request: timing, parity, and finances.

### RESPONDING TO TIMING EXCUSES

If your opponent invokes time as a reason for not meeting your raise request, perhaps by saying "You haven't been here long enough," respond with language such as: "I don't think you can fairly measure my achievement by the length of time I've been here," and then describe your successes once again.

## RESPONDING TO PARITY EXCUSES

If your opponent invokes parity as a reason for not meeting your raise request, by saying something like: "How can I pay you that much when I'm only paying your peers this much," come back with the following rhetorical question: "Am I to understand that no matter how hard I work or how well I do I won't be rewarded for it?" Then immediately say, "I was under the assumption that hard work and excellence would be rewarded."

## RESPONDING TO FINANCIAL EXCUSES

If your opponent pleads poverty, saying the company just doesn't have the money to meet your request, you should respond in one of three different ways: increase the nonmonetary elements of your compensation package; ask him to pay what he can afford now, but to agree to a retroactive increase that will take place at a later date; or agree to an interim raise, but also agree to have a renegotiation at a later date.

Let's see how Connie negotiated her increase. She began by asking others who worked for Truffles about the restaurant's policies. One waiter, who had been at the restaurant for nearly ten years, offered her a wealth of information. She then made some discreet calls to other people she knew in the restaurant business. She asked what the top salaries for assistant managers were and what kind of benefits were being offered. Next she sat down and made a list of all her achievements and the new responsibilities she had taken on in the past eight months. With her information all compiled, she prepared a request for a 15 percent increase in salary.

After eight months at Truffles, Connie understood where decision-making power on salaries resided: in the hands of the owner, not the manager. That meant she'd need to go over the head of her immediate supervisor and speak directly to the owner of the restaurant. Connie knew her actions risked causing some animosity between her and her manager, but she also knew that unless she went over his head she'd be limited to a meager increase. She explained the situation to her manager, in the process trying out some of her arguments, and while he wasn't thrilled by the prospects of her going over his head, he said he understood. Connie then scheduled a meeting with the owner of the restaurant for a Tuesday afternoon, after the lunch crowd was gone but before the dinner rush started.

Connie approached the meeting fearlessly, since she refused to look on her salary as an indication of her worth as a human being. Instead, she simply saw it as financial compensation for the tasks she performed. Connie maintained a warm but businesslike manner in the meeting. As soon as the owner of the restaurant agreed that she had indeed taken on these new responsibilities and, in fact, had been handling them very well, Connie knew she'd achieved the first part of her goal. She explained that she felt she deserved an increase of 15 percent due to her increased responsibilities. The owner, however, said that he couldn't give Connie the increase she requested since he didn't have the money right now. He said he could afford a 10 percent increase, but no more. Connie said she understood, but said that perhaps there were other things they could do. She asked for an extra week of paid vacation and tuition reimbursement. In addition, she asked that the owner agree to renegotiate her compensation again in six months, rather than waiting a full year. He agreed.

# Going to Bat for Yourself
## Asking for a Raise

- Aim to receive a pay raise of a specific percentage or amount.
- Present it as compensation for a change in facts.
- Negotiate with whoever has the power to make salary decisions.
- Your pitch needs a strong foundation of solid information.
- Remember, this is an economic judgment separate from your personal worth.
- Time your request by the cycles of the company.
- Maintain a warm and caring but businesslike manner.
- Get them to agree you're deserving of an increase.
- Response to seniority objections: you can't measure achievements by time.
- Response to fairness objections: hard work and excellence should be rewarded.
- Responses to poverty objections: increase nonmonetary elements, ask for a retroactive increase, or agree to an interim raise with built-in renegotiation.

# 20

# PARTING SHOTS

## Negotiating Severance Packages

*" 'You're fired!' No other words can so easily and succinctly reduce a confident, self-assured executive to an insecure, groveling shred of his former self."*

—FRANK LOUCHHEIM

One of the things Andy had always loved about working for Ajax and Nestor was the spirit in the office. Despite the hard work and long hours there was always a sense of teamwork, a feeling of mutual purpose, that flowed through the building. Supervisors didn't stand aloof from employees, and employees weren't afraid of voicing their opinions. The environment was open and democratic. That was why the sudden shift in atmosphere was so noticeable.

When he returned from vacation the company seemed to have changed. Office doors were closed rather than open. People gathered in little groups whispering. Sometimes when Andy entered a room the people in it would suddenly stop speaking. He found that he wasn't being given all the memos issued by his department head and that his own memos weren't being circulated widely. His supervisor, once his regular tennis partner and close friend, was now keeping him at arm's length. Andy couldn't figure out what was going on until Friday afternoon when he received a call to come see his supervisor. The secretary didn't look up as he walked into the office, and sitting there next to his supervisor was the head of personnel. Suddenly, everything made sense.

# THE TERMINATED EMPLOYEE'S
# SELF-EXAMINATION

In negotiating severance, as in every negotiation, the first step in the process is for you to analyze needs and weigh options, to know yourself. That's accomplished by asking three questions: "What do I want?" "Is it worth my time?" "Is it important to me?"

## *WHAT DO I WANT?—SETTING A SPECIFIC GOAL*

Being fired from a job is like suffering a death. Psychologically someone who's terminated tends to go through the same stages as someone who has lost a loved one. First there's denial: "This can't be happening." Then there's anger: "How could you do this to me?" And finally there's acceptance: "I've got to move on." In order to succeed in the severance negotiation, your final dialogue with an employer, you must at least superficially project yourself beyond the first two stages and into the third. Once you're told you're being let go you must get a firm grip on your emotions. Otherwise you'll be apt to set the wrong goal for this hybrid negotiation.

Terminators, at least those who have been trained well, know how to move you beyond the denial stage. This is usually done by giving the news quickly, honestly, and directly, with no room for misunderstanding. Their job, in this initial step, is to make sure you understand you've lost your job. However, once they've taken you beyond denial their next effort is to apply pressure on you to close the matter right here and now before the anger sets in. They present a meager severance package and urge you to sign a form waiving all potential claims against the company.

This quick attack on their part carries risks for both sides. While it sometimes works to the employer's advantage, it just as frequently backfires. Under such pressure, employees tend to instinctively react in one of two ways. Either their fear gets the better of them, re-sparks their denial instinct, and they press to be given another chance; or they move beyond denial into anger, explode with rage, and try to take revenge on the employer. When a fearful employee asks for another chance, his goal in the negotiation is simply to get his job back. When an angry employee rails against his employer, his goal is to get revenge; he has been hurt and he wants to hurt the company in return. Neither is an effective negotiating goal.

Even if you were able to talk the employer into giving you a second chance, what kind of future would you have in this company? You already know your job is hanging by a thread, and obviously you've no chance to get ahead. Anything you do or say could lead to dismissal. Why should you work for someone who doesn't want you? And while taking revenge on someone who has hurt you or wronged you is initially satisfying, that feeling of satisfaction won't pay your bills or put bread on your table. You need to take care of yourself and your family now. (If you can't put the desire for revenge out of your heart, try to funnel it into squeezing the employer for everything you can in severance.)

In order to be an effective negotiator in this situation you need to move beyond the emotional and establish a more rational goal. I know it's difficult, but as soon as you realize you're about to be fired, you need to put your emotions on hold and let logic rise to the surface. You need to focus on a two-part goal. First, you need to persuade the employer that the severance package offer is exactly that, an offer—the first round in a negotiation. And second, you need to improve the package as much as you possibly can.

### IS IT WORTH MY TIME?— DECIDING IF IT'S READILY NEGOTIABLE

Very few employees realize that severance packages are entirely negotiable. They've been so brainwashed by our employer-oriented culture that they honestly believe they've no right to severance, that it's something an employer does from the goodness of his heart. While there's a kernel of truth in that sentiment, it's really a misreading of the employer/ employee relationship.

It's true there's no *legal* requirement for an employer to pay severance to an employee who is let go (except in some states where there's a doctrine of implied fairness). However, an employer has a moral and ethical responsibility to do everything he can to compensate an employee who is fired without cause. (Being fired "for cause" means the employee has been let go for doing something illegal or against company policy.) In addition, an employer has a clear legal responsibility not to terminate someone for a discriminatory reason. And today that can mean anything from age to sexual orientation. The combined force of morality and ethics, potentially coupled with the possibility of discriminatory action, make the severance package eminently negotiable.

Of course there are degrees of negotiability. The longer you've been with a company, the older you are, the closer your relationship with your supervisor, and the better your previous work reviews, the more negotiable your severance package. That's because you'll have some leverage—either personal or legal—with which to negotiate. In fact, if you're a woman;

gay; disabled; a member of an ethnic, racial, or religious minority; over forty years old; or have worked for the company for over five years, you'll have substantial leverage because your employer will realize there is a possibility of legal action.

Another factor that affects the negotiability of a severance package is the number of firings taking place at the same time. If there are many people being let go at once, the company is under tremendous pressure to treat everyone equally, perhaps by paying a certain amount for each year's service with the company. If it deviates from this policy it leaves itself open to claims of discrimination. The only way to combat this pressure on the company to refrain from negotiating with you individually is to somehow separate yourself from the pack. I'll explain how that's done later on when I discuss tactics, but for now I'll just say that the more you succeed in separating yourself from everyone else in a mass firing, the more negotiable your severance package will be.

Remember, as long as you, the employee, treat the initial package as an offer, refuse to be bullied into accepting it as the final word, and separate yourself from the pack, your severance is readily negotiable.

## IS IT IMPORTANT TO ME?— MAKING SURE IT'S WORTH NEGOTIATING

Severance offers are always worth negotiating. If you look on this as a risk-versus-reward question, the reason becomes obvious. The potential reward is a larger severance package, encompassing either more cash or other noncash benefits. The potential risk is . . . There is no risk. You've already been fired. What more can your employer do to you? He has already used his ultimate power, the only power he had over you. He has no power left.

Sure, he may say he has the power to withdraw his severance offer if you don't accept it right away. But is that a serious threat? I don't believe so. If you're part of a mass layoff the employer will probably be forced to give you at least what everyone else is getting. He won't be able to justify withdrawing that offer simply because you tried to negotiate. And if you're not part of a mass layoff, all the employer is doing by threatening to withdraw his initial package is making a take-it-or-leave-it offer. As we've seen in other chapters in this book, take-it-or-leave-it offers are generally negotiating ploys rather than actual positions. And even if it is an actual position, it will still be in place if you respond with a counteroffer. Sure, negotiating a severance package will take some time. But it won't take so much time that it takes away from your looking for a new job. In the final analysis you've nothing to lose by negotiating a severance package—and you've got a whole lot to gain.

Let's see how Andy's self-examination went. As soon as he saw the director of personnel sitting with his supervisor Andy put two and two together and realized he was about to be fired. He couldn't believe it. After all he had done for the company and for his immediate supervisor he was going to get the ax. He didn't want to lose his job, especially in today's job market. He had friends who had been laid off and were still looking for work a year later. And he was angry—angry at his boss for not letting him know sooner, angry at the company for not reciprocating his own loyalty, and angry at himself for not reading the signs sooner. Yet despite all these feelings, Andy knew that the next few minutes would have an incredible impact on his short-term future. As he was sitting down he resolved to get as much as he could out of the company. He knew that severance packages were readily negotiable. He understood that it was clearly worth negotiating. There was nothing more the company could do to him. They'd used their ultimate weapon, and from here on he was the one with the power.

## LEVELING THE TERMINATION PLAYING FIELD

The second step in negotiating severance is to get to know your opponent and to use that information to level the playing field. This is done by answering four questions: "What do I need to know?" "With whom should I negotiate?" "Are there any potentially disruptive side issues?" "What do I share with my opponent?"

### WHAT DO I NEED TO KNOW?— GATHERING INFORMATION

In order to successfully negotiate a severance package you'll need to gather information as early as possible. In fact, it's best if you start gathering information before you're actually fired.

It's impossible for organizations to keep secrets. Signs of impending terminations leak out all the time. Sometimes the leakage is intentional: the organization would prefer to be spared the dirty job and wants the person or people in question to resign. Other times it's unintentional, simply a matter of gossip and a subtle shift in attitude. Subtle organizational signs often begin as far as three to four months in advance, and consist of vague urgings to cut budgets and expenses at the departmental level.

Eventually the signs shift to individuals as word filters out through the grapevine. You're left out of meetings. People stop talking when you enter a room. Responsibilities are taken away from you. Finally, the organization starts planting the seeds for dismissal. You're asked to compile a list of your projects. Your salary review is postponed or you receive your first negative review. You're told to postpone hiring an assistant.

I urge you to begin gathering information as soon as you see any of these signs. Take charge of the process. Grab control of your own termination. In today's workplace, where there's smoke there's fire. If you sense something is wrong, you're right. If you hear rumors, they're based on truths. The sooner you begin to gather information, the more successful you'll be in a severance negotiation. Let's go over the information you need to obtain, whether you go after it before or after you're actually terminated.

Many companies have employee handbooks that state exactly what a fired employee is entitled to. However, very few companies actually go by their stated policies. In most cases there is an informal tradition, an accepted pattern, for dealing with terminated employees, whether or not it has been written down, or whether or not it jibes with what has been stated formally. For example, a company's employee handbook may state that employees aren't eligible for any severance at all; however, it has been company practice to pay two weeks' severance for every year someone has been employed. You need to find out both what company policy is and what company practice has been. You can find out about official company policy from either reading the handbook or speaking with someone in Human Resources or Personnel. You can find out about company practice by speaking with someone who has been a long-term employee, someone who has a historical perspective on the company.

Don't be concerned about what will happen when others see that you're worried about your job. What is the worst that can happen? If you're mistaken you'll be told so and your worries will be over. If you're not mistaken you'll be sending a subtle reciprocal message for all the hints they're sending. It will demonstrate that you're aware of what's happening and capable of taking action. That will engender respect and perhaps even a little fear on the other side. Neither can harm you. Remember, all they can do is fire you. And if they've already reached that decision, or in fact have already done that, there's nothing else they can do to harm you.

The second important piece of information you need to gather is the reason for your dismissal. This is important for a couple of reasons. First, you need to make sure you're not being fired for cause—for stealing or breaking a company rule. That will insure that you're eligible for unemployment and for severance. Second, you need to determine who or what the company is going to blame for the situation. If blame is to be put on an external factor rather than your performance, you'll be able to use your being blameless as leverage in the negotiation. If blame is to be placed on you, you'll need to demonstrate the unfairness or inaccuracy of this, and then use your potential response to the accusation, as leverage in the negotiation. In other words, the stated reason for your dismissal determines what type of leverage you can use in the severance negotiation. In most instances you'll be given a reason for your dismissal. True or not, it will be the company's position. If you're not given a reason, ask for one. It's the least you're entitled to.

The third piece of information you need is an accurate description of the company's severance package. In sophisticated organizations, or when the package is complex, you'll often be handed a memo outlining the offer. In smaller companies, or when the offer is very basic, it will often be relayed verbally. In either case, make it your business to ask for it to be repeated verbally and then to take written notes about it. Taking notes offers you an opportunity to reduce their offer into language you can understand. It also plants the seed that you may be preparing to speak to a lawyer. If they question why you need it repeated or need to take notes, simply say that you're very upset and want to make sure that you get everything down on paper so you can review it later when you're feeling better. The calm, forthright, rational demeanor this demonstrates is an essential part of eliminating dissonance in the negotiation.

### WITH WHOM SHOULD I NEGOTIATE?— PUSHING THE UP BUTTON

Generally there will be two possible opponents for you to choose from when negotiating severance: your immediate supervisor or a representative from the human resources or personnel department. (Of course, if your company has no such department you'll be limited to dealing with your immediate supervisor.)

It's very difficult for a manager to fire someone. Not only is he firing that person, he's also firing his family. A manager isn't unmindful of the fact that he may be taking food out of the mouths of young children. In addition, he has probably worked closely with the person he's letting go and has come to know him as an individual, not just as a line in a budget. These difficulties often lead managers to extreme actions when they're forced to fire someone. Either they become angry and vicious in an effort to hide their own feelings or they become so compassionate that they don't clearly articulate the company line. The result is either a screaming match or an employee who isn't quite sure if he has been fired or not.

That's why most companies have a human resources person sit in on every termination meeting. These individuals are trained executioners. They know what to say, and what not to say, in order to make sure the termination is done quickly, mercifully, and, most important, legally. Human resources people are trained to couch terminations in such a manner as to avoid creating legal liability. Whatever the real reason for the termination, a human resources professional can put an entirely legal "spin" on the firing.

In addition, the human resources professional probably hasn't worked with the individual before. That insulates him from feeling guilty. The manager thinks back to all the times the employee has helped him out, and he remembers the employee's three little children who came to the company picnic. The human resources professional thinks only of the bottom line. In taking this team approach to firing, employers attempt to cover both their flanks simultaneously. However, it provides an opportunity for those savvy enough to exploit it.

Rather than choosing to negotiate with either the manager or the human resources person, or with both simultaneously, the most effective way to negotiate severance is to divide and conquer—to negotiate first with one, then with the other. Your best hopes for success in this negotiation lie in negotiating with each individually, using whatever leverage you have. For example: If you're a protected minority who has a personal relationship with your manager, you can use that relationship as leverage with the manager and your status as a protected minority as leverage with the human resources person. I'll get into this divide-and-conquer technique later on, but for now suffice it to say that, if possible, you should negotiate separately with both your manager and the human resources person.

## ARE THERE ANY POTENTIALLY DISRUPTIVE SIDE ISSUES?—ELIMINATING DISSONANCE

There are two major elements of dissonance that interfere with a successful severance negotiation: the terminator's distaste for the job and his fear that you'll react angrily, perhaps even violently. Terminators hate what they have to do, expect you to lash out verbally at them, and are deathly afraid you'll lash out physically as well. That's another reason there generally will be more than one person in the room at the time: companies believe the presence of a third party may keep you from going for your former boss's throat—and if you do, they want a witness.

Of the four primary techniques for eliminating dissonance, three don't apply to this negotiation. You can't affect the timing or location of your termination, nor can you do anything special to your appearance, since you had no role in setting up the meeting. (Just as an aside, professionals terminate people as early in the week and as early in the day as possible so the fired employee can apply for unemployment benefits right away and become proactive.) However, you can eliminate dissonance with your attitude. As ironic as it sounds, in order to eliminate the dissonance in this negotiation, you need to make the terminator feel comfortable and at ease. You do that by doing the exact opposite of what he expects.

Rather than reacting to the news of your termination emotionally, put on a mask of rationality. I know it's not healthy to keep your feelings inside, but in this instance it's in your best interest. Swallow your anger and your fear. Demonstrate that while you obviously aren't happy about the situation, you do accept it. Don't ask for your job back. In as businesslike a manner as possible go about gathering your information. Ask for a reason for your dismissal if it hasn't been given already. Don't argue with it now or express any opinion whatsoever. Simply write it down. Ask for a description of the severance package they're offering. Again, voice no opinion. Simply write it down. Treat this for what it really is, a business meeting. Granted, it's a terrible one to have to attend, but the more you turn it into an unemotional exchange the clearer it is that you've turned it into a negotiation.

Your businesslike, calm manner will be a godsend to the terminators. Their relief will be so great it may even be palpable in the room. Don't worry, you're going to ask for something in exchange for that relief you've given them. You're going to ask them to accept your version of the common ground between you.

### WHAT DO I SHARE WITH MY OPPONENT?— FINDING AND DEMONSTRATING COMMON GROUND

All too often the common ground between terminator and terminated is a speedy departure. The terminator wants the terminated employee out of the office as quickly as possible. He doesn't want the former employee's presence upsetting other employees, reminding them of their own job mortality and deflating morale. And terminators don't want the former employee's presence reminding them of their own responsibility in bringing about the demise. The former employee, on the other hand, often wants to get as far away from the scene of his "disgrace" as possible, as quickly as possible. Together, former employer and former employee work toward making the process as quick as possible.

However, in order to successfully negotiate a good severance package you're going to need to take a bit more time. And to get that time you'll need to define a different common ground between you and your former employer. Rather than aiming for speed above all else, use your businesslike demeanor as a demonstration that you want the separation to be as businesslike as possible. This is your common ground. The employer wants a businesslike process simply because the alternative is ugly and potentially dangerous. You want things to be handled in a businesslike manner because business decisions aren't made instantly—they're examined and thought about—and, yes, negotiated.

Directly say to your former employer that you want this to be handled in as businesslike a manner as possible and you know he does as well. He will already know that, due to your behavior. However, after having stated it you can go on to say that, therefore, you'd like to schedule another meeting in two days to go over the terms of your severance package and termination. In effect, you're saying that in exchange for your taking this well and not trying to kill him you want a second meeting.

Don't be surprised if you're pressed to accept the offer on the spot, perhaps even handed a waiver form to sign. DO NOT SIGN ANYTHING! Your signature on a waiver is your ace in the hole. Until you sign that form you and your former employer are linked physically, ethically, morally, and, most important in this instance, legally. Explain that you need time to think about what you've been told. Say you need to recover from the shock. If your back is pushed to the wall say you need to speak to your lawyer. But whatever you do, schedule a second meeting.

By forcing a second meeting to take place you've succeeded in the first half of your goal—making the severance package negotiable. The first part of the hybrid negotiation, the persuasion, is concluded. Implicit in there being another meeting is the fact that there's something left to discuss. And since you're all agreed that your employment is at an end, all that's left to discuss is your severance package. At the next meeting you'll be involved in a numbers negotiation over the terms of the severance package.

## INSIDER TIPS FOR TERMINATED EMPLOYEES

The third and final step in negotiating severance is to know the situation. That's accomplished by applying the lessons learned by those who are experienced with this particular situation. I've gained all too much experience negotiating severance packages for my clients in the past few years. In addition, I've spoken with labor law attorneys and personnel executives in researching this book. My experience and research leads me to offer you three insider tips. One is a general technique that can be used under any circumstances. The other two are specific techniques for instances when you've got legal or emotional leverage.

## *LAUNCH A PREEMPTIVE STRIKE*

The general technique is something I call "the preemptive strike." Rather than waiting to be told that you're about to be fired, you take charge. As soon as you begin to read the signs that there's trouble in the workplace, approach the human resources department. Explain that you love your job but have begun to sense there's something going on. Ask for help in clarifying the situation.

I've recommended you go to human resources rather than directly to your supervisor because I want you to get the truth. Supervisors have a tendency to put the best spin on the facts. Yours may be under pressure to fire you, but perhaps he's trying to fight the pressure. He'll then tell you he's doing everything he can and not to worry. He may already have decided to let you go but needs you to finish up your work. He'll then tell you not to worry simply in an effort to keep you productive. A human resources person, on the other hand, knows he could be in an awkward legal position if he lies to you. In addition, he may see your approach as an opportunity to avoid the dirty business of termination.

Once you've asked human resources for help in determining your situation, you've basically entered into a negotiation. From here on you're in a position to negotiate a "resignation" or "retirement" rather than a severance package. In addition, you've successfully separated yourself from any others who might be let go simultaneously, increasing your chances of negotiating a superior package. Yours will be a unique situation rather than just one more termination out of a handful or a hundred.

Whether you've instigated the negotiation through a preemptive strike or have been taken by surprise, you've two choices in how to handle your second termination meeting: you can rely on either emotional leverage or legal leverage.

## *USING YOUR LEGAL LEVERAGE IF YOU HAVE ANY*

If you're a member of a protected group (you're a woman, gay, disabled, over the age of 40, foreign-born, have worked for the company for five years or more, or are a member of a religious, ethnic, or racial minority), you've got legal leverage, whether or not you've actually been discriminated against. As soon as you know, or even suspect, you're being terminated, contact a labor lawyer. The attorney will be able to help you plan how to draw attention to your protected status without directly threatening legal action, and will assist in drafting a counteroffer. I believe the potential increase in severance as a result of properly wielding your legal leverage will far outweigh the cost of legal advice.

Remember, your goal isn't revenge. You're not interested in taking your employer to court, only in using the threat of legal action to increase your severance. Regardless of whether or not your employer has actually been guilty of discrimination, he will be willing to increase severance in order to avoid a lawsuit. Not only will he need to pay legal fees if you sue, he knows that most of these cases are settled by juries. And since juries are primarily made up of employees, not employers, he's running a big risk. In addition, under many of the protective laws you won't need to prove you were fired because of your protected status, only that your protected status played a role in the decision.

## USE YOUR EMOTIONAL LEVERAGE IF YOU HAVE ANY

If you have a personal relationship with your supervisor you can use emotional leverage—in other words, guilt. Since you don't have legal leverage, and therefore won't be enlisting the aid of an attorney, you'll need to do this on your own.

Draw up a counteroffer to the company's severance package. Your package should be based on your needs, not on the company's initial offer. As long as your offer is substantiated and explained, and presented without anger, it will be received as an honest attempt to reach an agreement, even if it's substantially higher than the company's proposal. Bear in mind that the company has already fired you, so there's nothing else it can do to you. Start with the cash element, which is probably the most important. Ask for one month's salary for every year you've worked for the company. The old rule of one week per year is no longer sufficient, especially with unemployment as high as it is right now. If the company's initial offer included outplacement counseling, ask for more. If it didn't, ask it to pick up the cost of career guidance—that could run anywhere from $1,500 to $5,000. Don't worry about it sounding excessive. Outplacement counseling would cost the company about 10 percent of your yearly salary. Next, consider asking for nonmonetary benefits such as the company's continuing to pick up the cost of your health coverage until you're covered by another employer, free use of the company's office equipment and secretarial staff, perhaps even the computer equipment in your office. In compiling your proposal keep in mind that the more items it contains the more opportunities you'll have to negotiate. All of this information should be summarized in a typed memo, addressed to both your former supervisor and the human relations person.

Once you've completed the memo contact your former supervisor. If you've been on a first-name basis with him before, make sure to address him that way now. The more you can do to reinforce the fact that the two of you had a personal relationship, the more successful you'll be. (If you can call him at home, for instance, by all means do so.) Explain that you're calling to get his advice about the upcoming meeting with Personnel. Say that you've always relied on his advice in the past and now you need it more than ever. Reiterate that you don't blame him for your dismissal— even if you do. Go over your proposal with him, taking the time to give a reason for each request. Make sure those reasons are personal ones. For example, when asking for continued health coverage remind him of your daughter's asthma. When asking for the equipment in your office explain that you'll probably need to do some free-lancing in order to keep your head above water. Tell him where you'll be setting up the home office, reminding him of his visits to your house. Be merciless in playing the guilt card. Conclude your conversation by saying that you know the company won't be able to give you all you're asking for but that you'd be grateful if he could put in a good word for you prior to the meeting.

By making this personal approach you've encouraged your former supervisor to intercede on your behalf. That intercession gives the human resources person an excuse to be less rigid. And by providing a wide-ranging proposal with many elements you'll give both your opponents an opportunity to craft an agreement they'll be able to sell to their superiors.

When you do appear for your second termination meeting, all those personal elements will be gone. You'll be back to the businesslike approach you took at the first meeting. Dress as you would for a job interview. Act cordial and calm. Begin by thanking them for seeing you again. Even though you forced them into it, it pays to be gracious. Say you've carefully gone over their severance proposal and would like to present your own proposal. Once again, go over each request and provide a reason. But this time, refrain from using personal reasons. Instead of specifically citing your daughter's asthma, cite the high cost of health insurance or the "special needs" of your family.

By shifting gears and going back to being the businesslike stoic, you'll accomplish a great deal. Rest assured your former supervisor has already told the human resources person of your daughter's asthma—he's been dying to relieve himself of guilt. However, by not referring to it yourself you play to the human resources person's weakness. He expected you to come in, beg for more, and offer a sob story. Instead you're being his dream employee, ascending the scaffold without tears, refusing even the blindfold. You'll rise in his eyes dramatically. In fact, he may wonder why the company is getting rid of such an intelligent and brave individual. By taking the personal approach with your former supervisor and the businesslike approach with the human resources person, you'll have played to both of their weaknesses and maximized your chances of succeeding.

Once you've completed your presentation, be prepared for some quick and hard bargaining. You want to resolve this matter at this meeting. Not only will you never get another one, but it's in your best interest to resolve this job so you can get to work finding another. Be willing to make sizable concessions in exchange for comparable concessions on the company's part. Bear in mind that noncash items, which can be absorbed into the company's operating budget and will have less of a perceived (or obvious) impact on the bottom line, may be easier to obtain than cash.

Once you've hammered out an acceptable package ask that it be documented in writing so all can sign it. Until you have both of their signatures on that memo, refuse to sign the waiver form. When all the paperwork is complete, sign your rights away, shake hands, and walk over to the unemployment office.

Let's see how Andy made out in his severance negotiation. He maintained his cool when told of his dismissal. He asked why he was being let go. It was tough to remain calm, especially since one of the reasons given was the company's losing the Achilles Soap account. Andy had warned his supervisor that would happen, but his advice went unheeded. Now he was being unfairly used as the scapegoat. Still, Andy remained businesslike. He asked what company severance policy was and what he was being offered. He wrote down everything that was said, and even had the human resources person repeat the meager content of their severance proposal—one month's salary for the four years he had worked here. When urged to agree and sign a waiver form, Andy explained that he needed time to think things over. He asked for, and received, an appointment for the next afternoon.

When he got home Andy drafted his own severance package proposal. He asked for four months' salary, $5,000 for outplacement counseling, continued health coverage until he was covered by another employer, use of his office and secretary until he found another job, and the computer system in his office. He telephoned his former tennis partner/supervisor later that evening, making sure to call him at home. He explained that he needed his advice and help as he had so often in the past. Andy reiterated that he didn't blame his former supervisor (even though he did). He explained his proposal line by line, giving a personal reason for each request. When Andy mentioned continued health coverage he spoke of his pregnant wife—whom his supervisor had met over dinner many times. When Andy talked about taking his computer system he told his former supervisor he'd set it up in his den—the den his former supervisor had helped him paint when he first moved in. Finally, Andy asked his former supervisor to intercede on his behalf to the human resources person prior to the next afternoon's meeting.

Andy arrived early for the meeting, dressed in his best blue suit. He greeted both his opponents cordially and thanked them for the meeting. He said that after carefully considering their severance offer he had prepared one of his own. He proceeded to go over his proposal line by line, but this time limiting his reasons to formal generalities. When he finished, the human resources person said he couldn't increase the cash portion of the package, nor could he give Andy money for career counseling; however, he was willing to continue picking up the cost of health insurance, would let Andy take his computer system, and would let him use the office facilities for one month. Andy agreed.

# Parting Shots
## Negotiating Severance Packages

- Turn the severance package into an offer and then improve it.
- Negotiate first with managers, then with Personnel.
- Remember, there's no risk—you've already been fired.
- Find out policies; why you've been fired; and the package terms.
- Act in a calm and businesslike manner.
- Force a second meeting, insuring it's negotiable.
- Try a preemptive strike, taking charge of your own termination.
- If you're a member of a protected group, use the threat of legal action.
- If you've emotional leverage, use it.

# 21

# FORBEARANCE REQUESTS

## Asking Creditors for More Time

*"Words pay no debts."*

—WILLIAM SHAKESPEARE

Hillary and David knew they were in for financial trouble when David lost his job. As sales manager of an auto dealership, David was paid very well. So well, in fact, that it had enabled them to live very comfortably, with Hillary working two part-time jobs—as an aerobics instructor and as a photographer for the local newspaper—neither of which paid well. Hillary and David had a big mortgage on their condo, traveled often, dined out weekly, and were frequent credit card users. They hadn't really lived beyond their means, but they had just about stretched those means to the limit. Now they'd be relying on Hillary's small paychecks and David's unemployment benefits. For two months they were able to pay all their bills by drawing on their savings, but then one day they sat down to pay the bills and found they just didn't have enough money to cover them.

## THE DEBTOR'S SELF-EXAMINATION

In forbearance requests, as in every negotiation, the first step in the process is for the debtor to analyze needs and weigh options, to know him or herself. That's accomplished by asking three questions: "What do I want?" "Is it worth my time?" "Is it important to me?"

## WHAT DO I WANT?—SETTING A SPECIFIC GOAL

There's nothing immoral about having a financial setback. It doesn't mean you're a failure or foolish. It won't ruin the rest of your life. You will not be marked for life or exiled. Almost everyone has some financial setback during their lives, so you aren't the first. Nor will you be the last. You can climb your way out of the hole, no matter how deep it is. Now that I've given you that little pep talk, and I hope have convinced you that all isn't hopeless, let me add one note of caution: you're still going to have to pay your bills.

While I'm sure that what you want from your negotiations with creditors is to be forgiven your debts, it's not going to happen. No one can work that kind of negotiating magic, no matter how skilled. And in order to get the most from your negotiations with creditors you need to understand and accept that fact. Your goal in these negotiations should be to get more *time* to pay back your debts—in effect lowering your monthly payments—not to get your debts forgiven. The magic word is *forbearance,* not *forgiveness.*

## IS IT WORTH MY TIME?— DECIDING IF IT'S READILY NEGOTIABLE

If you approach creditor negotiations as requests for more time they'll be readily negotiable. Most creditors, whether a bank that holds your mortgage or a sibling who loaned you $500, are concerned with one thing above all else: getting paid back. Even those creditors who hold collateral would prefer to have your money than sell your collateral. No bank, for instance, wants to sell your home and take the proceeds in settlement for the debt. Bankers know that they never receive market value for property sold at foreclosure. And no creditor, secured or unsecured, wants you to declare bankruptcy. A credit card company owed $5,000 would rather get the full $5,000, even if it takes five years, than settle for ten cents on the dollar today—and that might be all it would get if you declared bankruptcy.

I'll never forget the first time I realized how much leverage debtors had over creditors. I got involved with a client who was in debt to a local bank. My client's business had been excellent for years and years, and he had a long-term relationship with his bank. The worse business got the more money he borrowed. The bank was as convinced as my client was that the business would bounce back, and so kept pouring money into it. By the time I stepped in, the bank was into the business for around $7 million. My client was so important to the bankers by this point that they were sending limousines to pick us up and take us to meetings. The more my client owed the bank, the more afraid the bankers were of his going bankrupt, and the more willing they were to do whatever it took to keep the business up and running.

Some creditors are naturally more negotiable than others. Family and friends will obviously be the most flexible. Probably the next most flexible creditor, believe it or not, is the bank that holds your home mortgage. Utilities are fairly accommodating, especially those that provide essential services. Then will come credit and charge card companies, which are experienced at negotiating with debtors. Finance companies are among the least flexible creditors, topped only by landlords. Of course, the saving grace with a landlord is that it could take him four to six months to physically evict you. A subtle reminder of that fact makes even him somewhat flexible.

### IS IT IMPORTANT TO ME?— MAKING SURE IT'S WORTH NEGOTIATING

If you value your credit rating and your future relationships with your creditors, it's worth negotiating your inability to pay your bills. Remember that while your financial setback may be temporary, it won't go away unless you address it. Now isn't the time to hide under the covers and hope your problems will vanish. If you take charge of the situation you'll be better off in the long run.

Let's see how Hillary's and David's self-examination went. As soon as she saw they couldn't meet their bills, Hillary knew something had to be done. David, a bit shellshocked by his termination and subsequent inability to find another job right away, wanted to immediately declare bankruptcy and get out from under their debts . . . or, barring that, flee the country. Hillary calmed him down and explained that what they really needed to do was negotiate for more time. She explained that as long as they asked for forbearance rather than forgiveness their debts were negotiable. Hillary convinced David that negotiating was worth it if they wanted to maintain their future creditworthiness.

## LEVELING THE DEBTOR'S PLAYING FIELD

The second step in requesting forbearance of a debt is for the debtor to get to know his or her opponent and to use that information to level the playing field. This is done by answering four questions: "What do I need to know?" "With whom should I negotiate?" "Are there any potentially disruptive side issues?" "What do I share with my opponent?"

## WHAT DO I NEED TO KNOW?—
## GATHERING INFORMATION

There are really only two pieces of information you'll need to gather in this negotiation: your true financial status and your creditors' policies regarding forbearance. Sit down and make an objective, unbiased assessment of your financial situation. Calculate how much money you'll actually have coming in each month, at least until the temporary emergency is over. Then make an accurate list of all the moneys you owe, either monthly or in total. Draw up a master list of all the information for use during your negotiations. Next, telephone each of your creditors and ask about forbearance policies. In many cases you'll be surprised at how accommodating your creditors can be. In this first round of telephone calls, don't get into the specifics of your situation. Simply explain you're gathering information and will be calling back shortly.

Once you've gathered your information, analyze it. How best can you stretch your diminished income to cover your debts? Make sure you've trimmed your expenditures to a bare minimum. Then allocate your remaining income among your various creditors. Give priority to those creditors who offer essential services, such as shelter, utilities, and telephone. Finally, draw up a proposed budget outlining how much you can afford to pay each creditor.

## WITH WHOM SHOULD I NEGOTIATE?—
## PUSHING THE UP BUTTON

If a creditor is an individual, obviously you should negotiate directly with him. However, most creditors these days are institutions or corporations, making the selection of an opponent somewhat problematic. The solution is to find the organization's "work out" specialist. Every lending institution or company has either an individual or a department whose specific job it is to negotiate payment plans with debtors who are in trouble. The way to find them is to simply ask . . . you'll be amazed at how quickly you're connected. You see, one of the "work out" specialist's biggest fears is that you'll simply become incommunicado. Now that he has a chance to speak with you he wants to make the most of it.

## ARE THERE ANY POTENTIALLY DISRUPTIVE
## SIDE ISSUES?—ELIMINATING DISSONANCE

There is one prime element of dissonance surrounding negotiations with creditors: their fear that you won't be repaying the money you owe. This can only be eliminated by demonstrating your good faith and commitment to meet your obligations.

Handle your discussions with individuals who are creditors as you would negotiate with a family member. Since you'll be relying to a large measure on the strength of your relationship with this person, this is no time to distance yourself from him by using the telephone. Speak to him in person. Your attitude should be one of contrition: you've made a mistake and need his help in rectifying it. Explain the reason for your setback in as much detail as possible and describe how you'll be trying to overcome it.

Since most of your creditors are probably institutions, however, you might not be able to have many such face-to-face discussions. Instead, you'll probably be forced to handle most of these negotiations over the telephone. That means you won't be able to draw on physical tools to demonstrate sincerity and explain your situation. Instead it will need to be conveyed verbally.

First, state that you're calling because you don't want to cause the organization any harm or undue alarm. You wanted the "work out" specialist to know as early as possible that you'll be paying your debt late. Never say you won't be paying a bill or that you're unable to pay. Remember, you're asking for forbearance, not forgiveness. Any hint, no matter how slight, that you may not be paying your debt will be taken poorly.

Creditors aren't really interested in hearing a sob story, so don't feel you need to go into detail about your problems. It's often sufficient to say you've had a temporary financial setback and give a general reason for it. Just for your information, it will be received better if the setback doesn't appear to be your fault. For instance, being laid off always evokes more sympathy than being fired. A medical emergency is always very heart-rending, particularly if it happened to someone other than yourself and you were needed to help foot the bill. If it's clear the setback will be temporary, stress that fact.

Finally, tell him you'll be keeping him informed of your financial situation on a regular basis. This will reinforce the notion that you won't be disappearing.

By the way, don't let creditors' comments about your credit rating being adversely affected create dissonance. Your credit rating isn't the issue you should be worrying about right now, it's your ability—or inability—to pay your bills. If you successfully negotiate forbearance now, you'll have time to repair your credit rating later.

### WHAT DO I SHARE WITH MY OPPONENT?— FINDING AND DEMONSTRATING COMMON GROUND

The most important thing you can do in this conversation is to establish and directly state the common ground between you and the "work out" specialist: that you're 110 percent committed to repaying your debt fully as soon as possible. In exchange for this unflagging commitment, however, you need his help in arranging more manageable payment plans.

## INSIDER TIPS FOR DEBTORS

The third and final step in requesting forbearance is to know the situation. That's accomplished by applying the lessons learned by those who are experienced with this particular situation. I've been a banker and a venture capitalist, and as an attorney I've represented literally hundreds of individuals and businesses asking for forbearance from creditors. I've also written articles and books on borrowing and have lectured on the topic at more than a hundred major universities. All that experience, as well as research I conducted for this book, leads me to offer you three insider tips: one for short-term problems; one for long-term situations; and one for either.

### ASK TO SKIP OR MAKE PARTIAL PAYMENTS IN THE SHORT TERM

If it's clear this will be a temporary or short-term problem—one to three months—ask if you can skip one or two payments or just make partial payments of the amount you outlined in your budget. For example, when speaking to a credit card company ask if you can pay only the interest for a couple of months; when speaking to a landlord ask if you can pay a percentage of the rent, promising to make up the difference once your problem has been resolved.

### ASK TO RESTRUCTURE PAYMENTS FOR THE LONG TERM

If your financial setback may be a long-term problem—more than three months—ask to restructure the monthly payments based on your new budget. While such a restructuring should be amenable to most institutional and individual creditors, some, such as your landlord, who don't have a long-term commitment to you, may not be willing to go along with this. In that case, ask him to bear with you for as long as he possibly can, and say you'll look to make other living arrangements.

## BE OPEN TO CONCESSIONS

Whether your problem is short-term or long-term, you must be prepared to make some concessions in exchange for creditor forbearance. For example, tell a credit or charge card creditor that you won't be using the card again until you've paid your balance off. You probably wouldn't be allowed to use it anyway, but your offer will be seen as a positive step. However, if you're asked to take some irrevocable action, such as returning your credit card, do everything possible to resist. Of course, if you must give it back, do so.

You may not be able to get every creditor to agree to your proposed new payment plan. Each will understandably try to get the maximum amount from you. The secret to minimizing such compromises is to impress on the creditor that you've truly calculated your finances objectively and have cut every other debt payment down an equivalent amount. Stress that your goal is to pay your debts fully and that if you're unable to stick to the budget you've drawn up you may be forced into bankruptcy. Remember, your ace in the hole is your willingness to continue to pay off your debt. In most cases, as long as you pay something rather than nothing—as long as you show a willingness to meet your responsibilities—you'll find your creditors willing to work with you.

Let's see how Hillary and David dealt with their creditors. They sat down and drew up an accurate list of exactly how much they owed and how much income they would have until David landed a new job. Hillary then contacted each creditor simply to gather information about forbearance policies and to get the names of the "work out" contacts. Then Hillary and David sat down and drew up a proposed budget, outlining exactly how much they could afford to pay each of their creditors. With this in hand, Hillary telephoned each creditor. In her conversations she explained in a calm but forthright voice that she was calling because she and David had suffered a temporary cash flow shortage and wanted to let their creditors know that they would need some help. She stressed their commitment to paying back their debts entirely as soon as possible and to keeping their creditors fully and regularly informed. She explained that they had sat down and drawn up a very frugal budget and wanted to lower their monthly payments. Hillary noted that they were approaching all their creditors and asking each to accept an equivalent reduction until the temporary problem was alleviated. The bank that held their mortgage agreed to let them skip two payments entirely, and then make interest-only payments for the following four months, by adding a balloon payment to the end of the mortgage. The credit card they owed money on allowed them to pay interest only for up to six months, as long as they made no additional purchases. They would, however, be required to pay off the entire balance at the end of six months. The telephone and utility companies both worked out monthly payment plans for the amounts in arrears.

## Forbearance Requests
## Asking Creditors for More Time

- Get more time—forbearance, not forgiveness.
- If the creditor is an individual, negotiate with him face-to-face.
- If the creditor is an institution, negotiate with the "work out" specialist.
- Calculate a budget for paying back debts.
- Demonstrate good faith and a commitment to meet obligations.
- State your commitment to complete repayment as soon as possible.
- Short-term problem: ask to skip one or two payments or make partial payments.
- Long-term problem: ask to restructure the monthly payments.
- In all cases, be open to concessions.

# 22

# SELLING YOURSELF

## Negotiating Fees for Your Services

*"The price of wisdom is above rubies."*

—THE BOOK OF JOB

Jim had been having a slow season. His housepainting business always tailed off in the winter months. Not only couldn't he do exterior work during the winter, his marketing wasn't as effective, since people driving by didn't see him hard at work on a home and start to think about painting their own houses. That meant it was very important for him to land as many jobs as came along. It was with this eagerness to get work that he approached his negotiation with Mr. and Mrs. Robb, who had telephoned him saying they'd like an estimate on having the interior of their small home repainted.

## THE SERVICE PROVIDER'S SELF-EXAMINATION

In selling a service, as in every negotiation, the first step in the process is for you to analyze needs and weigh options, to know yourself. That's accomplished by asking three questions: "What do I want?" "Is it worth my time?" "Is it important to me?"

### *WHAT DO I WANT?—SETTING A SPECIFIC GOAL*

When you're selling your own services it's easy to set the wrong goal. For too many people such negotiations become attempts at getting people to like us, or to approve of what we do. Sure, such personal elements are part of selling your own services, but taking an entirely personal approach can lead to disaster. That's because this is, at its core, a business transaction. The fee you're paid for your services is more than the physical manifestation of a person's affection or approval—it's your stream of income as well. It's the money that pays your business's bills and then puts food on your table, a roof over your head, and clothes on your back. That's why, regardless of the potential ego boost involved in landing a job, the fee must make sense. Therefore, your goal in this negotiation should be to sell your service for a fee that's profitable. Therefore, not only do you need to convince the other party that you're the best man for the job, you want him to agree to pay the fee you've set. And that's what makes this a hybrid negotiation for you, even though for your opponent it's an incremental negotiation.

### IS IT WORTH MY TIME?— DECIDING IF IT'S READILY NEGOTIABLE

Fees for services are perhaps the most negotiable prices in capitalism. If done correctly, they are set first to cover overhead costs. But after that the entire process is subjective. The service provider, if he's smart, will charge as much as people are willing to pay. He generally comes up with this number through consultation with other service providers and through trial and error. How does the potential client decide what he's willing to pay? Once again it's largely subjective. The only objective factor is affordability—no one has bottomless pockets. But beyond being able to afford a fee, potential clients base their estimation of value on their perceptions of the service provider's skill. Sometimes they can look for tangible evidence of skill (such as Jim's previous painting jobs), but in many cases there is no evidence, or whatever evidence does exist is sufficient only to demonstrate competence. That means all they can go by are subjective factors. They will assume that experience and/or education translates into knowledge. They will assume that having a good reputation means being responsible and reliable. They will assume that professional behavior and appearance lead to professional results. The only factors possibly limiting the negotiation over service fees are the provider's cost and the client's affordability.

### IS IT IMPORTANT TO ME?— MAKING SURE IT'S WORTH NEGOTIATING

Service fees are worth negotiating for someone who relies on them for a stream of income. If you don't need the work you can afford to take the position that your fee is nonnegotiable—take it or leave it. But if you've got bills to pay and need to generate cash flow, negotiate.

Let's look at Jim's self-examination. He knew he needed to negotiate a fee that afforded him some profit. He also knew that the only things limiting the negotiability of his fee were his costs, below which he couldn't drop, and the Robbs' affordability, above which they couldn't go. Since the address they gave him was for a very affluent part of town, Jim didn't think they'd have a problem with affording his fee, so the only issue would be his convincing them that he was worth it. Finally, since Jim needed to generate a stream of income to pay his professional and personal bills, he new it was worth negotiating for the job. That's why he started leveling the playing field right away.

## LEVELING THE SERVICE PLAYING FIELD

The second step in selling a service is for the service provider to get to know his or her opponent and to use that information to level the playing field. This is done by answering four questions: "What do I need to know?" "With whom should I negotiate?" "Are there any potentially disruptive side issues?" "What do I share with my opponent?"

### WHAT DO I NEED TO KNOW?— GATHERING INFORMATION

Generally you'll need to uncover three things about potential clients when selling services: their ability to pay your bill; their willingness to pay your bill; and the nature of their prior experiences with providers of this service. The first two are the pieces of information any lender needs to know about a potential borrower—and make no mistake about it, a client is a borrower.

In most service transactions payment comes only after the service has been provided. That means the service provider is, in effect, serving as the client's banker. There are some ways to minimize the risks of this— such as asking for an advance or requiring payment in stages—but the nature of the transaction requires that the service provider take a chance. Let's not forget, however, that the client is taking a chance as well. He is hoping the service provider will competently do what is required, for the sum agreed to, within the time allowed. Before the client takes that chance he will research the service provider's past history for signs of reliability. The service provider should do the same and investigate a potential client's financial history. That could mean speaking with the client's banker, examining current financial statements, or obtaining a credit report, which is the best indication you can find of a person's willingness and ability to pay back a debt. The cost of such a formal investigation makes it unrealistic to conduct one for small jobs. But some research, even if it's informal, should be done nevertheless. At the least, ask other service providers you know if they've ever dealt with the client and how things went.

Once you've finished researching your potential client's finances, turn to his prior experiences. The best way to find out about how he has fared with your type of service in the past is to ask. During one of your initial conversations, ask him if he has ever hired someone else like you. If he has, find out if he was satisfied with the service or if he had any complaints. Rest assured the client will tell you everything your predecessor did wrong. If nothing else he will use the opportunity to stress whatever he considers important. And that's exactly what you need to know in order to close the sale.

## WITH WHOM SHOULD I NEGOTIATE?— PUSHING THE UP BUTTON

Obviously it's best to negotiate with the individual who will be using your services. That way you'll be able to directly demonstrate how he will benefit from your services and explain why you're worth what you're charging. But sometimes you may be forced to negotiate with a representative of the end user. The user may be incapacitated. He may not be readily available. Or perhaps he wants to maintain his privacy. In those instances you'll need to convince the user's agent that the user will benefit from your services and that you're worth what you're charging. If that's the case, remember that the agent's perceptions of the user's needs are more important than the user's actual needs.

## ARE THERE ANY POTENTIALLY DISRUPTIVE SIDE ISSUES?—ELIMINATING DISSONANCE

There are two possible areas of dissonance in this transaction: the client's prior bad experiences with other providers of your service and anything negative in your own reputation. In order to eliminate the former you'll need to demonstrate how you're different from your predecessors— that can be done by providing positive references and other evidence of your abilities. Eliminating the latter will be a little more difficult. It's difficult to overcome a bad reputation—whether it's deserved or not. You can steer the client to positive references, but that will, at best, blur the issue. It won't clear things up. The best thing you can do to overcome a bad reputation is to address it directly. Own up to prior mistakes. Explain them. And then show how you've learned from your past and have incorporated the lessons into your current business. Make your case with humility and honesty and it just might convince potential clients. After all, it's the American way to give people a second chance.

### WHAT DO I SHARE WITH MY OPPONENT?—FINDING AND DEMONSTRATING COMMON GROUND

The common ground in this negotiation is respect for the quality of whatever the service is you'll be rendering. The client wants the job done right and so do you. The best way to demonstrate common ground with a potential client is to show that you can do the job right by discussing your experience. Tell him about all the times you've handled similar tasks for similar people. Impress upon him that you understand his worries, needs, fears, and desires, and have successfully addressed these same worries, needs, fears, and desires for other clients. You want to portray yourself as someone who has been through it all before, who won't be surprised by anything that happens. The more confidence you can generate, the firmer the common ground you'll share with a client.

## INSIDER TIPS FOR SERVICE PROVIDERS

The third and final step is to know the situation. That's accomplished by applying the lessons learned by those who are experienced with this particular situation. I've been selling my services as a professional for more than thirty-five years. In addition, I've interviewed hundreds of service providers in the process of researching this book. My experience and research lead me to offer three insider tips, which I call "the testimonial," "the credential," and "the ironclad fee."

### PROVIDING TESTIMONIALS

Have a mutual friend or acquaintance of both you and the client endorse your character. It's the business equivalent of having someone "put in a good word" for you. The closer the mutual friend is to the client, and the more enthusiastic the endorsement, the more likely you'll be to get the job.

### POINT OUT YOUR CREDENTIALS

Try to tell every client about some special achievement or accolade that marks you as truly being an expert in the field. You're trying to back up the character endorsement you received from the testimonial with an endorsement of your abilities. Some of the better credentials are having taken a special class or having graduated from a particularly impressive institution; receiving an award for excellence from a prestigious organization; writing a book or article on the subject; or being cited by the media as an expert.

## SAY YOUR FEE IS IRONCLAD

When presenting your fee don't treat it as a subject for negotiation. Your motto should be "The fee is the fee." Act as if it is an objective fact. Explain that the only way you can change the fee would be to change the nature of what you're doing. That leaves the door open for you to negotiate everything other than the dollar amount.

Let's see how Jim handled his negotiation. Since the job wouldn't be for a substantial amount of money—the Robbs had a very small home—Jim decided not to bother checking their credit formally. He telephoned the Robbs and asked them about their prior experiences with painters. Mrs. Robb told Jim that the painter they had used to paint the exterior of their home two years ago was a nice fellow but a little sloppy. Jim knew the other painter (he was indeed a sloppy worker), and after finishing with the Robbs gave the fellow a call. The other painter said that while the Robbs were picky, they paid promptly. Jim had an impeccable reputation—he was known as being a bit expensive but worth the money—so there was no dissonance to eliminate on that score. However, since the Robbs were apparently very concerned with neatness, Jim made sure to show up at their home dressed in his suit rather than his painting clothes.

While there was no intermediary standing between Jim and the Robbs, there were two people on the other side of the negotiation. Jim would need to figure out which of the Robbs he should be negotiating with, since it is difficult to deal with two people at the same time. From his telephone conversation with them, it appeared to Jim that the Robbs' relationship was very traditional. That led him to assume he'd probably need to first persuade Mrs. Robb that he could do the kind of job she wanted, and then negotiate his fee with Mr. Robb.

In his meeting with them Jim spoke to Mrs. Robb of his careful work and concern for neatness. In the course of conversation Jim discovered that the Robbs used the same accountant as he did. Jim made a note to ask the accountant to call the Robbs and offer a testimonial to his good character. When Jim returned with his price estimate he gave it to Mr. Robb. Jim said that while Mr. Robb might be able to get lower prices from other painters, Jim wouldn't be able to give the job the level of personal attention and care he normally does for anything less. Mr. Robb pressed him to lower the fee. Jim said that the only way he could charge less was to farm out the work to one of his assistants. He, of course, would stop by once a day to supervise the job. Jim stressed that if they wanted him personally to do the work the Robbs would need to pay his fee. Three days later Mrs. Robb called to give Jim the go-ahead.

# Selling Yourself
# Negotiating Fees for Your Services

- Convince the other party you're the best and he should pay your fee.
- The only limiting factors are your costs and the client's affordability.
- With agents, their perceptions are more important than the user's actual needs.
- Find out about the client's willingness and ability to pay your bill.
- Learn the nature of clients' experiences with other providers of this service.
- Demonstrate how you're different from your predecessors.
- Own up to mistakes, explain them, and show how you've learned from them.
- Demonstrate experience at solving the client's problem.
- Have a mutual friend or acquaintance endorse your character.
- Point out credentials that establish expertise.
- When presenting your fee, don't treat it as a subject for negotiation.

# 23

# OTHER HYBRID NEGOTIATIONS

## A Guide to Six Other Important Situations

Just as it was impractical for me to go over every possible number or persuasive negotiation in great detail, so too it's unrealistic to go over each potential hybrid negotiation with the depth of the previous five chapters. But as I've stressed throughout this book, my goal is to make you a total negotiator. That means I can't just leave you completely on your own when it comes to these other hybrid situations. In this chapter you'll find brief capsule guides for six other common hybrid negotiations. In keeping with the total negotiator approach, each of these capsule guides, like those in the two earlier capsule chapters, is built around the three main steps in total negotiating: know yourself; know your opponent; and know the situation. And as in earlier chapters, I provide insider tips for each situation—based on my personal and professional experience as well as research conducted for this book—so you won't need to rely on experience. In this chapter, I've focused on specific situations, just as I did in the capsule chapter on persuasive negotiations.

## ASKING YOUR PARENTS FOR MONEY

### *KNOW YOURSELF*

- *What do I want?* Your goal should be to obtain a specific, finite amount of money for a particular reason.
- *Is it worth my time?* It's readily negotiable if it's framed as a loan rather than a gift.
- *Is it important to me?* It's worth negotiating if you can't obtain money you desperately need from an institutional lender.

## KNOW YOUR OPPONENT

- *What do I need to know?* You need to first make sure your parents can afford to make the loan. Next, you need to carefully consider what financial ramifications this could have on them. Finally, you need to consider whether any third parties, such as other children, could be adversely affected.
- *With whom should I negotiate?* In this instance you need to negotiate directly with the parent who has the power to make financial decisions, not both parents (unless, of course, they share financial power).
- *Are there any potentially disruptive side issues?* There are three possible areas of dissonance for your parents. First, that other children will have a problem with the loan. Second, that the loan could be used for something capricious. And third, that it won't be repaid. You can remove these by speaking to your siblings ahead of time and obtaining their consent, demonstrating that the loan is for something logical and necessary (preferably dealing with your health, education, or welfare), and outlining exactly when and how you will be paying the money back.
- *What do I share with my opponent?* The obvious common ground in this negotiation is your well-being. If you can show that the loan is needed for that purpose, and you can successfully eliminate dissonance, you'll be on firm footing.

## KNOW THE SITUATION

- Insider Tip: Before asking for a loan from a parent, make sure you've mended all your fences. Do so as far in advance of the actual negotiation as possible so any changes in behavior or attitude don't look phony.
- Insider Tip: Be prepared to discuss exactly why you need the money and why you're unable to obtain it elsewhere. While the information may have no bearing on whether or not you receive the loan, your parents are likely to feel they have a right to the answers. Any hesitancy on your part to provide the whole truth, whether or not it's relevant, will derail the negotiation.

# PRENUPTIAL AGREEMENTS

## *KNOW YOURSELF*

- *What do I want?* Your goal should be a mutually acceptable plan for the division of marital assets in case of a divorce or death.
- *Is it worth my time?* It's readily negotiable in second marriages where one or both spouses have children from a prior marriage; it may also be negotiable in any marriage in which there is a large discrepancy in the wealth of the parties.
- *Is it important to me?* It's always worth negotiating a prenuptial in a second marriage with children, since it's their future that is at issue. In first marriages, the possible ramifications of asking must be weighed against the protection of financial assets.

## *KNOW YOUR OPPONENT*

- *What do I need to know?* The key to an equitable prenuptial agreement is for both parties to have complete and total access to all financial information. There must be total disclosure of every single dollar in assets.
- *With whom should I negotiate?* You should negotiate with whoever controls the other party's wealth. In most cases that will be the future spouse. In some instances, however, that may be a parent or the trustee of an estate or trust.
- *Are there any potentially disruptive side issues?* In second marriages where one or both parties have children from previous marriages there's usually no dissonance—it's understood that the agreement is primarily intended to protect the children, not the individuals getting married. In all other instances there's an understandable fear that the agreement, in effect, plants the seed for divorce and that the party advocating the agreement doesn't quite trust the future spouse. The only way I know of to at least minimize this dissonance is to make sure the agreement becomes null and void upon certain events, such as the birth of a child, after five years of marriage, or upon death.
- *What do I share with my opponent?* Family and friends.

## *KNOW THE SITUATION*

- Insider Tip: Timing is essential in this negotiation. The subject must be brought up as soon after the engagement, and as far prior to the marriage, as possible. It's vital that it not be seen as a last-minute ultimatum.

# RENEGOTIATING BUSINESS LOANS

## KNOW YOURSELF

- *What do I want?* Your goal should be smaller monthly payments, resulting either from an extension of the loan term or from the addition of a large final balloon payment.
- *Is it worth my time?* Ironically, the more you owe the more readily negotiable the loan is. When a lender is owed a great deal of money it wants to make sure it gets something rather than nothing.
- *Is it important to me?* If the renegotiation will result in a necessary improvement in your business's stream of income, then it's well worth doing.

## KNOW YOUR OPPONENT

- *What do I need to know?* First, you must investigate the size and nature of the lender's problem loan portfolio. If the lender already has many problem loans you'll need to present a more persuasive case than if it has few problems. And second, you need to prepare a loan proposal that does four things: shows your business's inability to pay the current loan without going bankrupt; illustrates its ability to repay the recast loan; explains that the current problem is only temporary; and demonstrates that your business is still viable.
- *With whom should I negotiate?* Negotiate with a loan officer, not the "work out" specialist. That way the loan stays current. The loan officer will serve as your advocate before the lender's loan committee.
- *Are there any potentially disruptive side issues?* The main element of dissonance in this negotiation is surprise. Lenders can be very accommodating if you approach them with the news that you're having problems repaying. If they find out themselves, because you're paying late or you miss a few payments, they'll be afraid you're unreliable and will be less apt to be flexible.
- *What do I share with my opponent?* The common ground is keeping you in business. If you're out of business the lender won't get its

money back. Show that you need the renegotiation to stay in business and to continue to pay back the loan and you'll have established common ground.

## KNOW THE SITUATION

- Insider Tip: If all else fails, consider providing the lender with a co-signer, additional collateral, or a personal guarantee. Any one of these three devices should break down resistance to recasting the loan.

# RENEGOTIATING PROFESSIONAL FEES

## KNOW YOURSELF

- *What do I want?* Your goal should be to reduce your overhead without losing needed professional advice or service.
- *Is it worth my time?* Professional fees are entirely negotiable in these slow economic times. In addition, the more important a client you are to the professional, the more room you'll have to negotiate.
- *Is it important to me?* As long as you won't receive a reduction in quality, it's worth negotiating since it will take little time or effort and every penny you save will go right to your bottom line.

## KNOW YOUR OPPONENT

- *What do I need to know?* Learn the going rate for services in your area by asking friends and other professionals.
- *With whom should I negotiate?* Negotiate with the professional directly, not a secretary, deputy, or bookkeeper.
- *Are there any potentially disruptive side issues?* Never attack the fee as being too high or the services as not being worth their cost. Instead, stress that your appeal is based on affordability and your need to reduce expenses.
- *What do I share with my opponent?* Firm up the natural common ground present in a mercantile transaction between buyer and seller by implying that, despite your appreciation of the professional's skill, you'll be forced to shift your business unless costs are reduced.

## KNOW THE SITUATION

- Insider Tip: One way to compromise over fees is to ask for a reduction to be retroactive. This lets the professional save face by not reducing the fee as much, while offering you an opportunity to get the same savings.
- Insider Tip: You can also ask that the professional pass more of the work along to his or her associates, whose time may be billed at a lower rate.

# RENEGOTIATING RENT

## KNOW YOURSELF

- *What do I want?* Your goal should be to reduce your shelter costs without having to move to another location.
- *Is it worth my time?* If you have been a good tenant, and the market for rental properties in your area is soft, then the rent is readily negotiable.
- *Is it important to me?* It's worth negotiating if the resulting reduction in rent will ease the pressure on your stream of income.

## KNOW YOUR OPPONENT

- *What do I need to know?* Investigate the rent market in your area and try to find as many examples as possible of comparable locations that are rented for less. The idea is to provide your landlord with proof that you could move to a similar location for less money if this negotiation doesn't work out.
- *With whom should I negotiate?* Negotiate with the landlord directly, not a real estate agent or building manager.
- *Are there any potentially disruptive side issues?* The landlord's fear is that you'll either leave without notice or will stop paying rent entirely. It's very difficult to find good tenants, and it's even harder to evict a bad tenant. By presenting your case in a businesslike manner you should at least minimize some of this fear.
- *What do I share with my opponent?* The common ground here is the desire to continue the financial relationship. By stressing your love of the location and your eagerness to remain, you force the landlord to choose between continuing the relationship, albeit at a

lower rent, and taking the chance of finding another tenant as good as you.

## KNOW THE SITUATION

- Insider Tip: If the landlord brings up the lease agreement, just say that you hope the discussion won't get to that point. Without even mentioning the word *court* you'll have conjured up images of protracted and expensive legal proceedings.
- Insider Tip: Offer a rent figure you can afford. If the landlord comes back with another number, ask for it to be retroactive as a compromise.

# RENEGOTIATING YOUR OWN FEE

## KNOW YOURSELF

- *What do I want?* Your goal should be to increase your fee without losing the client.
- *Is it worth my time?* The degree to which you can renegotiate your own fee depends on the client's affordability, how much he or she needs you, and how happy he or she is with the service you're providing.
- *Is it important to me?* As long as your request isn't unreasonable, it's worth negotiating, since the risk can be minimized and every additional penny you earn will go right to your bottom line.

## KNOW YOUR OPPONENT

- *What do I need to know?* Try to gauge the three factors that go into making your fee negotiable: the client's affordability; your value to him or her; and his or her happiness with your services.
- *With whom should I negotiate?* Negotiate with the client directly, not a secretary, deputy, or bookkeeper.
- *Are there any potentially disruptive side issues?* Stress that your wish to renegotiate your fee has nothing to do with your personal relationship with the client, that you're spreading the increase among all your clients, and that you'll be doing everything possible to become more efficient—minimizing the number of hours you need to put in while maintaining the same level of service.
- *What do I share with my opponent?* Firm up the common ground present in the negotiation by stating how much you value the rela-

tionship and that you don't want to lose the person as either a friend or a client.

## KNOW THE SITUATION

- Insider Tip: State that your upcoming fee increase is a fact rather than a possibility: "As of next month I'll be raising my hourly fee to $250" rather than "I'm thinking of increasing my fee 20 percent." Blame the increase on your increased costs of doing business.

# THE TOTAL NEGOTIATOR'S CHECKLIST

## Step #1

### Know Yourself
### Analyzing Needs and
### Weighing Options

- What do I want?—Set a specific goal.
- Is it worth my time?—Decide if it's readily negotiable.
- Is it important to me?—Make sure it's worth doing.

# Step #2

## Know Your Opponent
## Leveling the Playing Field

- What do I need to know?—Gather information.
- With whom should I negotiate?—Push the up button.
- Are there any potentially disruptive side issues?— Eliminate dissonance.
- What do I share with my opponent?—Find and demonstrate common ground.

# Step #3

## Know the Situation
## Learning the Lessons of Experience

- Absorb the insider tips offered throughout the book.
- Become a student of the process and do your own research.

# AXIOMS OF THE TOTAL NEGOTIATOR

- The more specific a goal, the more likely it will be achieved.
- When preparation time is limited, goals should be limited.
- Don't negotiate for things that aren't readily negotiable.
- It's worth negotiating if the potential rewards and the outcome of not negotiating outweigh the costs of negotiating.
- Any discrepancies between the real and perceived powers of opponents should be eliminated or minimized.
- Negotiate only with someone who has the power to make a decision.
- Prices are invitations to buy, not statements of value.
- Terms are as important as dollars when negotiating numbers.
- A number can be negotiated only with the person who set it.
- Everything possible should be done to depolarize persuasive negotiations.
- Authority figures' decisions shouldn't be appealed; instead, the results of the decisions should be mitigated.
- Peers should work toward mutual goals.
- Hybrid negotiations involve persuading someone to act and then quantifying the action.
- The more powerful a persuasive argument, the more value will be obtained for the action.
- The more a proposed action is linked to its proposed value the more likely the value will be obtained.
- If linkage between actions and value is dangerous, discussions should be expanded to include things other than dollars.

# INDEX

# "IF YOU REALLY WANT TO WHEEL AND DEAL—THIS BOOK IS FOR REAL. DON'T NEGOTIATE WITHOUT IT."

David Horowitz, bestselling author of <u>Don't Get Ripped Off</u>;
creator/host of TV's "Fight Back! With David Horowitz"

Nearly everything in life is a deal, a persuasion, a battle of wits and wills—and to come out on top, a person must be a combination diplomat, snake-oil salesman and strong-arm enforcer. It takes more than right to win an argument or successfully conclude a transaction—whether in business or your personal affairs. But negotiating is a fine art that isn't taught in any school.

One of America's foremost experts on business, real estate and personal finance, **Stephen M. Pollan**—with the assistance of co-author **Mark Levine**—now offers clear, practical, nuts-and-bolts strategies for gaining and *keeping* the upper hand. Here is invaluable help for any everyday situation—from securing a loan to easing family tensions to talking your way out of a traffic ticket—a powerful philosophic approach to successful bargaining PLUS a *specific*, step-by-step guide to dealing with virtually *any* negotiational circumstance that might arise.

# "REMARKABLE...AN INDISPENSABLE GUIDE...NOT JUST A TOOL FOR BUSINESS, BUT FOR EVERYONE WHO WANTS TO ENHANCE THEIR LIVES...<u>THE TOTAL NEGOTIATOR</u> LEADS THE WAY TO SUCCESS IN COUNTLESS REAL LIFE SITUATIONS."

Scott DeGarmo, Publisher/Editor-in-Chief, <u>Success</u> Magazine

BUSINESS

ISBN 0-380-77019-9

77019

0 71001 01000 8